BRONX PRIMITIVE

BRONX PRIMITIVE

KATE SIMON

HARRAP
London

Grateful acknowledgement is made to the following for
permission to reprint copyrighted material:
Irving Berlin Music Corporation: Excerpts from *Because I
Love You*, by Irving Berlin, page 77; copyright 1926 by
Irving Berlin, renewed. Excerpt from *Always*, by Irving
Berlin, page 77; copyright 1925 by Irving Berlin, renewed.
Excerpt from *Remember*, by Irving Berlin, page 93;
copyright 1925 by Irving Berlin, renewed. Used by
permission, all rights reserved.

First published in Great Britain 1989
by Harrap Books Limited
19-23 Ludgate Hill, London EC4M 7PD
First published by Harper & Row Ltd 1982 and 1986 as
two separate books

ISBN 0 245-54744-4

Designed by Jim Weaver
Phototypeset by Falcon Graphic Art Ltd
Wallington, Surrey
Printed and bound in Great Britain by
Mackays of Chatham Limited

Contents

PORTRAITS
IN A CHILDHOOD

For Alex and Mark Kajitani

1

Lafontaine Near Tremont

We lived at 2029 Lafontaine, the last house on the west side of the street from 178th to 179th, a row of five-story tenements that ended at a hat factory. To the north and solidly, interminably, along the block to 180th there stretched a bitter ugliness of high walls of big stones that held a terminal point and service barns of El trains. (It may be that my recoil from early Renaissance palaces, their pugnacious blocks of stone and fortress grimness, stems from these inimical El walls.) Across from the factory were a garage and the Italian frame houses that lined that side of the street down to 178th Street. At the corner of 178th Street, on our Jewish-German-Polish-Greek-Hungarian-Rumanian side, was Mrs. Katz's candy store. The only other store I knew at first was the grocery run by a plodding elderly couple at the corner of 179th Street and Arthur Avenue, the street to the east. In spite of their lack of English and my frail Yiddish, I eagerly ran errands there to watch their feet slide and pat in their brown felt slippers and to admire the precision with which the old man cut once, twice, into a tub of butter to dig out exactly a quarter pound. And on their side of 179th Street, about midway between Arthur and Lafontaine, there was a big tree, the only street tree in the neighborhood, which showered me, and only me, with a million white blossoms. It was my tree and I watched and touched it as carefully as the Italian grandfathers watched and touched the tomato plants in their backyards.

Our station of the El was Tremont, which was numerically 177th Street, and Main Street. Between dark Third Avenue and its changing grids and slashes of light and Lafontaine, there was Monterey Avenue, on its west side a row of tenements and on its east, running from 178th to 179th, a resplendent, high empty lot,

as full of possibilities as a park. It had patches of daisies and
buttercups, plumy and scratchy bushes; on its eastern edge and
below our fire escapes, seductive glittering objects thrown from
Lafontaine windows – a shining knife handle, red glass and
blue glass, bits of etched cut glass. Once my brother and I found
a seltzer bottle nozzle and once a Chinese record, a wonderment
we played over and over again on the Victrola, until our parents,
impatient with the repetition of high thin notes with startling starts
and stops, caused it to disappear. There were two ways of getting
onto the lot: 178th Street was an easy, gradual slope; 179th Street
was jutting rock for a height of two stories. The few girls who
managed it were never quite the same again, a little more defiant,
a little more impudent.

To the west of Lafontaine was Arthur Avenue, a mixture
of Jewish tenements and frame houses in which lived Italian
families and a number of Irish. Beyond was Belmont, whose only
significance was that it held, at its meeting with Tremont, the movie
house we all trooped to on Saturday after lunch. The other movie
house, which offered a combination of films and vaudeville, was a
rare pleasure; it cost more and was saved for special occasions, a
birthday or a report card that said A for work, A for effort, A for
conduct.

This theater for celebrations was also on Tremont, toward
the west, not far from Webster Avenue, beyond Bathgate and
Washington. Bathgate, moving southward from Tremont toward
Claremont Parkway, was the market street where mothers bought
yard goods early in the week, as well as dried mushrooms and
shoelaces. On Wednesdays they bought chickens and live fish to
swim in the bathtub until Friday, when they became gefilte fish.
Most women plucked their own chickens. A few aristocrats, like
my mother and Mrs. Horowitz (who spoke English perfectly, the
only Jewish woman we knew who did), paid a little dark bundle
in a dusty red wig ten cents to pluck fast, her hand like the
needle of a sewing machine, up down, up down, as a red and
black and white garden of feathers spread at her feet. On the
next block, Washington, was the public library, and a block north
of it, on the corner with Tremont, the barber shop where I went
for my Buster Brown haircut. Tremont west of Third also held the
delectable five-and-ten, crisscrosses of rainbows and pots of gold.

Our suburbs, our summer country homes, our camps, our
banks and braes, our America the Beautiful, our fields of gaming

and dalliance and voyeurism were in Crotona Park, whose northern border fronted on Tremont Avenue.

Our apartment, 5B, was a top-floor railroad flat, with most of the rooms strung off a long hall. The first room nearest the outer door was a small bedroom with a large bed in which my brother and I slept, a chair on which we were to put our clothing rather than drop it on the floor, and, shortly after my sister's birth, her crib. From the bed I could see a hallway picture of the explosion of Vesuvius, a red horror of flames and fleeing bodies toward which I felt quite friendly when I was very young, not then knowing what it meant except bright color and lively lines. The next room off the hallway was the bathroom, all our own and a luxurious thing, with a tub, a sink, and a toilet that didn't have to be shared with neighbors. On Wednesday and Thursday nights we watched the big, vigorous carp in the tub, to be killed on Friday (when we were, unfortunately, in school) and chopped, in concert with the chopping that sounded from a dozen other kitchens, for Friday night's meal. The toilet had constantly to be pumped with a plunger to disgorge the inventive matter – spools, apple cores, a hank of wool – my brother threw in to see the water swirl and swallow, which it often didn't. The bathroom was also the torture chamber. It was here, after a long lecture explaining that the act was essential to the improvement of our conduct and we would be grateful for the lesson later on, that the strap was slowly, very slowly, pulled out of the loops on my father's pants while we bent over the lidded toilet bowl to be whipped, my brother much more often than I. He was an adventuresome explorer and breaker, while I was already well practiced in the hypocrisies of being a good girl. Furthermore, there was something shameful, except for extraordinary infractions, in beating a girl; a girl was for slapping rather than whipping.

The next room along the hallway was the kitchen where we chattered, ate, fought over who had more slices of banana in his dish and who was the biggest pig, the one who ate fast or the one who ate slowly, savoring each delicious bit when the other had long finished. Here we watched my mother peel, for our pleasure, a potato or an apple in one long unbroken coil. It was in the kitchen that we learned to understand Yiddish from my father's accounts of union news read from the socialist paper, the *Freiheit*. My mother read from the *Jewish Daily Forward* the heartbreaking stories gathered in the 'Bintel Brief' (bundle of letters) that wept of abandoned wives, of 'Greene Cousines',

spritely immigrant girls who were hanky-pankying with the eldest
sons of households, set to marry rich girls and become famous
doctors. The stories moved me deeply, as all stories of betrayal
and abandonment did, while my mother laughed. We loved to
watch her laugh, big tears rolling down her face as the laughter
rocked her plump body back and forth, but I found her humor
chilling, heartless. She told one laughing story that appalled me
for years: there was a man who could neither sit nor stand nor lie
down (this with elaborations of voice and gesture), so he found a
solution – he hanged himself. Another story concerned an old
man who had trouble peeing – great effort and pain contorted
her face and body – and consulted a doctor for relief. The doctor
asked the man how old he was. Eighty-three. 'Well,' said the doctor,
'you've peed enough. Go home, old man.' We were constantly told
to respect the old; here she was being amused by a sick old man. It
wasn't until I picked up the fatalistic ironies of Jewish humor that
I understood and almost forgave her the cruel jokes.

Beyond the kitchen the hallway opened to the 'living room',
almost always unused because we had few relatives and they
visited rarely. We might look at the things in it but must not
touch, except to practice the piano when that inevitable time came.
The room was my mother's art museum, her collection of treasures.
In the china closet a few pieces of cut glass, an etched pitcher, two
little china bowls. On the round oak table a machine-embroidered
cloth covered with fat red and pink roses and thick green stems
with thorns; a mighty work I thought it, and so did she, since she
paid the Arab peddler who sold it to her endless weekly quarters
for its ebullience. On a sideboard stood my favorite piece – a
marble bowl on whose rim rested two or three pigeons (a copy of a
famous Roman mosaic repeated in many materials throughout the
centuries). The pigeons could be lifted off and set back into little
holes in the rim, a loving, absorbing game and a rare privilege
never at all permitted my brother. He could not resist inventive
variations on any theme, would try to place the pigeons where there
were no holes and they would certainly crash, and he would get a
beating and – just better not. It was in such circumstances that
our parents used an odd phrase for both of us: 'They have to know
from where the feet grow', an amused reference to our curiosity, a
phrase that my mind moved from feet to knees to genitals, where
the ancient phrase with its sexual connotations probably found its
origins. Not for the first or the last time I wondered why words and

suggestions allowed grown-ups were forbidden children. There was no answer, it was just another example of 'walking on eggs', words I found felicitous to describe our delicately balanced lives.

The end room was my parents' bedroom with its big bed, chests of drawers, and my mother's talented sewing machine. Her feet rocking the treadle that said in metal letters 'Singer', her hand smoothing the material taut as the needle chased her fingers, the turning, turning spool of thread feeding the jumping needle were a stunning show. Equally remarkable were the narrow long drawers, three on each side of the machine. You pulled a knob and out came long open boxes full of papers of shining, meticulously spaced pins, empty spools to string as trains, full spools that spilled baby rainbows, bits of silk and matte cotton to mix and match in myriad combinations, the dull with the shiny, the yellow with the blue, the white with the red, the square with the round; endless. Whether it was because of the dignity of the parental bed or the multitude of treasures in the sewing machine, it was in this room that my brother and I played most peaceably, most happily, a room I still see, rain softly streaming down its windows, when I hear Mozart quartets. That end room was also the room of the fire escape. The balconies that jut out of modern apartment houses are empty stages, staring and lifeless compared with the old fire escape and its dynamic design of zigzag stairs and the teasing charm of potential danger when the metal stairs were wet with icy rain. Our fire escapes were densely inhabited by mops, short lines of washed socks, geranium plants, boxes of seltzer bottles, and occasional dramatic scenes. Skinny Molly, whose mother had an explosive temper, could escape by running down the fire-escape stairs where her fat mother couldn't follow, forcing her to expend her rage by threatening, 'Wait till your father gets home, you crazy thing!' The fire escape was our viewing balcony down on the eventful lot we shared with Monterey Avenue, and it became our minute bedroom on hot nights when we slept folded on each other tight as petals on a bud, closed from the perilous stairs by a high board.

My family arrived on Lafontaine the summer before I was six and ready to be enrolled in the first grade, my brother in kindergarten. As I had learned to do in European trains and stations, in inns, on the vastness of the ship *Susquehanna* when I was an immigrant four-year-old, I studied every landmark, every turning of our new surroundings.

On the day we registered for school, P.S. 58 on Washington Avenue at 176th Street, my mother pointed out each turn, the number of blocks to the left or right and here we were at the big red building, the school, across from the little white building, the library. On the first day of school we went unaccompanied – hold his hand, don't talk to strange men. He complained that I was squeezing his hand and I probably was, tense and worried, avidly searching for the places I had marked out on our route: first to Tremont Avenue and right to the cake store, cross Third Avenue under the El, pass the butcher's with the pigs' feet in the window, cross Tremont at the bicycle shop to the barber's pole, continue on to the white library, and cross Washington Avenue to the school. It was a long walk, and I reached the school confused and exhausted, with just enough presence of mind to thrust the papers my mother had given me at the first teacher I saw, who led us to our respective rooms. We made the trip three more times that day, home for lunch and back and home again at three, and I was so bloated with triumph on the last journey that I varied the turns and crossings while my brother pulled in the directions he had memorized, as frightened as I had been that morning. With no memory of the feeling and no sympathy, I pulled him along, calling him a crybaby.

Except for those journeys, all that remains of P.S. 58 is a Mrs. Henkel, a brown old lady addicted to Spencerian handwriting. She pushed our hands around and around on the ridged, worn desks, grinding dust into our skin so that a number of us developed abscesses. Somehow the practice stopped; we were never told why. Certainly it could not have been complaints from our awed mothers, to whom schools were sacred citadels, except maybe English-speaking Mrs. Horowitz, who navigated comfortably in the alien worlds.

As the street, the shops, the people became more familiar, there were rules to learn, accumulated gradually and hardened into immutability like big pink patches always England in geography books, like Italy always the shape of a boot. Rumanian ladies used rouge and laughed a lot and ran around too much. Hungarian men were stuck-up and played cards late into the night and all day on Sunday. Bad girls who didn't go to school and who hid with tough boys were invariably the daughters of Polish janitors. Saturday night thumping and crashing and loud Victrola records came exclusively from Irish houses. The Jews stuck together, the

Neapolitans and Sicilians stuck together, altogether apart from the northern Italians. Yet, in spite of momentary flare-ups, a mutter of anti-Semitism, 'savage' thrown at a Sicilian, they clung to one another, arranging and rearranging the symbiotic couplings of the poor and uncomprehending in confrontations with the enemy, the outsider who spoke English without an accent. Except for a few entertaining, itinerant drunks, unaccented English was the alarm for the wary silence and the alert poise of the hunted. Not that it was a troublesome block. Most of the inhabitants were inert with timidity, but some of them had had and all of them had heard fearsome stories of brushes with truant officers, visiting nurses, people from naturalization offices, *Them* of the bewildering powers, and uncomfortably close. The Bronx County Building was stuffed with policemen, judges, immigration officials, women who looked like nurses or assistant principals. This confident, inimical enclave that spoke fast English and ate peanut butter sandwiches on white bread sat at our edge of Crotona Park, dourly in our line of vision almost everywhere we went. We children couldn't imagine them in ordinary tenements or frame houses, like ours, so we pushed them all into cold cubicles in the big-bellied building, like sides of beef in a huge butcher's icebox.

2
Forebears

As they leave few vestiges of dwelling places, not a slab of house wall standing, only subterranean caves that eat into the earth rather than vault the sky as places of worship, the ancient poor shed their ancestors, leaving them to become nameless dust when they fled plagues and famines and wars. This was particularly true of the Jews, almost constantly in flight, forced or cautionary; Jerusalem to Rome under Titus, burned out of York to settle in Lincoln, to be driven to London and expelled to wander southward where their skills were needed, and then no longer, by the Spanish kings. From Spain to Salonika, to Amsterdam, to Venice, to Lyons, to Cologne. Several centuries later, the great exodus from central Europe to America to escape conscription and pogroms and to find 'ah Jahb,' the first word in most immigrant vocabularies. They dragged their large down puffs like fat clouds, their burnished samovars, the candlesticks and hand-embroidered cloths for the Sabbath table, the old men their prayer shawls, the women their *shaytlin* (wigs worn by married women) and cotton headcloths and slips of paper supplied by HIAS, the guardians of the Golden Gates, whose formal name, rarely used, was Hebrew Immigrant Aid Society.

They brought with them Moses, Esther, Abraham, Isaac, Joseph, Sarah, David, Solomon, miracle rabbis, and old stories gentle, magical, and bawdy. But, as if they could carry no more baggage, they left their closer ancestors in a thousand scattered cemeteries from which a few vivid flowers grew, to be pressed by each family in its Old Country Book. There were few who did not have, somewhere among their ancestors, a bride so beautiful that she was strewn with rose petals on her way to the *chuppa* (the bridal canopy), her dainty little feet lightly treading the red velvet rug that was her path. As she shone under the canopy, one despairing young man ran from the happy crowd to drown himself in the nearby river. Another went home to develop brain fever, struggling with the Angel of Death for months and never the same again. When Zuleika Dobson appeared in my life, she, too, stood pink-cheeked and glittering under a canopy while young men in side locks languished and fell before her. Another graveyard flower was an ancestral rabbi of unerring wisdom who knew how to rekosher an unkoshered pot, how to frighten the tongue of a lying shrew, and who, at least once, had exorcised a dybbuk.

My family was unfortunately free of these engaging ghosts, no learned Gaon, no village Esther. My parents were skeptics and, bored with the spates of *bubbe meises* (grandmother's tales), preferred to tell pointed little stories about each other's relatives. My earliest known ancestor was my mother's grandmother, Kaila, for whom I was named. All I know about her is that she was an entertaining grandmother and the wise woman of her Warsaw ghetto street, the Tvarda Gass, where I was born. My mother's father – I think he was Kaila's son, but I'm not sure – was a tinsmith, a quiet, passive man who died early, after falling off a roof on which he was working. He left twelve children – a thirteenth had been smothered in infancy lying between its sleeping parents, a not uncommon incident. Most of the children, like my mother, had one year's schooling, from the age of seven to eight, and then went out to work, running errands, moving barrels and sacks in markets, selling shoelaces and buttonhooks, sweeping up the floors of dressmaking establishments, each learning enough to progress into an apprenticeship and a better-paying job. The youngest girls stayed at home to help my grandmother. About her I know singularly little except that she was religious, apparently colorless, and possibly not overly bright. My mother, a gifted raconteur and mimic, rarely spoke of her, in itself a strange fact, and strange still since it was in her house that I spent my earliest years and it was in her house that my brother was born. We have pictures of two young aunts, arms around each other's shoulders, a coquettish silk rose on one bosom, a swirl of black hair on the other's head, winsome, girlish half-smiles fixed as their immortality. There are no other pictures, an effect of poverty or superstition that might have been a lingering whisper of the biblical injunction against graven images.

The exodus from the Warsaw ghetto that brought us to America took three aunts to Buenos Aires, one uncle to Paris, another to London. I have made sporadic efforts to locate them, with no success. The only relative on my mother's side whom I actually met was a cousin, chic and multilingual, a functionary with the Free Polish in England and married to an Englishman. I've lost her, too, as I've lost a large number of unknown relatives of two or three generations destroyed in the Warsaw ghetto. From what little I know of some of them, the spirited, the courageous, they might have taken part in the ghetto uprising. I don't know, I hope.

My paternal ancestors are much more vivid, brought to life largely by the quick eye and tongue of my mother. Perhaps the best way to introduce them is in the person of my father just arrived on Ellis Island.

Having installed my pregnant mother and my one-year-old self in the flat of my grandmother and my young aunts with the promise that he would send for us soon, he went off to America. He arrived an unencumbered princeling, twenty-six and handsome, with fine shirts and handmade shoes in his real leather valise, no peasant bundle of sentimental odds and ends to embarrass him, no pink-eyed crusty-headed child to threaten his entry. He had an uncle's promise of a bed and an introduction to a 'landsman' whose occupation was sniffing out jobs. And he had the freedom to taste girls again. It would be as easy as picking flowers in a summer field, the white candid daisies, the yellow buttercups peering out of the grass, the round pink clover, all the little 'Greene Cousines.' Their song, one of the most famous among the many immigrant songs, described their teeth as matched pearls, their eyes as doves, their cheeks as pomegranates; their feet never walked, they skipped and danced. They were optimistic and courageous; a new life meant several kinds of new life, free of the frowning bearded father worlds away, the mumbling scowling aunts erased. It was not my father's habit to pursue; he stood grand and unsmiling while the pomegranate girls in their starched shirtwaists and pearly buttoned shoes did him obeisance, and a few, to use the lovely chivalric euphemism, 'did him solace.' A highly skilled craftsman who could make the whole sample shoe, decorations and all, to be shown to a Fifth Avenue buyer, my father got a job quickly. He moved out of the niche in a wall in his old uncle's railroad flat and found a younger, more raffish family who provided a room, robust Polish-Jewish meals, and the company of several spirited boarders. It took almost three years to bring us to America. World War I was drawing to a close but still tearing Poland apart: communications were erratic; Warsaw, dismembered by Germany and Russia, was a corpse. Yet, knowing something of my father's upbringing and vanity, I suspect that caused him little concern or disappointment.

He was a royal baby, his birth a gift of immortality. He was a miracle, a sudden kindling of cold ashes stirred by God's hand. All privilege was his. Year after year my grandmother had produced girls and only girls, a few stillborn, one or two victims of diphtheria or scarlet fever, but five or six thriving as big, marriageable maidens. The menopause years were approaching while my embittered grandmother muttered over the *cholent* (a stew of potatoes, carrots, meat, and prunes) that she shoved into the oven on Friday afternoons to cook slowly through the night and provide a warm meal on Saturday when no stove might be lit. She mumbled angrily while she ironed, spitting the dampening water as if it were venom. Someone, maybe an old witch who envied her her good house, her gold watch, her silky new *shaytl*, had cursed her with the Evil Eye, depriving her of a son, a *Kaddish* to pray for her after her death. The girls' prayers, if they prayed at all, counted for nothing; like animals, they had no souls and no voices to God's ear. My grandfather was indifferent to the whole matter, heartily sick of the Evil Eye and the sacrificial fasts his wife imposed on herself and him, when he allowed it. He was impatient with her charities, which involved her in quarrels with other women about what orphan should or should not be given a wedding dress and a dowry, and impatient with the superstitions among which she moved fearfully. He enjoyed the noisy gaggle of girls who racketed around in his house as he enjoyed being the most important Jew in his village near Lodz. When the manager of the big tobacco factory, the principal source of local employment, died, my grandfather was moved up from foreman, an almost incredible appointment for a Jew, and he earned enough to buy his rangy house and feed the girls as well as a number of orphans and any traveling Jew who was far from home during the holidays. He was curious and gregarious and handed out cigarettes and advice with broad profligacy; a lovable man, my mother said, in spite of the fact that he reeked of tobacco, and under his light and sometimes foolish quips – just to keep the talk going – a smart man.

Several of my aunts grew into marriage and brought their young husbands to the house. One opened a dry-goods store with help from my grandfather, another was given a job in the tobacco factory, a third was a scholar, required to do nothing but study and be an honor to the family. As my aunt, Teibele, the Little Dove, grew rounder and rounder with pregnancy, my grandmother grew thinner and more dour, her bleeding had stopped, the menopause had taken her, sterile of sons. Teibele's baby was born, thank God a girl, and Grandma began to look a little better, her cheeks less gray, her back straighter, a belly pushing out between the lean hips. The belly ultimately became my father and my grandmother's ecstasy. No infant was ever so brave at his circumcision, no baby so quick to walk and speak, never a child so beautiful as her Yukele. The house and everything in it belonged to her miracle. She awoke each morning at four-thirty to listen for the baker's wagon and raced down the stairs to greet him as he dropped the sack of bread and rolls at the back door. She carefully examined each roll, rejecting those not quite baked enough, those too well baked; squeezed each for the proper mixture of resilience and softness, took the best three or four, went back upstairs to put them under her pillow to save for her little King David, and went back to sleep. At dinner, eight or ten adults, a couple of adolescents, a few younger children at table, no one made a gesture, not even Grandpa, toward the platters of chicken and boiled beef until Yukele, from his infancy to his early manhood, had made his choice.

My father's shirts, cut of Paris silks, were made by a Warsaw shirtmaker. The local cobbler would do for the rest of the family, but my father's shoes were made to measure by the best establishment in the capital. There was talk of sending him to a yeshiva in Warsaw, where he might pick up a little Russian or German as well as Talmud and Gemorrah. Grandma wouldn't have it and insisted that he be tutored at home. My philosophical grandfather agreed. (Suddenly it seems dreadful that I do not know his first name or that of my other Old Country relatives or what they looked like except for the slanging little contests of wit and malice between my parents. He spoke of my mother's family as *knaydlach*, round dumplings, all fat cheek and ass and no neck. My mother spoke of his favorite sister, a tall lissome beauty according to him, as a board with a hole. He said she had a vulgar Warsaw mouth; she said he spoke like a coarse provincial drover, the most foulmouthed of Jews. And so on, while we listened, entranced, silent, hardly breathing, our backs bent hard with the feigned virtue of homework. It is still not possible, and probably never will be, for me to see Picasso's flat wooden women without hearing my mother's laughing voice, '*A brate mit a loch.*')

Having agreed that Yukele could stay at home, Grandpa insisted that he learn a trade as well. Sulking, wailing, shrieking that the silken hands must not be defiled, while Grandpa hummed happy little songs about merry tailors and lusty drovers, my grandmother reluctantly accepted this commonplace for her golden son. At twenty, my father was ready for a bigger world. He was a fast reckoner, read and wrote Yiddish and Polish well, and could follow Hebrew prayers and texts competently, all my carefree grandfather asked for. Pitifully little for my grandmother, who wanted a radiant rabbi with the beard of Abraham and the side locks of David, the wisdom of Solomon and the enlightenment of Maimonides, and – even if he was a heinous apostate – Spinoza's renown among learned *goyim*. The actual spur, according to the meager, somewhat apocryphal family history, that sent my father into an apprenticeship with a skilled cobbler in Warsaw was my mother. He, when he was fond of her, romanticized their meeting – a wedding where he watched her dance, a gathering of young people where she sang and played the mandolin. She insisted that their meeting was forced on her by her mother, who had begun to speak of her as 'already a girl in the years' (she was twenty-two or twenty-three) and had enlisted a matchmaker who also had dealings with my grandfather. He was beginning to sicken with cancer of the lungs and was eager to see his spoiled son under the control of a competent girl before he died.

It was a lackluster courtship. My father pursued casually, on instructions from the matchmaker and the urging of his father. My mother eluded, without a touch of maidenly coyness. She was earning well, helping to support her younger siblings from the proceeds of her own corset shop. She enjoyed not only the independence but also the fun of making a lace-trimmed black corset with a tight waist for the mistress of a banker. She liked talking and joking and listening to the confidences of the prettiest *shiksas* around town, invariably referred to by my father as 'prostitutkes', which was invariably countered by my mother with a reference to one of his idiot cousins who had willingly spread for a saddler, the price a glass ring.

My mother mentioned it once and only once, as part of a lecture on female independence and the overrated charms of marriage, that she was in love with a Gentile for a number of years and for that reason thoroughly resistant to all marriage offers, several from prosperous businessmen to whom an appealing, playful girl with a good business head was markedly attractive. The love story was left there; no continuation, no end. One can assume that the anticipated shock and pain of a mixed marriage to both families, sharpened by the notorious anti-Semitism of the Polish and the fear of Poles in every Jew, forced the ultimate separation.

The desultory courtship went on while my father developed fine skills and a keen eye for the English suits in elegant shop windows, while my mother's business flourished and her rounds of songs and mazurkas widened, often with *goy* friends, a shame for the neighbors, my grandmother complained. My paternal grandmother had heard about this, too – the grapevine among Jewish communities was as dense a meshwork as Renaissance politics – and greeted my mother on her first visit with her eyes firmly cast down. To look at her would have been to burn her up, this *shiksa* with the Polish name (Lonia Babicz) who worked and collected money on the Sabbath and had declared that she would never wear a *shaytl*. The grandfather addressed her with courtliness, conducted her to the best chair, said that he had heard it was becoming the fashion for women to smoke in Warsaw, would she care for a cigarette? He admired her pretty dress and how small her feet were and continued to seduce her for his son. She married the son, my mother said, because she loved the father. His unremitting flattery was entertaining but nothing more. It was his patience with his dotty wife, the inventive games he played with his grandchildren, the courage that hid his pain, his generous interest in everyone, and the love that shone on her like the sun that made her accede to his delicately expressed dying wish. She married his Yukele shortly before her old true love died.

I was born a year later. The year after my father left for America. It should have been a happy infancy, dandled and sung to by young aunts, near my mother, who worked at home after her shop was confiscated with the outbreak of war. Among the few Polish words I remember are references to me as 'a pretty doll'; obviously I didn't lack attention. But I missed my father and looked for him constantly, behind doors, under tables, in the street. I was told that he was in a place where everything was good and where we would soon go. If a toy broke, he would buy me another, a better one, when we got to America. If there was no sugar to put in my milk, I would have lots of sugar, heaps as tall as trees, in America. As wartime supplies of food diminished to coarse bread and potatoes, my life was filled with images of raisins and chocolate, cookies and dolls, white slippers and pink hair bows, all waiting for me in a big box called America, which would be mine soon, very soon.

3

Voyage and Discovery

When my brother was born, I was eighteen months old. My father, for whom I was still searching, had been in New York for six months. Our Warsaw apartment turned dark, the singing stopped. It need hardly be said that I was jealous, felt abandoned, unloved, coldly shadowed while the full warm light that was mine now circled him. It cannot have been that my grandmother and aunts and mother suddenly stopped loving me, and I might in time have grown interested in him, beginning with the gallant way he peed, upward in a little shining arch, out of a finger in a peculiar place. But he was a very sick child and the household alternated between sad, quiet staring and frantic dashing to rescue him from death. His head was bright, alert, and very large compared to the arms and legs that would not develop beyond thin, boneless ropes. He was a classic picture of the rachitic famine child who still tears the heart of the newspaper reader, the television viewer. We were not too poor to buy the food he needed; it was simply unavailable, grabbed up by the military for its soldiers. My mother took the baby from doctor to doctor, all of whom gave her the same short answer: 'All this child needs is a steady, normal diet.' Because her food intake was meager, the milk she gave him was insufficient; my aunts scoured the city, offering large sums for an orange or two, an egg, a pint of milk, with no success. I grew thin and listless.

The last doctor my mother saw in Warsaw, made blunt by the misery he could not remedy, shouted at her, 'Leave the boy, he's going to die anyway. Take the girl to America while there's still time. Or do you want to sit with two dead children in this graveyard city?'

We left for America. My brother was two and a half, a babbler in several languages, a driven entertainer and flirt. His arms and hands were weak but usable, his legs not at all; he moved with amazing, mischievous rapidity by shuffling on his behind when he wasn't being carried. I was four, grown silent and very capable. I could lift him to the pot, clean him, and take him off. I could carry him to bed and mash his potato. I knew where he might bump his head, where he might topple, how to divert him when he began to blubber. It was a short childhood. I had my first baby at not quite four, better trained in maternal wariness and responsibility than many fully grown women I later observed. At four I also knew one could intensely love and as intensely hate the being who was both core and pit of one's life.

The month-long journey across devastated Europe to reach our ship, the *Susquehanna*, in Rotterdam remains with me as snatches of dream. I am sitting with my brother on my lap, in a room full of heavy dark furniture that I have never seen before. I am telling him that our mother went to buy food and will be back soon. I hope that she will come back, but I'm not sure; over and over, in every dark dream, I am not sure. I don't say this to him but wonder what I will do, where we will go, if she doesn't come back, as our father didn't. I continue to talk to him. We'll soon be on another choo-choo train and then the big, big ship that will take us to our father in America. He is silent in these dreams, his face old, serious, as if he were listening to the fears under my bright optimistic patter.

The next vision is actual recollection: a long cobbled quay marching into a world of water, more water than I had ever imagined. On the side of the quay a stall at which a woman shining with smiles and sweat stands frying small cakes. My mother buys three and hands me one. I expect it to be sweet and it tastes like fish. The vomit leaps out of my mouth, down my clean dress, and into the cracks around the cobblestones. What do they do in this place to girls who vomit on their streets? Will they keep me off their ship? The pink sweaty lady washes it away with a bucket of water. My mother thanks her in the Dutch she has picked up, I say my best Polish thank you, my smarty brother dazzles her with a '*Merci beaucoup*' someone had taught him on a train, and we go to look for the *Susquehanna*, my mother carrying my brother and one big valise and I two big bundles.

Just as I find it a great loss not to know my grandparents' first names, I feel deprived of what should have been an unforgettable sight: the big ship as it swayed on the waterfront, and, later, the endless corridors, the stairs, the crowds of people, the disorder, the shouting, the weeping in terror, in relief, in joy, that my mother described. We were on the ship a full month, listed in steerage. I don't know where my brother and I actually stayed, however. As if our lives were designed to fill every requirement of the classic immigrant hegira, typhus raged through steerage, my exhausted mother one of the victims. We children must have been taken care of in some other part of the ship by strangers whom I cannot remember except as sensations of pleasure: an India rubber ball whose lovely colors played hide and seek with each other and the man who gave it to me, a slight man in a brown hat who limped. I searched for him for years after. A slight man in a brown hat who limped was the dream lover of my adolescence, a steady image through the short, searing crushes, the unbuttoned blouse and the frightened crawl of boys' fingers.

Knowing that there would be a long wait at Ellis Island, my father had equipped himself with a couple of Hershey bars to nibble on, and when he finally picked me up to kiss me, I tasted the chocolate and announced to my mother, 'Our father has a sweet mouth.' It was frequently quoted as an example of my dainty, feminine grace, and only four years old, mind you. I have often thought it was an act of propitiation: I am eager to love you; love me, please.

At Ellis Island we were questioned and examined by immigration officials and told our English names. Because my Polish birth certificate said 'Jew-child Carolina' I was dubbed and registered as 'Caroline', a barbed-wire fence that divided me from myself throughout my school years. I hated it and would never answer my father when he tried to be fancy and American in public, addressing me by a name that belonged entirely to P.S. 58, P.S. 57, P.S. 59, to Theodore Roosevelt High School, to James Monroe High School, to Hunter College, not to me. How we got to Kate I don't know. My mother must have sought it out to keep as clear as possible the link to her grandmother Kaila, not realizing how intensely Catholic a name it then was. Being serenaded as 'K-K-K-Katy, my beautiful Katy' was a flattering bewilderment until I realized it was not written for me and then grew bored and irritated with the repetition from elderly relatives. (As bored as I later became with their descendants and their witty greeting, 'Kiss me, Kate.') My brother, the master mimic, learned 'K-K-K-Katy' immediately and learned, too – our weaponry of injuries that were deep and yet unpunishable was uncannily sophisticated – how much it annoyed me, and he sang it constantly to the admiration of the old uncles and aunts who never ceased to wonder at the speed with which he picked up English songs and the pretty, true voice on which they floated clear, loud, and incessant.

Instead of a city of silver rivers and golden bridges, America turned out to be Uncle David's flat on Avenue C in which my father had first lived when he came to America. We walked up several flights of dark stairs and knocked on a door pasted over with glazed patterned paper of connecting rectangles and circles in blue and red and green, whose lines I liked to trace with my eye while the others talked. That door led to a large kitchen with a round table in the center, a few chairs around it, and, off to a side, a brown wooden icebox. At another side, a shining black stove whose cooking lids were lifted by a clever long black hook when pieces of coal had to be added to the waning fire. From the kitchen ran a narrow dark alley with divisions that made niches for beds and then opened into a small living room at whose end there were two windows with views of clouds and chimneys. Only once were we held to look down to the street below; never were we to try on our own, and we couldn't, so thoroughly were we watched by our entranced Uncle David, who looked like god and Moses and, more often, Old King Cole. He had a long white beard and puffs of white hair leaping from the edge of his skullcap and a magical skill of putting his finger inside his cheek and pulling it out to make a big popping sound. He laughed a lot, told incomprehensible stories about Italians whose only English was 'sonnomabitz,' drank great quantities of tea, sipped from a saucer and drained through a cube of sugar held in his teeth. Everything about him was wonderful: the black straps and boxes he wrapped on his arms and forehead and the rhythmic bowing of his prayers when he was God; the fluttering old fingers and light touch of his gray carpet slippers as he paced a Chassidic dance when he was Old King Cole.

The rest of his household consisted of two middle-aged spinster daughters. Rachel was a plump, bustling, talkative woman who addressed us as her little sheep, which made us feel pathetic and affecting and sure we could get anything out of her – another candy and yet another – and we played her. In spite of her bounty and mushy vulnerability, I was afraid of her. She wore glasses so thick that her eyes were invisible behind concentric circles of shine. Though her cheeks were high-colored and her teeth strong and yellow, she looked like a mechanical woman, a machine with flashing, glassy circles for eyes. The third member of the household was completely apart from us and truly fearsome. Yentel (a name, I was later told, that derived from the Italian 'Gentile') was tall and gaunt, blind and deaf. She moved through the small apartment deftly, measuring her spaces with long, constantly moving fingers. She made the beds, pulling, smoothing, lining up the edges with her subtle, restless fingers. She shelled peas, she peeled potatoes and plucked chickens. While my brother sang and shuffled around Rachel and Uncle David, I watched her out of the corner of my eye. I didn't know what blind really meant; anyone who was so dextrous could not be entirely without vision and I was afraid she would see me staring at her if I watched her with my eyes wide open.

Though I was relieved of some of the care of my brother, I still had to be in charge many times. Uncle David and Rachel could keep him from banging into Yentel and would prepare his food, but we had confusing language difficulties that I had to unsnarl when my parents went out, my mother wildly eager to see everything and now, particularly while she had such devoted baby-sitters. My brother and I spoke Polish, Uncle David and Rachel had been brought up in Yiddish with a few Polish words they no longer remembered accurately. When my brother sleepily mumbled '*Spatch* [sleep]' they briskly rushed him to the cold toilet in the hall, vaguely remembering a similar Polish word that they thought meant shit, *sratch*. Unable to explain, I resorted to rough pantomime: run into the toilet, shake my head vigorously, pull him, confused and weeping, off the seat, and carry him to one of the beds, where I dump him and his lush glorious howling, to let them take care of the rest. Conversely I had to watch for the suffused worried face and the shifting buttocks that they tried to settle in bed while he yearned for a toilet. The story of bed and toilet was frequently told in our household to considerable laughter; my brother and I were never amused, it gave us both anxious bellyaches.

Force-fed like a Strasbourg goose by everyone who looked at him, my brother began to strengthen and even to take a few tentative steps now and then. An early talker, his only strengths his brain and speech, he was prodigious at three. He might easily have learned to read but he preferred talk, preferably oratory. The first time we were taken out on a sled one winter afternoon, he declared when we came home that so small a child (as he) must not be taken out in snowy cold. People had to realize that a small body got colder

faster, that snow was for animals with fur and not for people with
skins. And so on and so on, in his adept combination of splashing
guilt as he charmed. And how he could cry, high wide luxuriant
wails to which his whole body danced, and to which everyone
responded anxiously, except one time when we were taken on an
elevated train and, at one station, a black man walked in and sat
opposite us. I didn't know how to feel: maybe he was a charred man,
darkened like wood in a fire and I must be sorry for him, maybe he
ate coal, maybe he was some sort of monkey like those in a picture
book and I should be afraid of him. While sorting it out, I admired
the light palms of his hands against the dark backs, the big purple
lips, and the wide holes in his nose. My brother shrieked in terror,
screaming – in Polish, fortunately – 'Take him away, take
that black giant away! He's going to eat me! Kill him, Papa, kill
him!' It was a crowded train; to give up our seats and move to
stand in another car would have been foolish. My father slapped
the small pointing finger and with his hand stifled the howling.
The child thrust his head into my mother's armpit and, shuddering,
rode that way the rest of the journey.

My brother's fear of blacks dispelled itself in the stellar
entertainment we found on 98th Street, between Lexington and
Third avenues where we had moved from the Lower East Side. At
the top of the street there were three tall-stooped narrow tenements
and below, running to Third, small houses with crooked porches.
These were black houses and to us places of great joy and freedom.
My brother was already walking quite well and we were allowed the
street – I was always to hold his hand and watch that he didn't
go into the gutter and see that he didn't get dirty and not to talk
to strange men and not wander around the corner. We watched,
at a distance, the black children fly in and out of their houses,
calling strange sounds, bumping, pummeling, rolling, leaping, an
enchantment of 'wild beasts' my father never permitted us to be.
The best of the lower street were the times when everyone, adults
and children, marched up and down, carrying bright banners, and
to the sound of trumpets and drums sang, 'Ohlly Nohly, Ohlly
Nooo. Bumpera bumpera bump bump bum, Ohlly Noooo.' Ohlly
Nohly became our favorite rainy-day game, my brother banging
on a pot with a clothespin, I tootling through tissue paper on a
comb, high-stepping jauntily, roaring from hallway to kitchen to
bedroom our version of a revival hymn that must have begun
with 'Holy Lord, Oh Holy Lord.' We never could reconstruct the

bumpera bumpera words though we never forgot the tune.

It was on 98th Street, across from the tall long sinister stone wall on which the Third Avenue El trains came to rest, that I began to know I would never get to America. Though I learned in the kindergarten on 96th Street, among the many other English words that I taught my brother with a prissy, powerful passion, that I lived in America, it was not the America promised me in Warsaw or by the chocolate sweetness of my father's mouth. There were no sacks of candy and cookies, no dolls, no perennial summer that meant America. America was a stern man whose duty it was to cure us of being the cosseted spoiled little beasts our mother and her idiot sisters had allowed to flourish. At the far remove of decades, I can understand how infuriating it was for this indulged semibachelor to be saddled with a wife and two noisy children whom he hadn't the courage to abandon nor the wish to live with. Nothing to do but mold us with speed and force into absolute obedience, to make his world more tolerable and, I often suspected, to avenge himself on us for existing.

It was his habit to take a constitutional after dinner every night, a health measure he clung to all his life, as he clung to the bowel-health properties of the cooked prunes he ate every morning. One autumn twilight, when my brother was about four and I five and a half, we walked down 98th Street, toward Third Avenue, I averting my eyes from the tall black wall that deadened the other side of the street. Somewhere on Third Avenue we slowed at a row of shops, one of them a glory of brilliantly lit toys. Carefully, deliciously, my brother and I made our choices. He wanted the boat with big white sails to float in the bathtub or maybe the long line of trains that ran on tracks or maybe the red fire engine with a bell. I chose a big doll whose eyes opened and closed and a house with tiny beds and chairs and a clothes wringer in the kitchen. Or, maybe, the double pencil box crammed with coloring pencils, serious school pencils, a pen holder, and three pen points. As my brother lilted on in gay covetousness, the wariness that was already as much a part of me as blue eyes and wild blond hair made me suddenly turn. It was night. There was no mother, no father, on the dark street and I didn't know where we were. Feeling my fear, my brother turned, too, and began to cry heartbreakingly – no imperious shrieks for attention now, this was deep sorrow, the sorrow of the lost and abandoned. I felt, too, the cold skinlessness, the utter helplessness, the sickness of betrayal. I wanted to cry but I must not. As in the heavy rooms of my later dreams, as on the ship when we were separated from our sick mother, I told him not to worry, I would take care of him. Look – I wasn't afraid, I wasn't crying. By the time – and I cannot possibly estimate its length because the overwhelming fear and the effort to control it filled all dimensions – my mother burst out of a doorway to run to us, I had become, in some corner of my being, an old woman. It didn't matter that she hugged and kissed us and that my father carefully explained that it was merely a lesson to teach us to walk with him and not linger. I held them to be bad strangers and would not talk to either for days.

My brother sloughed off the incident, as he did many others; I remembered and judged, accumulating a sort of Domesday Book on my father's deeds. He sensed and feared it, and it was that fear on which I battened, the tears he could not make me shed freezing as an icy wall between us.

4
Fifth Floor

Our fifth-floor landing resembled in mood the *castellare* of old Italian towns, a cluster of dwellings capable of closing itself off as a fortress against invasion; no one passed our doors or walked our stairs to the roof without our knowledge and consent. We four families were thus somewhat isolated from the hamlet of 2029, special people, and as frequently happens with the isolated and special, we became a close tribe.

One of the neighbors on our landing was Fannie Herman, a skinny little sparrow, hopping, restless, a bewildered child in a strange room. Attached to the nervous spareness were large red hands and enormous bunioned feet, almost always bare. I became clearly aware of her – before that she had been, like most adults, an object in my landscape, like trees and street lamps – when I heard my mother speaking to her on the landing, in Yiddish and as to a child: 'Fannie, the holidays are coming soon. Let's clean your house, you and I together. Buy a broom and a scrubbing brush for the floors and lemon oil for the furniture. I'll give you some rags. We'll wipe off the dust and sweep away the feathers. We'll make it nice, you'll see.' I had come out of our apartment and could see Fannie's meager face sharpen in terror. 'Where will I buy? They talk English in the hardware store. I can't.' 'All right, Fannie, don't worry. Give me the money and I'll buy.'

Fannie rarely went out; the street was Gehenna. She had seen her first child, a little boy, smashed by a truck on the street. Her daughters ran wild and howled on the street, the street was where Mr. Herman's car shone and lured his girls away from their homework and piano practice. Like his wife, Mr. Herman was illiterate, but under his lumbering silence, my father said, there were courage and shrewdness. In a community of factory workers he was an entrepreneur, the owner of a small kosher slaughterhouse. More amazingly, he owned, drove, and washed a car like an American. It was he who ordered the milk to be delivered, bought the children their shoes and winter coats, and supplied the bread and chickens they ate each night.

Their night meal was a fairy ritual, incomprehensible, exotic, anarchic, very seductive to the child of a reasonably well-ordered household prickly with rules. Since the Hermans' day started at dawn, the children were shooed off to bed early in the evening, long before the rest of us were, and were asleep when their father arrived carrying two paper bags, one full of large rolls, the other wrapped around a headless chicken, eviscerated but still feathered. Without a greeting, he put the bags on the kitchen table, took off his cap and coat, and put a record of cantorial music on the Victrola in the next room. Fanny set herself firmly, purposefully, on a kitchen chair, and tucking the chicken into her lap, began to pluck it with impassioned speed, her thin arm like a fast piston. The feathers soared up and spiraled down to the floor, rocked and floated into the air and onto the table, little pin-feathers danced toward the sink where they settled, quivering like winged dandelion seeds. Fannie then took the chicken to the stove where she turned and turned it over an open flame to burn off remaining stubble. The smell was fatty and bitter, as satisfying as hot tar; the smell of incantations.

Singed and stippled, the chicken was dropped into a large pot of salted boiling water. There was none of the usual busyness of preparing a table, no place settings, no napkins, no plates, no tablecloth, nothing but the bag of rolls and a feather or two. Fannie kept poking impatiently at the chicken while Mr. Herman changed the records on his Victrola, from melancholy Hebrew liturgy to melancholy Yiddish folk songs. When Fannie decided the chicken was done, she scurried toward the children's bedroom shouting, 'Come eat!' The sleepy baby drooped in his high chair while the two girls in their underclothes (nightgowns were worn only by Lillian Gish) became quickly alert and plunged into the rolls, chewing them in big-cheeked mouthfuls while the chicken cooled in its pot on the table. Fannie poured off some of the soup for the next day's lunch and then, adroitly, marvelously, the chicken was torn apart. Fannie was first, plunging two fingers into the pot to pull out a wing for her baby, her miraculous resurrection of the dead boy. Then it was the father's turn; with a quick twist he had a leg and thigh. The practiced hands of the girls plucked out shreds of breast in the smooth, steady rhythm of picking buttercups in the park. There was no conversation; the only sounds were the chewing and the ululations of Yosele Rosenblatt from the Victrola. When the chicken and rolls were finished, the children went back to bed, their mouths and hands still silky with chicken fat. Fannie then fished for her own dinner – a back, a gizzard, a foot, the neck bones to suck, standing over the pot when everyone else had finished, in the habit of most of the neighborhood women. It was hard for me to leave, though it would soon be my bedtime, but Mr. Herman gave me his sign, pulling his suspenders off his shoulders, getting ready for bed. I shuffled through the feathers, scraped a few off my shoes at the door, and crossed the landing to 'wash your hands', 'clean your teeth'.

Miriam Herman was a quiet, neat child who read library books and did her homework promptly. She was the same age as my brother and was his playmate until he decided at seven never again to play with girls, who were more disgusting than snot. Her older sister, Tobie, was my age, a gangling, rawboned girl, tall like her father, skinny and jumpy like her mother. She was taut with belligerence, her very presence threatening. Rarely admitted to jump-rope games, she would kick at a rope in its snapping rounds to trip a jumper. She would stoop suddenly, and with the big hand of her mother, grab two marbles from the games of boys who protested but were too afraid to counterattack. Some of the Jewish women said she had a 'gilgul', a troublesome imp, in her. Others dismissed her as a 'wild beast'. Tobie should have hated me more actively than she did as the paragon of the prime neighborhood virtues. I practiced the piano, I was never fresh to my mother or father, I took care of my brother and baby sister (I was, in short, a coward), and Fannie kept shouting my praises at her wayward daughter, who wiped me off her earth, circling me as if I were a stump. The wrath she might have turned on me thundered around her mother instead.

The high dramas between Fannie and Tobie that pierced the Herman door and shot into the hallway mounted to frenzy when Tobie was left back in school while I skipped a class and, shortly after, won a bronze medal in a music contest. Fannie had insisted that like me – like Ruthie, like Rosie, like Sarah, like Beckie, et al – Tobie must learn to play the piano. Good-natured and affluent Mr. Herman bought a piano, a baby grand, one of the wonders of our lives. Miriam practiced but Tobie could no more be tamed to music than to spelling or arithmetic. She kept on running and kicking, her long stick legs clattering down the five flights of stairs and onto the sidewalk to kick balls, cats, garbage pails; her only pauses of quiet were the minutes she sat in her father's car waiting for him to take her for a ride. The conflict between the piano and the car became a monumental struggle. Having satisfied Fannie with a baby grand, Mr. Herman cared little how and when it was used. He didn't work on the Sabbath but he wasn't particularly observant since no one had bothered to teach him the elaborate rules. So, on Saturday mornings while the prayers of downstairs Mr. Liebowitz crackled out his window, Mr. Herman drove his car around the neighboring streets, and when he grew lonely, called for his girls. Miriam had usually finished her practicing, Tobie hadn't started and wouldn't. When the auto horn sounded its signal, Fannie ran to bar the door. Tobie was not to go before she finished practicing. The girl, taller and strong with rage, tore the door open, and leaning long-necked and poisonous toward her mother, like a snake about to spit, yelled, 'Crazy mother! Teeny mother! Teeny, crazy mother with the big feet! Teeny mother with the big bunions! Crazy mother with the big ugly bunion feet!' continuing the howling litany as she rocketed down the stairs. Fannie dashed back to the street window of her flat, flung it open, and screamed her spate of curses to the street and the heavens. 'May the piankele be buried in the earth! May the machinkele be swallowed by the earth! May black cholera carry off both the piankele and the machinkele! May they suffer of boils! May they succumb to a dark fate!' until my mother stopped her, reminding her that she would soon have to nurse her baby and she didn't want to sour her milk, did she.

The next day Fannie would be extraordinarily subdued. She was afraid, she had cursed and would be cursed. It was on those days that an unexpected breeze, a touch that lifted the hem of a curtain, would bring her weeping to our door, the baby in her arms. The Angel of Death had flown in! And then the rocking chair had begun to rock itself! The Angel of Death was sitting in it, sitting and waiting! He was waiting to grab her baby as he had grabbed her other boy. My mother took her back after a while to her own apartment, explaining a breeze, a careless push against a rocker. Reason worked but never for long. Though she trusted my mother almost slavishly, the Angel of Death was closer to Fannie, possibly her most intimate relation.

It might have been because I felt banished by my mother's

absorption with my new baby sister – no time to make me a
new pongee sailor dress, no time to hear me sing 'Over the Hill'
with heartbreaking quavers – that I spent more and more time
with Fannie. I told her about the stories I read and complained
about my teachers; sometimes I played a sad Chopin waltz on her
baby grand. She told me in Yiddish and her few English words of
her childhood. She was orphaned at six in a small Polish town and
taken into a big house as the most minor servant whose job it was
to scrub all the outside stairs in all weathers. Her bed was a pile of
sacks in the cellar and her food was bread and a potato or apple she
stole from the cellar bins. Mr. Herman was a stable boy for the same
house, also an orphan, so they got married. It was an awful story to
me – the imagined cold, the imagined hunger – like a story
of starvelings in Grimm. But she spoke without anger or sadness;
these were her facts, neither just nor unjust.

One late holiday afternoon, while her baby was sleeping and
Miriam and Tobie were out for an auto ride, Fannie said to me,
words and hands mumbling, 'You know, Katie, you know what I
want more than anything, except my children should be healthy?
I would like to know how to write my name.' She couldn't find a
pencil or paper but there was the great expanse of the dusty piano.
Guiding her finger, I traced with her 'Fannie, Fannie, Fannie,'
countless times through the wide gray space. She was enchanted
and indefatigable. From time to time I did try her with a pencil
on paper but her hand was too awkward for the small, tight
movements. She became discouraged, bleakly defeated. So back to
new accumulations of dust on the piano, on the big unused dining
table, on the chests of drawers. Best, when the frosts came, was
melting her name into the icy windows, her finger skating along
fairly briskly without my help. When she had traced 'Fannie' in
dust and frost thousands of times, I suggested 'Herman.' No
success at all, she wouldn't even try. When I asked her why not, she
looked at me worriedly and said after a long silence, 'It's his name
and I don't know my own other one. So maybe Fannie is enough.'
I tried 'Herman' again and she tried a bit to please me but it went
poorly.

I had to spend more time with our new baby when my mother
began to work at selling corsets from door to door in the late
afternoons, and my father complained I wasn't practicing enough.
There was talk of moving out of Lafontaine Avenue and ultimately
we did. I don't know if Fannie ever wrote her name again, although

I liked for a long time to picture her, and still do, etching the dust with her forefinger, curve after careful curve.

The Haskells lived next door to the Hermans. He rarely spoke, which didn't matter (we children rarely connected with the men, the voices that filled our world were those of women, the Mothers, large stoves to warm at, sofas to read on, home base, an apple after school), but he did have one godlike gesture. He and his wife, whom I liked to look at because she resembled a melting vanilla cone, had no children and spent much of their Sundays reading the Sunday *American*. On Sunday evenings Mr. Haskell rapped on our door and without a word, like a lord, handed us the 'jokes' and the delectable magazine with its tales of high society, curly pictures, and horrifying medical stories illustrated in toothsome detail.

Mrs. Haskell avoided the Herman children. Tobie was beyond her understanding; her gentle, cowlike decorum knew no defense against such ferocity. She found us easier, especially myself; my brother moved too fast and erratically. She was, I now realize, lonely, and being shy of the bustling women around her, welcomed the snooping of a curious little girl. One Indian summer day when the four doors of the landing were open for cooler air, she invited me into her neat apartment, the furniture still and stolid, the curtains in stiff, regular folds, standing like school monitors. She told me to sit down and gave me a Lorna Doone and a Fig Newton, asking politely how school was and was my father going on strike. She had read about it in the papers and hoped it wouldn't happen. And did I know the world was going to end on October 20? Mr. Anderson, the leader of her Pure Christian Believers meetings, had said so and that God would take only his special people with him while he destroyed the rest. I believed her; I believed everything that was strange, preferably cataclysmic. Was Mr. Haskell going, too? No, he wasn't a Believer and so God couldn't, of course, include him among the Protected. I wanted yearningly to be taken, not to have to suffer a terrible holocaust like the people trying to flee the blood-red eruptions of Vesuvius that hung in our hallway. I doubted, though, that her Christian God with his blond hair and soft blond beard would take a Jewish child. We had to depend on the dour old man with the blazing eyes and windy white beard, like Moses who was inclined to favor few, if any.

Mrs. Haskell also told me that she was beginning to prepare for the Coming. Everything in her house, every salt shaker and frying pan was to be scrubbed, the sheets and towels boiled, every fork and knife polished – rather like Yom Kippur preparations. And then she was going to get herself ready, a bath every day for two weeks, her hair washed every other day, her toenails cut, the wax taken out of her ears, all of her clean and pure.

For several days I looked for her when I returned from school but she, almost always housebound, was away. I waited and watched, running out one evening as I heard her unlock her door. She was carrying fancy boxes like the kind Barbara La Marr opened when a rich, infatuated admirer sent her a present. The boxes bore the noble letters, MACY's, a legendary world where no one else I knew had ever wandered. She invited me to come in and, still in her hat and coat, opened the large box from which she lifted, very daintily, a long white nightgown with long sleeves and a high neck. It was beautiful. I wanted one like it and to live among blond angels who sang all day and not to die as part of a mountainous garbage heap. Still, I couldn't ask her to take me along, worried and quiet as she showed me her new pair of white laced oxfords like those the school nurse wore. A few days later she arrived with two smaller Macy boxes, one with a white nurse's cap in it and another that held the whitest cotton gloves. I asked her if she would go to bed to wait, in her new shoes and cap and gloves, seeing her laid out like a corpse. She said no, she was going into Eternal Life, not ordinary death, and would sit on her sofa covered with its new white sheet.

The anxious days went by, very slow and too fast. I could hardly speak to Mrs. Haskell, who had become as awesome as the Statue of Liberty. My mother was annoyed with me, inattentive, restless, brooding, darting toward the hallway whenever I thought I heard the Haskell door opening. Once my mother asked me, 'What's the matter with you?' The answer was, 'Nothing'. We learned early to keep worries about God and sex to ourselves.

The tremendous day came. I awoke very early and slipped quietly out of our apartment and down into the street to observe warnings: people falling about, dogs trembling, cats dead, the sky glowering menace. The sky was blue, the clouds were tumbling like clowns, two sparrows picked at the manure left by the old-clothes-man's horse, Grandpa Paladino in his droopy pants and Old Country undershirt was frowning at his tomato plant. In school that day I kept watching the sky, waiting for it to crack open like an immense ripe plum and pour fire and black smoke. I ran home from school at lunchtime, the October wind snapping at my bare knees. Mrs. Haskell's door was closed but I saw her clearly in her white clothing on her white sofa, docile and patient as always. Lunch was my favorite, broad noodles with pot cheese and white raisins, sugar and cinnamon sprinkled on top, and the pleasure it gave brought solace and relief as well. Maybe this End of the World, like Christmas and Easter Sunday, was for Christians only, the good ones flying gently up to Heaven, guided by God's hand, and the bad stabbed by lightning and dropped into the ocean. The Jews would go on doing their homework, cooking, scolding, working in factories.

What about Mrs. Polanski, our janitor? What about the black Gypsies who wandered through the streets, begging like cursing? Would Miss Monahan, my favorite teacher, be in school the next day? Mr. Jameson the principal, Mr. Keenan who opened the school doors? Where would all the *goyim* of my life be? I would miss the picture in Christian kitchens of the fat-legged baby who sat in the lap of the pale lady with the golden ring around her head. Who would keep a little goat tied to a stake in a backyard? Would I ever be able to touch, very lightly (it might be a sin), a real Christmas tree? Who would talk like singing, as Patrick the milkman did? Would I never again see the thin blue eyelids, fine as butterfly wings, of Jimmy and Mary O'Neill? The world would be as full of holes as an old blanket but, nevertheless, I would stay triumphantly alive.

The night of the 20th disappeared and so did the following days and nights. I saw Mr. Haskell go to work and return, but no Mrs. Haskell. All the Christians were in school and the Italians sat on their porches, but I wasn't worried much about them because they were just Jews who didn't talk Yiddish. They didn't go to synagogues, either, but a lot of Jews didn't. Most of them went to church only on their high holy days, like Jews. They bothered their kids, kissed them and shouted at them, like Jews. Their old people, mumbling in old languages, also sat in the big chairs and were listened to. The clinching proof of this conviction was a rumor – I could hardly believe it – that the fat-legged baby who grew up to be a sad man wearing a circle of thorns was a Jew. Killed by other Jews. (That I couldn't believe at all; Jews didn't kill, they were killed in pogroms.)

Much happened during the next few days. My brother broke two front teeth, somehow my fault. The nurse with the terrible boiling face found nits in my hair and I walked home from school wrapped in flames of anger and humiliation. I hated the nurse, I hated my mother, I hated my brother who danced around me singing, 'She's got nits. My dirty sister's got nits.' When we reached the outer stairs of our apartment house, I ran ahead and turned to kick him full in the face, intending to kill him, or at least break his taunting mouth. There were, of course, consequences, and for days I seethed, forgetting Mrs. Haskell, until her door opened one afternoon as I arrived from school. With her usual courtesy, she asked me to visit with her for a few minutes. She offered me a Tootsie Roll and a new penny from the pocket of her pink flowered housedress and then turned to polishing her furniture, slowly, carefully. While she polished, she told me that God had come on October 20th. Not really, actually, come into her house but she had seen his long, pale hand in the sky pointing toward her and heard his gentle voice say, 'Patience', 'Soon', 'Keep ready'. Mr. Anderson had said the same thing at last night's meeting and would let them know when to start their purifications again, when to put on their white robes. Would she let me know the next time? No – she gave me a Fig Newton – this time it would have to be a secret for the Pure only.

Whenever we met, we avoided each other's eyes, although Mr. Haskell nodded politely. Then came a roaring Sicilian wedding, came the funeral of a grandfather who had a gnawing crab in his belly, came Rudolph Valentino in *The Sheik*, came the first bitter winds and conflicts over wearing lumpy, itchy, shaming winter underwear, came the flu whose fever made beautiful pictures swim in my head. Fannie Herman found pink worms in little David's anus and almost tore our door down in her panic. Esther Goldstein, sixteen and incandescent, so luminous that I could hardly look at her, said I was 'odd' and killed me. Time erased and destroyed its events to make room for others, while Barney Google, the Captain and the Kids, and Mutt and Jeff kept coming every Sunday evening from the Haskells'. No news, ever again, of a Visitation.

Immediately to the left of us lived the Silverbergs. Manya Silverberg was dashing and pretty, younger than my mother and more stylish, with an impressive repertory of clothing that she made herself. She cooked well and made cookies that were more 'American' than my mother's little pockets of hard tack known as cheese cookies. Like my mother, she was soft-spoken, a reader and a learner; both moved like debased aristocrats through the slatternly street of dented garbage cans on their way to English classes at the local public library. I loved Mrs. Silverberg as I loved Lillian Gish, as I loved the pretty young aunts, still in Warsaw, in the photographs I stared at for long times, trying to invent voices for them, improvising dialogues with them. She became a substitute aunt. And then she disappeared, after a midnight explosion. Since the bed my brother and I shared was nearest the door, we reached it first when we heard loud voices in the hallway. We were quickly shooed back to bed, our bedroom door closed on us firmly. But I had already seen the high color, the brown burning eyes, the waterfalls of earrings, brooches, and layers of pearls heaped like a five-and-ten counter on the ordinarily chaste neck. On the disordered dark hair a wide, swooping, arrogant hat and a big shawl draped around her shoulders like a movie star's evening cloak. High, loud, without a pause, in a torrential rain of words she spoke of going out to a fancy restaurant, of men, many men, waiting for her, of meeting with her lover, Rudolph Valentino, of dancing to cabaret music. She shrieked happiness hideously.

It was difficult after that to be absolutely certain of what was sane or insane, one world slid in and out of the other with confusing ease, particularly confusing when the word '*meshugge*', crazy, was used so profligately for stamping and hollering with a Victrola record, for begging for new skates, for destroyed Mrs. Silverberg.

The lower landings were more remote, shaping their own looser tribes. A number of our friends lived in various sections of the house and we knew some of their parents, of little consequence to us unless they were unusually hospitable or unusually forbidding. The only fourth-floor family that steadily interested me were the Liebowitzes. Ida Liebowitz, who was in my class, wore long stockings and long sleeves winter and summer, a cruel piece of religious fanaticism according to the other mothers. She had no skates, wasn't permitted to go to the movies, ever, and on Saturdays read her library books on her fire escape away from the eyes of her father, Yontiff ('Holiday'), who would not permit the handling of *goyish* books on the Sabbath. He once caught her at it and tore the book out of her hands, thrusting it far onto the empty lot. There were fierce, unspecified punishments for losing library books, a sin as terrible as stealing or playing doctor. Ida might be sent to prison or left back in school or made to stay in every afternoon writing a hundred times 'I must not lose library books.' We all worried. Ida was not permitted to leave her house, the free-roaming boys would not stoop to search for a girl's book, and the girls, eager for the drama of the search, were told to 'stay home and mind your own business.' In any case, we hadn't much time. Last night's gefilte fish wrapped in its quivering coat of jelly and the chunks of *challa* were already on the table to be gobbled fast so we could get to the Belmont movie theater when it opened.

We almost immediately lost interest in the book and in the Liebowitzes, who soon moved to what the women called a more 'kosher' neighborhood, with more piety, fewer *goyim*, and fewer of the even more dangerous Jewish *goyim* who let their children skate on Saturday and go to libraries and movies on Saturday, handling money to view the abominations of Sodom and Gomorrah. All we ever knew of Mrs. Liebowitz was that she wore a dull brown wig and never joined the conclaves of women and baby carriages on the street; she was as cloistered as a nun. He was bearded and frowning, like a picture-book pirate, except that he wore a dark hat. The Liebowitzes' door was always tight shut, even in the heat of August, and we kids who were free with several houses, running in and out except of course when floors were being washed or a new baby had been born, never saw the inside of their apartment. Nor did we play much with the Liebowitz children, who were not allowed in the corrupting street except to go directly to school and come directly home. Although I hardly knew them, I liked them or rather the idea of them, their secret lives, their fierce separateness, a cave people, a woods people like those who glowered out of fairy-tale darknesses. I missed them after they moved, very briefly.

5
The Movies and
Other Schools

Life on Lafontaine offered several schools. School-school, P.S. 59, was sometimes nice, as when I was chosen to be Prosperity in the class play, blond, plump, dressed in a white pillow case banded with yellow and green crepe paper, for the colors of grasses and grain, and waving something like a sheaf of wheat. The cringing days were usually Fridays, when arithmetic flash cards, too fast, too many, blinded me and I couldn't add or subtract the simplest numbers. (For many years, into adulthood, I carried around a sack of churning entrails on Friday mornings.) The library, which made me my own absolutely special and private person with a card that belonged to no one but me, offered hundreds of books, all mine and no tests on them, a brighter, more generous school than P.S. 59. The brightest, most informative school was the movies. We learned how tennis was played and golf, what a swimming pool was and what to wear if you ever got to drive a car. We learned how tables were set, 'How do you do? Pleased to meet you', how primped and starched little girls should be, how neat and straight boys should be, even when they were temporarily ragamuffins. We learned to look up soulfully and make our lips tremble to warn our mothers of a flood of tears, and though they didn't fall for it (they laughed), we kept practicing. We learned how regal mothers were and how stately fathers, and of course we learned about Love, a very foreign country like maybe China or Connecticut. It was smooth and slinky, it shone and rustled. It was petals with Lillian Gish, gay flags with Marion Davies, tiger stripes with Rudolph Valentino, dog's eyes with Charlie Ray. From what I could see, and I searched, there was no Love on the block, nor even its fairy-tale end, Marriage. We had only Being Married, and that included the kids, a big crowded barrel with a family name stamped on it. Of course, there was Being Married in the movies, but except for the terrible cruel people in rags and scowls, it was as silky as Love. Fathers kissed their wives and children when they came home from work and spoke to them quietly and nobly, like kings, and never shouted or hit if the kids came in late or dirty. Mothers in crisp dresses stroked their children's heads tenderly as they presented them with the big ringletted doll and the football Grandma had sent, adding, 'Run off and play, darlings.' 'Darling', 'dear', were movie words, and we had few grandmothers, most of them dead or in shadowy conversation pieces reported from At Home, the Old Country. And 'Run off and play' was so superbly refined, silken gauze to the rough wool of our hard-working mothers whose rules were to feed their children, see that they were warmly dressed in the wintertime, and run to the druggist on Third Avenue for advice when they were sick. Beyond that it was mostly 'Get out of my way.' Not all the mothers were so impatient. Miltie's mother helped him with his arithmetic homework; my mother often found us amusing and laughed with and at us a lot. From other apartments, on rainy afternoons: Joey – 'What'll I do, Maaa?' His Mother – '*Va te ne*! *Gherradi*!' (the Italian version of 'Get out of here'); Lily – 'What'll I do, Maaa?' Mrs. Stavicz – 'Scratch your ass on a broken bottle.' I sometimes wished my mother would say colorful, tough things like that but I wasn't sure I wouldn't break into tears if she did, which would make her call me a '*pianovi chasto*' (as I remember the Polish phrase), a delicate meringue cake that falls apart easily, which would make me cry more, which would make her more lightly contemptuous, and so on. Despite my occasional wish to see her as one of the big-mouth, storming women, I was willing to settle for her more modest distinction, a lady who won notebooks in her English class at the library and sang many tunes from 'Polish operettas' that, with later enlightenment, I realized were *The Student Prince* and *The Merry Widow*.

Being Married had as an important ingredient a nervous father. There must have been other kitchens, not only ours, in which at about seven o'clock, the fathers' coming-home time, children were warned, 'Now remember, Papa is coming home soon. He's nervous from working in the factory all day and riding in the crowded El. Sit quiet at the table, don't laugh, don't talk.' It was hard not to giggle at the table, when my brother and I, who played with keen concentration a game of mortal enemies at other times, became close conspirators at annoying Them by making faces at each other.

The muffled giggles were stopped by a shout of 'Respect!' and a long black look, fork poised like a sword in midair while no one breathed. After the silent meal, came the part we disliked most, the after-dinner lecture. There were two. The first was The Hard Life of the Jewish worker, the Jewish father, the deepest funereal sounds unstopped for the cost of electricity (a new and lovely toy but not as pretty as throbbing little mazda lamps) for which he had to pay an immense sum each time we switched it on and off, like the wastrels we were. Did we think butter cost a penny a pound that we slathered it on bread as if it were Coney Island mud pies? Those good expensive shoes he bought us (he was an expert shoe worker, a maker of samples, and tortured us with embarrassment when he displayed his expertise to the salesman, so don't try to fool him), which were old and scuffed and dirty within a week, did we know how much bloody sweat was paid for them? The second lecture was the clever one whose proud, sententious repetitions I listened to with shame for him, wanting to put my head down not to see my handsome father turn into a vaudeville comic whose old monologues strained and fell. This lecture was usually inspired by my brother who, in spite of the 'nervous' call, dashed at my father as soon as he heard the key in the lock with 'Hello, Pa. Gimme a penny?' That led it off: 'You say you want a penny, *only* a penny. I've got dimes and quarters and half-dollars in my pockets, you say, so what's a penny to me? Well, let's see. If you went to the El station and gave the man four cents, he wouldn't let you on the train, you'd need another penny. If Mama gave you two cents for a three-cent ice cream cone, would Mrs. Katz in the candy store give it to you? If Mama had only forty-eight cents for a forty-nine-cent chicken, would the butcher give it to her?' And on and on, a carefully rehearsed long slow aria, with dramatic runs of words and significant questioning pauses. Once or twice I heard my mother mutter as she went out of the room, 'That Victrola record again,' but her usual policy was to say nothing. She was not afraid of my father, nor particularly in awe of him. (I heard him say frequently how fresh she was, but with a smile, not the way he said it to us.)

In none of my assiduous eavesdropping on the street did I ever hear any mention of unhappy marriage or happy marriage. Married was married. Although a Jewish divorce was a singularly easy matter except for the disgrace it carried, the Jewish women were as firmly imbedded in their marriages as the Catholic. A divorce was as unthinkable as adultery or lipstick. No matter what

– beatings, infidelity, drunkenness, verbal abuse, outlandish demands – no woman could run the risk of making her children fatherless. Marriage and children were fate, like being skinny, like skeletal Mr. Roberts, or humpbacked, like the leering watchman at the hat factory. *'Es is mir beschert,'* 'It is my fate,' was a common sighing phrase, the Amen that closed hymns of woe.

My mother didn't accept her fate as a forever thing. She began to work during our school hours after her English classes had taught her as much as they could, and while I was still young, certainly no more than ten, I began to get her lecture on being a woman. It ended with extraordinary statements, shocking in view of the street mores. 'Study. Learn. Go to college. Be a schoolteacher,' then a respected, privileged breed, 'and don't get married until you have a profession. With a profession you can have men friends and even children, if you want. You're free. But don't get married, at least not until you can support yourself and make a careful choice. Or don't get married at all, better still.' This never got into 'My mother said' conversations with my friends. I sensed it to be too outrageous. My mother was already tagged 'The Princess' because she never went into the street unless fully, carefully dressed: no grease-stained housedress, no bent, melted felt slippers. Rarely, except when she was pregnant with my little sister, did she stop for conversations on the street. She was one of the few in the building who had gone to classes, the only mother who went out alone at night to join her mandolin group. She was sufficiently marked, and though I was proud of her difference, I didn't want to report her as altogether eccentric. In the community fabric, as heavy as the soups we ate and the dark, coarse 'soldier's bread' we chomped on, as thick as the cotton on which we practiced our cross-stitch embroidery, was the conviction that girls were to marry as early as possible, the earlier the more triumphant. (Long after we moved from the area, my mother, on a visit to Lafontaine to see appealing, inept little Fannie Herman who had for many years been her charge and mine, met Mrs. Roth, who asked about me. When my mother said I was going to Hunter College, Mrs. Roth, looking both pleased and sympathetic, said, '*My* Helen married a man who makes a nice living, a laundry man. Don't worry, your Katie will find a husband soon.' She knew that some of the boys of the block wound up in City College, but a girl in college? From a pretty, polite child, I must have turned into an ugly, bad-tempered shrew whom no one would have. Why else would my marrying years be spent in college?)

I never saw my mother and father kiss or stroke each other as people did in the movies. In company she addressed him, as did most of the Jewish women, by our family name, a mark of respectful distance. They inhabited two separate worlds, he adventuring among anti-Semites to reach a shadowy dungeon called 'Factory', where he labored ceaselessly. In the evening he returned to her world for food, bed, children, and fighting. We were accustomed to fighting: the boys and, once in a while, fiery little girls tearing at each other in the street; bigger Italian boys punching and being punched by the Irish gangs that wandered in from Arthur Avenue; females fighting over clotheslines – whose sheets were blocking whose right to the sun – bounced around the courtyard constantly. The Genoese in the houses near 178th Street never spoke to the Sicilians near 179th Street except to complain that somebody's barbaric little southern slob had peed against a northern tree. To my entranced ears and eyes, the Sicilians seemed always to win, hotter, louder, faster with *'Fangu'* – the southern version of *'Fa' in culo'* (up yours) – than the aristocrats who retired before the Sicilians could hit them with *'Mortacci'* – the utterly insupportable insult. My brother and I fought over who grabbed the biggest apple, who hid the skate key, and where he put my baby picture, I lying on a white rug with my bare ass showing, a picture he threatened to pass among his friends and humiliate me beyond recovery. I would have to kill him.

These sorts of fighting were almost literally the spice of daily life, deliciously, lightly menacing, grotesque and entertaining. The fighting between my mother and father was something else entirely, at times so threatening that I still, decades later, cringe in paralyzed stupidity, as if I were being pelted with stones, when I hear a man shouting. The fights often concerned our conduct and my mother's permissiveness. My father had a rich vocabulary which he shaped into theatrical phrases spoken in a voice as black and dangerous as an open sewer. The opening shot was against my brother, who was six or seven when the attacks began. He was becoming a wilderness boy, no sense, no controls, dirty, disobedient, he did badly in school (not true: with a minimum of attention he managed mediocrity). There was no doubt that he would become a bum, then a thief, wind up alone in a prison cell full of rats, given one piece of bread a day and one cup of dirty water. He would come out a gangster and wind up in the electric chair.

When it was my turn, I was disobedient and careless; I didn't
do my homework when I should, I didn't practice enough, my
head was always in a book, I was always in the street running
wild with the Italian and Polish beasts. I didn't take proper care
of my brother, I climbed with boys, I ran with boys, I skated with
them on far streets. Mr. Kaplan had seen me and told him. And
how would this life, this playing with boys, end? I would surely
become a street girl, a prostitute, and wind up being shipped to a
filthy, diseased brothel crawling with hairy tropical bugs, in Buenos
Aires. My mother's response was sharp and short: we acted like
other children and played like other children; it was he who was at
fault, asking more of us than he should. And enough about prisons
and electric chairs and brothels. He went on shouting, entranced
by his gorgeous words and visions, until she left the room to wash
the dishes or scrub the kitchen floor. We, of course, had heard
everything from our bedroom; the oratory was as much for us as
for our mother. When the big rats in the windowless cell came to
our ears, my brother began to shake with terror beyond crying. I
tried to comfort him, as accustomed a role as trying to maim him.
I didn't know what a street girl was, and I certainly didn't know
what a brothel was, but I wasn't afraid – I was too angry. If
our father hated us so, why didn't he go away? I didn't examine
consequences, who would feed us and pay the rent. I just wanted
him out, out, dead.

Other fights were about money, and that, too, involved us. How
dare she, without consulting him, change from a fifty-cent-a-lesson
piano teacher to another – and who knows how good *he* was?
– who charged a dollar? What about the embroidered tablecloth
and the stone bowl with the pigeons that she bought from the Arab
peddler, that crook. Did she realize how hard he had to work to pay
for our school supplies each fall? And add to that the nickel for
candy to eat at the movies every Saturday, and the ten cents each
for the movie and the three cents for ice-cream cones on Friday
nights. And God only knew how much money she slipped us for
the sweet garbage we chewed on, which would certainly rot our
teeth, and where would he get the money for dentists? Maybe she
thought she was still in her shop in Warsaw, dancing and singing
and spilling money like a fool. And on and on it went. These
tirades, too, were answered very briefly. Our lives were meager
enough. Did he ever think of buying us even the cheapest toy, like
the other fathers did, instead of stashing every spare penny in the

bank and taking it out only for his relatives? The ignorant Italians he so despised, they had celebrations for their children. Where were our birthday presents?

Long silences followed these fights and we became messengers. 'Tell your mother to take my shoes to the shoemaker.' 'Aw, Pa, I'm doing my homework. Later.' 'Tell your mother I have no clean shirts.' 'Aw, Pa, I'm just sitting down to practice. I'll tell her later.' We used the operative words 'homework' and 'practice' mercilessly while he seethed at our delays. My mother heard all these instructions but it was her role neither to notice nor to obey. Those were great days and we exploited our roles fattily, with enormous vengeful pleasure.

One constant set of squabbles that didn't circle around us concerned her relaxed, almost loose judgments of other people. She showed no sympathy when he complained about the nigger sweeper in the factory who talked back to him, when he complained about the Italian who reeked of garlic and almost suffocated him in the train. Most loudly he complained about her availability, spoiling his sleep, letting his supper get cold, neglecting her own children, to run to any Italian idiot who didn't know to take care of her own baby. Let them take care of their own convulsions or get some Wop neighbor to help. It was disgraceful that she sat on Mrs. Santini's porch in open daylight trying to teach her not to feed her infant from her own mouth. If the fat fool wanted to give it germs, let her. If it died, she'd, next year, have another; they bred like rabbits. Why didn't my mother mind her own business, what the hell did these people, these foreign ignoramuses, mean to her? The answer was short and always the same, 'Es is doch a mench,' yet these are human beings, the only religious training we ever had, perhaps quite enough.

There were fights with no messengers, no messages, whispered fights when the door to our bedroom was shut tight and we heard nothing but hissing. The slow unfolding of time and sophistications indicated that these were fights about women, women my father saw some of those evenings when he said he was going to a Workmen's Circle meeting. There was no more 'Tell your mother,' 'Tell your father,' and except for the crying of our baby, no more evening sounds. No Caruso, no Rosa Ponselle, no mandolin practice, no lectures. My father busied himself with extra piecework, 'skiving' it was called, cutting with breathtaking delicacy leaf and daisy designs into the surface of the sample shoes to be shown to buyers. She, during one such period, crocheted a beaded bag, tiny beads, tiny stitches. We watched, struck dumb by their skill, and because it was no time to open our mouths about anything, anything at all. The silence was dreadful, a creeping, dark thing, a night alley before the murderer appears. The furniture was waiting to be destroyed, the windows to be broken, by a terrible storm. We would all be swept away, my brother and I to a jungle where wild animals would eat us, my parents and the baby, separated, to starve and burn alone in a desert. School now offered the comforts of a church, the street its comforting familiarities, unchanging, predictable. We stayed out as long as we could, dashing up for a speedy supper, and down again. On rainy nights we read a lot, we went to bed early, anything to remove us from our private-faced parents, who made us feel unbearably shy.

One spring evening, invited to jump Double Dutch with a few experts, uncertain that I could leap between two ropes whipping in rapid alternation at precisely the exact moment, and continue to stay between them in small fast hops from side to side, I admitted a need, urgent for some time, to go to the toilet. I ran up the stairs to find our door locked, an extraordinary thing. Maybe they had run away. Maybe they had killed each other. Sick with panic, I kept trying the door, it wouldn't give. Then I heard the baby making squirmy, sucking baby noises. No matter what, my mother would never leave the baby, and anyway, maybe they were doing their whispering fighting again. Still uneasy, I knocked on the Hermans' door and asked to use their toilet. When I came out, I asked Fannie Herman if she knew whether my parents were at home. Yes, she said. Her door was wide open and she would have seen or heard them come out, but they hadn't. The Double Dutch on the street was finished when I got down so I joined the race, boys and girls, around the block, running hard, loving my pumping legs and my swinging arms and my open mouth swallowing the breeze. When most of the kids had gone home and it was time for us, too, I couldn't find my brother, who was hiding from me to destroy my power and maybe get me into trouble. I went up alone. The door had been unlocked, and as I walked uneasily through the long hallway of our railroad flat with wary steps, I heard sounds from the kitchen. My mother was sitting on a kitchen chair, her feet in a basin of water. My father was kneeling before her on spread newspaper. Her plump foot rested in his big hand while he cut her toenails, flashing his sharp work knife, dexterous, light, and swift. She was splashing him a little, playing the water with her free foot. They were making jokes, lilting, laughing. Something, another branch in the twisted tree that shaded our lives, was going to keep us safe for a while.

6
Summer Fruits

One of the summer pleasures was to sit at the kitchen window and listen to the polyphony of courtyard noises out of twenty other kitchens. Early in the morning came the screech of clotheslines being pulled to and from the big pole at the back of the yard that supported the lines of both 2029 and 2027, an admirable grandfather pole sustaining so many children. At that time there wasn't much talk across the yard; there was too much to do, like getting the kids' breakfast, a nice collection of noises: 'Finish your breakfast, you can't go out before you do'. '*Schloch* [slob]! Look what you did to the dress I just ironed'; 'Tie your laces so you don't fall'; in several weary tones, 'Don't bother me. Get dressed first and then you'll talk'; 'No, you can't go to Mannie's house, his sister has chicken pox'; 'Here's a nickel for a new ball; if you lose this one, you won't get another.' The heavier sounds of exasperation came later with the heavier heat of the day: a crash, a slap, and 'I'll break your hands if you touch that china closet again,' and as leitmotif, a broken chorus of '*Geddade*', also pronounced '*Gerrare*' and '*Gherradi*', depending on the national origin of the shouter. The litany of Jewish curses, calls, and wisecracks that became bright spots in immigrant literature were lacking in our courtyard. We never heard the famous bread call: 'Ma, cut me off and butter me up and throw me down a piece of bread.' Ours was the less colorful, less musical, 'Ma, I want a piece of bread.' (Not from 5B in 2029, though; this was too much country manners for my parents and strictly forbidden.) Of the numerous references to trolley cars quoted in the literature, we never heard the gorgeously picturesque 'May a trolley car grow in your belly that you may piss nickels and shit transfers [or vice versa].' My father would answer my mother's conjectures when he was in a playful mood with 'If, if.

If my grandmother had wheels, she'd be a trolley car,' and better yet, 'If my grandmother had a penis, she'd be my grandfather.' The most stimulating local curse came from Ruthie Rosen's kitchen, on the third floor of 2027: 'May you grow like an onion with your head in the ground and your feet in the air.' During my early encounters with this image, I examined Rosie to see if her head was bending to the ground and her feet flying off the sidewalk, as her mother said they must be. She stayed the same mouse-faced little girl, skinny and erect as a ruler – another ground for skepticism.

The afternoon sounds were 'Practice. Go practice. Now, I say,' and the assembled pianos cranked out the wobbling sounds of an immense broken merry-go-round. From three pianos the thumping, sure or tentative, of 'Für Elise' competing with tortured gropings from everyone's primer, 'Bayer's Book.' From the first floor of 2029, a merry reckless bumbling through Tchaikovsky's 'Troika' colliding with a comet of scales from the first floor of 2027. When it all faded out, the crickets on the long Monterey lots covered the afternoon with their rustling taffeta sound. The 'Ole Close' men called as the sun began to pale, never doing a brisk trade. Old clothes were sent to relatives in the Old Country. The yard singers did better with their mixed repertoire of 'O Sole Mio', 'Eli Eli', 'Delia, Oh Delia', and 'Daisy, Daisy'. It wasn't only the singing and the romantic presence of a street singer but the luxury of giving away money for something intangible that spurred us kids to hop around our mothers nagging for two pennies, three. We wrapped them securely in large wads of newspaper and flung them down, feeling like lords. The hour of clanging pots and 'Wash yourself, you look like the coalman,' was the hour of the opening and closing doors and 'Hello, Pop,' followed by threnodies of complaint. They were short bursts, stifled by a large, round 'Shut up. Let me sit and have my supper first.' During the quiet of supper, the birds who had been hiding from the kids on the lot all day began to call and sing a little, timidly, as if they were still scared of boys with sticks. The later hours were parents' time, a rich tapestry – if one could stay awake long enough – of Victrola horns spilling jigs and reels, Alma Gluck, Yosele Rosenblatt, Caruso, 'When You and I Were Young, Maggie', Sousa marches, flowing through and over and around the banging of chairs and doors, the weeping and shouting of adult quarrels, never quite clear enough for the clouds of music around them. Very late and the yard's final 'Good night', the small gasps and whistles of snoring from open bedroom windows.

The shapes of things changed in the summertime. The smoke from the hat factory next door became fat and slow, oozing like a chorus of fat ladies in pink, blue, yellow, purple dresses. The edges of buildings shook and melted. Cold, dry faces opened and glistened with sweat. The spikey park flowers bent and hung. The sidewalks sweated, the walls sweated, and out of the heat and wetness came heavily ornate, lazy bunches of grapes, the opulent shine and swell of plums, the rubies of pomegranate seeds set in their yellow embroidery. (When I came to know Keats' 'Ode to Autumn' and the Ingres women in his 'Turkish Bath', they became again the languid airs and shapes of my childhood summers.)

Summertime was life, wide and generous, fat King Cole lolling on his throne listening to his fiddlers three, a smiling dolphin turning, playing in big, shining waters. Summer was another country whose fathers had, suddenly, bare, shy arms, whose mothers padded like cats on bare feet. Time was still summer air, as slow and round as pregnant women. In the mornings, time sat quietly, waiting for me as I commanded it to, watching me think, shape, arrange the world. The breakfast farina and milk should be mountains and rivers and I heaped mounds and scraped tunnels with my spoon to make it so. The sun that lit up the rung of a chair, if it hid behind the cloud, would the chair become something else? And if I decided to call the chair a table and said it many times, would the back disappear and the seat broaden to become a table? My brother's pinches (he was still asleep; I hated sleeping, it stole things from me) hurt me. Why didn't I feel anything when I pinched him, just as hard? (I still find myself searching for that answer.)

Cloaked in the royal robes of omnipotent childhood, I went down – it was very early – to check the condition of my domain and my subjects. I was the queen of my block. No one but I knew it and I knew it well, each morning making a royal progress on my empty street, among my big garbage cans, my limp window curtains, my sheet of newspaper slowly turning and sliding in the gutter, my morning glory on Mrs. Roberti's porch vine, my waiting stoops fronting my sleeping houses; my hat factory on the corner of 179th Street, resting from its hours of blowing pink and blue and purple dye smoke; my Kleins, my Rizzos, my Petrides, my Clancys safely in bed, guarded by my strength and will. Even after

I had been heavily assaulted with school proofs that very little of the world was mine, that history existed of itself and not as a huge crowded stage hurriedly arranged the day I was born, I maintained a deep interest in my subjects, moving out of absolute control to the more subtle control of observer and critic. (My father, no fool, sensing the menace inherent in the long stares half hidden by my thatch of flaxen hair, accused my mother of having brought forth a silent white snake.)

Early one July morning, the sidewalk already soft and steamy like the bed I had left, I made my usual surveillance, this morning the good fairy tiptoeing through the sleeping castle in the sleeping forest. All was well: the De Santis garage door was locked; the factory door was locked. The Morettis' gray cat was stalking a sparrow, and I hoped she would get it since she wasn't a good mouser and must have a disappointing life. As I watched the cat – a dummy, not good at sparrows either – the clanking of bars and the rumble of turning bolts told me that the factory doors were opening. The oldest De Santis boy, still chewing on a breakfast roll, came out of his stucco house to set a chair on the porch for his grandmother. Annie's father in his working cap, carrying a brown paper lunch bag, ran down the stairs of their house and turned briskly in the direction of the El station. Windows and doors shot open, the trickle of voices thickened, and the legs of the fathers on their way to work became a jumble of zigzags on the sidewalk. I watched my show, contented with its expectedness, hoping a little for the unexpected. Maybe Mr. Kaplan would be wearing his new hat to work, like the gentleman and hero he was. Two Sundays ago he had shouted up at a towering *goy* who wouldn't let him sit on a nearby park bench, 'Because I'm a Jew and you're a Christian, I should kiss your ass? You can kiss *my* ass.' If not Mr. Kaplan's hat, maybe Mrs. Santini would come out on her porch, chewing yesterday's spaghetti and pushing it into the mouth of her new baby, like what birds did, and then nurse it from a pale flood of breast. Maybe, with luck, I might see one of the sleek men who looked like knives, nobody's fathers or immigrant uncles, run quickly out of the houses of '*nafkas*', a word whispered by the mothers as they rocked their baby carriages in the street, a word, like many, I didn't quite understand yet sensed fairly accurately.

The stage was filling nicely. The milkman was coming around the corner, little boys – not my dopey brother, thank God – were tumbling into the streets. Suddenly, from around the corner, at the back of the factory, the sounds of yelping, wailing, shrieking. I ran, to see something Lon Chaney might have invented as a mad doctor. Dogs, back to back stuck together, trying to pull away from each other, screaming as they pulled. They snapped their teeth at the air, their eyes rolled in anguish, their legs arched and pawed in a crazy dance, their rumps rubbed and twisted, but they couldn't separate. Two factory workers stopped for a moment, watched, exchanged a phrase and a smile, and walked on. I couldn't understand why two grown men couldn't, wouldn't, separate the dogs who must have sat in some glue that was tearing their skins and fur as they pulled.

I ran back to my house and leaped up the tenement stairs, past the open doors that drew relief from the cool stone landings. Past Mrs. Petrides' floor, past Mrs. Schwartz's, past Mrs. Szekely's and up to our own, where Mrs. Haskell, with no children to feed or dress, sat reading love advice, fanning herself with the rest of the *Graphic*. I gasped 'Hello' and dashed into our apartment. 'Mama! Mama! Come down quick. There are two dogs stuck together, maybe some mean person glued them. They can't separate and it hurts them. They're screaming. Please, Mama, it's terrible, get them apart.'

The expected move to the door didn't happen. Even with her new big belly, my mother would run down the four flights when Marie Moretti shouted up from the stairwell that her mother's new baby was twisting funny, or when Mrs. Bernstein called across the yard that her stinking old father was sick and needed cupping. Now she stood at the stove and continued stirring the soup as she poured in barley. 'Please, Ma, please hurry.'

'No. I'm staying here and so are you. Mind your own business. Play in the house.' The round face and the mouth like summer fruit had become dry and flat, she looked like the assistant principal, an iron lady. Another 'Please' would have been useless, I knew. I must have done something wrong and I went away from the strange woman as far as I could, to the back fire escape to watch the colored smoke from the factory fade into the sky. I counted the mattresses flopping out of the open windows on Monterey Avenue, across from the empty lot below. I took out my box of cloth scraps to try the pink with the blue; no, the yellow with the blue, the shiny with the dull; two shinys. I was going to stay on the fire escape forever, burn in the sun, freeze in the snow, never go back into the kitchen with the woman with the stone face and the ugly humpback on her belly. She called me in for a glass of milk. I went and drank it in the kitchen, both of us very quiet, a nervous quiet like the first day in a new class. I shouldn't have told her about the dogs. I didn't ask her why. She didn't tell me.

The day of the glued dogs led off many watchful days, days of going out only with Mama. I was her helper, her monitor, much, much older now than my brother, in gray shade while he darted and dazzled in the full sun of the street. They were slow troublesome walks. I didn't want to be with her when her belly burst open and spilled a hundred tiny babies like watermelon seeds. Or it might crack open and a skinny little blind chick would fall to the sidewalk, or out of the crack would slide the long, shining blue of a skinless rabbit like those on the hooks of the Italian butcher shop. I couldn't say I wouldn't go with her, but I hated this swollen person who used to be as lively as jumping rope and never scared. Now she was scared when she stepped off the sidewalk, scared of the boxes flung around in the market, scared of crippled people and Mary Sugar Bum, who staggered around singing like a penny whistle. Once her skirt caught in a band of metal on the stair rail. She tripped, lost her footing, but didn't fall, nothing to make a fuss about. But she sat down on one of the steps and burst into tears. I couldn't understand why, nothing had happened, she hadn't even torn her skirt or scraped her knee and I hadn't ever seen her cry except when she laughed very hard. She was becoming a big ugly crybaby, and lazy. She had to rest a lot and I didn't really know what 'resting' meant. She told me to go down and play but I wouldn't. I sat in the kitchen reading about and envying the Dutch Twins who clomped around in noisy wooden shoes – and people let them – or ice-skated and ice-skated all day through the winter. Sometimes I would take, very careful with the latch, a few cherries from the icebox. I ate them slowly, stroking the silk skin, looking at the way the stems jumped up like dancers, crunching into the juicy blood red and sucking the pit until it, too, felt like silk. While I examined and bit and sucked, I heard from across the courtyard Ruthie rumbling her way through scales on her new piano and the sighs of steam from the factory.

Our walks grew shorter, the descent down the stairs slow and careful, I gripping her hand, bracing myself against the pull of the belly, maybe ready to fall and bounce like an enormous ball, thudding down, down, along the four flights of stairs and into the street. As the descent became more difficult – and frightening, I suppose – my mother stopped for a few minutes of what the

men referred to as 'women's talk' with the neighbors before we
went on toward the park or around the block. While they talked,
I bounced my ball, staying as close as I discreetly could to the low
words. 'They had to pull the baby from her with instruments. She
screamed for two days.' 'She always lost them in the fourth month.'
'The cord got twisted around the neck, so it died.' Bounce, bounce,
bounce, foot over the ball on the fourth bounce, waiting for the key
words, how a baby got into a belly and just how it got out, but they
never came. There was repeated mention of nine months. Did that
mean that it took nine months for a baby to ripen like a banana to
be peeled, a peach to be sliced when it was ready? It must hurt,
otherwise the women wouldn't be whispering about screaming. As
I bounced the ball, a heat of terror and guilt burned through me and
turned to icy nausea in my stomach. I had done this to my mother,
made her shout with pain for hours and hours, while doctors dug
and ripped at her with 'instruments', big pliers and saws that tore
her flesh and skin. No wonder my mother could get so mad at
me sometimes for reasons I didn't understand. Bouncing, still
bouncing the ball, I wondered why she didn't fight this baby off?
Or maybe she didn't know it was coming in, like nits in hairs, like
worms in puppies and babies? I kept waiting for words that would
unlock the door the women guarded, for the light that would make
everything clear and nice, like the neat gardens and the clear people
with clear smiles in books.

Instead, the women moved into the commonness of headaches
and sore throats, a winding, boring exchange of symptoms and
cures I'd heard before. But old Mrs. Rabinowitz was usually there
and she said odd things. I bounced the ball and listened. Mrs.
Rabinowitz was a kind of witch who, some of the women said,
put curses on people. She had appeared one late Friday afternoon
at the door of the Rosenbergs, asking for a match for her candles.
Matches in hand, she looked in toward the dining room where
the gleaming candlesticks and the shining *challa* rested on the
table, sniffed the scrubbed smell of the house, the lemon oil
on the furniture, the golden smell of chicken soup, watched the
children rolling marbles down the apartment hallway, stared at Mr.
Rosenberg reading his paper in his comfortable chair. In her rough,
deep voice as steady as her burning eyes she intoned, 'I also had a
husband. I also had children. Be careful. With God one makes no
contracts.' Mrs. Rosenberg pushed her out the door and ran from
child to child, making three spitting sounds over the head of each

to dispel the Evil Eye the old witch had brought in. Mrs. Rosenberg avoided her, would never talk to her after that. The other women were just as afraid of Mrs. Rabinowitz but preferred to keep on her good side because she was also a powerful healer; she might be useful someday. Who knows what God might send? So the women listened patiently as I did above the dull, light rhythm of the ball, as she told them what to do for the inflamed throats many of the children suffered each winter. 'The mother must take her own stocking. It must be her own, it must be cotton, it must be black, no other color, only black. Then the mother must make water on it, and while it's still warm, wrap it around the child's throat. And she should do that each time she makes water until the child is better and that's in a day, always.' My mother, a big-city girl and herself a reputable healer and not much concerned with the Evil Eye, asked, 'But wouldn't warm water on a cloth do the same thing?' 'No, never. How can water from a sink and a piece of old sheet be as good for a child as its mother's water and a stocking from her body? Foolish woman.'

Fighting the stinking, wet stocking I imagined around my neck, fighting the horrors of birthing, I shouted in my head a powerful curse I had just read: 'You're only a deck of cards!' They were all crazy, all those old people, peeing on black stockings, letting themselves have babies that hurt, whispering dumb secrets, and getting mad for nothing. I blew them away and ran to join a potsy game (books called it 'hopscotch') chalked out on the sidewalk.

At the end of August that year, the temperature rose to near 100 and stayed, motionless, thick. It was too hot to walk, too hot to go to the library, too hot to play in the street. My brother took his train of spools down to Jimmy Petrides' house; Bianca's grandmother was sick so I couldn't swing in her yard, and I was mad at Becky, who stole my best pencil and denied it. I had finished reading the Belgian Twins and French Twins. I couldn't play with the big doll in the closet that had been there for two years. It was mine, bought for me by old Uncle David, but my father said I couldn't play with it, it was too good. (My brother broke it a year later, climbing up into the closet and down awkwardly, smashing her gorgeous, staring face to bits. He accused me of egging him on, and he was probably right, but I denied it, screaming anguish and hatred.) My mother suggested that if I was very careful, I might play with the bowls in the china closet and the basket of tiny flowers, but I must put them back very carefully. I didn't feel like being careful, so when she went to her room to lie down, I just sat and waited. I looked at the light behind the drawn window shade, listened to the crickets on the green lot, traced with my pinkie the red roses and green leaves stitched into the tablecloth in the dining room. When I heard my mother's light snoring, I slipped into the hall, through the open door and up the stairs to the roof.

This was my second kingdom, a continuous black, romantic terrain of tar and low brick dividers that marked off the houses, which stretched from one end of the block to the other. Here I could walk high above the street, in the sky and unshadowed sun. It was here that my subjects spent the hottest nights, when it became a place of dark figures dragging white sheets that billowed like sails and waves as they sank on spreads of newspaper. The sleepy children were put down to curl on each other, fitting like sections of orange. At one side of the pale patches of sheet, the fathers talked quietly while the mothers sat whispering on the other side. From the factory at the end of the row, dye vat vapors stained the thin, smoky dark of the summer night. On this slow-breathing afternoon there was no one around. The hot tar squeaked under my feet as I practiced stepping like Mae Murray with dainty, pointed toes over the brick dividers. I picked some of the hot shining tar from between the bricks and chewed it, a forbidden thing. It tasted of sun and dust, stiffer and better than bubble gum, better than rubber bands. As I chewed and pointed my toes, wondering how close I could get to the edge of the roof before I became too frightened, I heard funny little sounds. They seemed to come from behind a skylight of the middle houses. Like an Indian scout I moved carefully, watching out for the pebbles that might slide under my feet and, rattling, give me away. Following the little gasps and moans and giggles, I reached a side of the skylight from which I could peer around to the front. A man and woman were squirming together like big, tangled worms. Their clothing was all mixed up, open, closed; some off, some on. Clasping, turning, legs and arms grasping and lashing like an octopus, a behind thumping like an angry gorilla, they were stuck as the dogs were but not hurting. I watched for a while as their gasps and moans became shuddery little 'Oohs' like being splashed with cold water. More crazies, getting dirty and sweaty, messing up their clothing, hugging, digging, twisting on the hot sticky tar.

I ran back to my skylight, forgetting the twinkle-toe steps, laughing and laughing. Down the stairs and into the apartment

to tell my mother about this funny thing I saw. She was still on
her bed, awake now and smiling. 'What's so funny? What are you
laughing at? What happened?' I was about to tell her when I looked
at her face, the face that had turned to stone when I asked her to
help the dogs. I looked at her belly; maybe the people on the roof
were making a belly. Quite easily, smoothly, I began to play the
secrets game, as comfortable in my evasions as grown-ups were.
'Nothing much, Mama. Sarah was trying to imitate Nita Naldi. She
was trying to slink vampy with her fat behind and pigeon toes.' 'Did
she say anything? Tell me.' 'Nothing, Ma, honest.' 'She probably
said dirty words, that Sarah, didn't she?' 'Yes, Mama.' 'Don't tell
me then, don't repeat them.' 'All right, Mama, I won't.'

All that day I could feel the laughter bubbling in me, I could see
the whipping bodies of the dogs and the people mixed up with the
swell of my mother's body. I washed my face and combed my hair
without being told to; I cut the cucumbers neatly, in even slices,
almost as well as my mother did, when I helped with supper. The
tall door to their secret gardens was beginning, maybe just a crack,
to open to me. I didn't know just what I knew, but I knew I was
closer to knowing.

7
Birthing

He looked so much like a story character – the gentled Scrooge of a *St. Nicholas Magazine* Christmas issue, a not-too-skeletal Ichabod Crane – that it is difficult to say how he really looked. And he was ephemeral, his visits timed for the hours we were in school so that we caught only occasional glimpses of him as he strode around a corner, immensely tall (something we were not accustomed to in our Mediterranean street) and thin, wearing a long, skinny black coat and a shapeless black hat, carrying a black doctor's satchel. We knew Dr. James had visited when we found our mothers in bed 'resting', an odd word, an odd event. When we left for school, they had no symptoms of cold or cough or pain; preoccupied perhaps, but that was common among women who worried about getting the rent paid on time, about shoes for the children, about husbands who habitually came home late from work. There was never an explanation for Dr. James's visit, what he did, what he said; only the mother on the bed, a peculiar worrisome thing, like finding the library or school suddenly, without warning, closed. By suppertime the mothers would be chopping, cutting, cooking, sometimes more quiet than usual, sometimes more irritable, nothing more.

When I became a member of a medical family that had practiced in the Bronx for decades, I once mentioned Dr. James and his unexplained short visits to mothers only, and never to deliver babies. A spate of enthusiastic information poured over the dinner table. Dr. James was, even when I knew him as a child, quite an old man, retired from a prestigious and lucrative practice in Boston, they thought. His was a prosperous intellectual family, the famous New England Jameses that produced William and Henry, but to the older Bronx doctors, *the* James was the magnificent old driven scarecrow. Having educated his children and seen their arrival into respected professions, he dedicated himself to poor immigrant women for whom there was no sex information, no birth-control clinics, nothing but knitting needles, hat pins, lengths of wire, the drinking of noxious mixtures while they sat in scalding baths to prevent the birth of yet another child. At times one woman would inflict these well-meant injuries on a sister, a neighbor; sometimes they were solitary acts of desperation. Some women died of septicemia; some of those who could not kill the fetus had to wait out the nine months and the delivery to let the infant die of exposure or suffocation.

To prevent such suicides and murders, Dr. James went from one immigrant neighborhood to another, performing abortions. (How he was informed where he was needed no one seemed to know; there must have been one woman in each area who transmitted messages.) He lived to be quite old and, according to my informants, worked vigorously at his self-appointed job until he died, having performed thousands of abortions, the fee a dollar or two or nothing, depending on the degree of poverty he met. Every adult in his neighborhoods knew him and his function, including cops and Board of Health people, who usually let him be. It was during the periodic sweeps of new brooms in office that he was arrested and imprisoned. He succumbed to it all very calmly, didn't call lawyers or his family, nor offered bail. Apparently he got in touch with one or two colleagues who called others, who in turn called others, and together they stormed the court where he was being tried. They pleaded, they argued, they shouted; they accused the police and the court of ignorance and inhumanity, and had him released. This drama was repeated several times, memorable times for the doctors who could thus demonstrate their admiration for the old man with the courage and independence to act as they might, if they but could.

Dr. James was a careful gynaecologist as well as a skilled abortionist. There were women he would not abort. My little sister was much more gently handled, more eagerly cosseted, than my brother and I were because, my mother told me when we had become close adult friends, the baby was unwanted and was allowed to be born only because Dr. James refused to perform another abortion; she had had too many and another could be hazardous. How many she had I found out when I checked her into a hospital a few years before she died. Thirteen. I asked her

again when we were alone in her hospital room whether I had
heard correctly. Thirteen? And three children besides? Yes, and
that was by no means the neighborhood record, she said. How
could I account for the fact that a number of our Italian neighbors,
urged by the Catholic Church to produce large families, had no
more than two or three children? Certainly it wasn't the abstinence
of Italian husbands, no more controlled than Jewish husbands. It
was the work of the blessed hands of that wonderful old *goy*.

When school started in September before I was quite eight, the
walks with my swollen mother – watching her skirt so that she
didn't stumble on the stairs, pacing my steps, skipping in place to
her lumbering, rocking walk, like the elephant in the zoo –
stopped. When we came home from school there was a quiet in the
house that seemed to tremble against the walls, no lilting greetings,
no apples and crackers on the table, in the sink a cold half cup of
tea with milk. She was resting, and resting meant sick, like the
times when Dr. James had come and gone. It also meant trouble.
I kept glancing surreptitiously at her ankles to see if they were
swollen. In scraps of eavesdropping I had accumulated something
about women swelling and having convulsions before babies were
born. My mother had swelled but didn't have convulsions when
I was born, a difficult delivery, 'with instruments' that dented
my forehead. (Tracing the dent in my forehead, I wondered if
it would squeeze my brains and someday make me crazy, like Mrs.
Silverberg or my father's sister Surrele, whose name was thrown
at me when I threw shoes and slammed doors.) 'Instruments' were
enormous black pincers, like those the iceman used to pull blocks
of ice from his wagon, stuck in my mother's belly, ripping through
the flesh and searching among her bleeding bowels until it hit my
forehead and grabbed me, pulling up and out again through the red,
messed flesh into the air, and dropped me, a doll covered with pee
and shit, into hands that slapped me to make me breathe. And now,
in our house, a few paces from the kitchen, fewer from the dining
room, it was probably all going to happen again; tonight, tomorrow
night, the next night. It always happened late at night, a shameful,
secret thing, too dark and terrible for open day.

One afternoon in early October we came home to find Mrs.
Nagy and Mrs. Kaplan bustling around the kitchen and Fannie
Herman standing in the hallway wringing her hands. Mrs. Nagy
gave us a piece of strudel and told us brusquely to go down and

stay in the street until our father came home. We hung around the stoop feeling uncomfortable, lost. We had to go to the toilet, we were getting cold in the falling light, we didn't feel like playing. Something was happening to our mother and why couldn't we see her? It had to do with her belly and the baby. I wanted to watch and at the same time wanted to be far, far away; to be someone else in another place, a girl who lived in a book.

When our father arrived and asked us what we were doing in the street so late, my brother mumbled something about the baby and we ran upstairs. We could hear Mrs. Kaplan's voice in the far big bedroom as my father walked into it and closed the door. Mrs. Nagy was in the kitchen putting stuffed cabbage and pieces of cornbread on the table. Our father called to us to eat and do our homework in the kitchen, he would eat later. We were to be quick and quiet and go to bed – and close the door – as soon as we were through. We didn't talk, as we often did, in bed; there was no point at which to start a discussion of something so large and forbidding, and words might betray our fear.

During the night we were awakened by a shriek and then another. Our door was pushed shut and we knew we were not to open it, not to get out of bed, not to see what was happening. People bustled in the hallway, to and from the kitchen, to and from the bathroom. Someone rang the doorbell and was admitted, probably the doctor. Through the sound of feet and the hushed voices, another scream and more, louder, more piercing, like ambulances. This I, too, had done to my mother, distorted her good-natured, singing person into a howling animal. I imagined her hair wild and swept across her staring green eyes, her pretty mouth torn by the screams, the doctor pushing the immense pincers into her belly and searching, searching for the baby, ripping her to pieces as my birth had done. My brother was asleep or pretended to be. I was alone in a guilt that made me want to disappear, to die.

Not knowing how to die, I separated myself from myself, one girl not there, one girl going through familiar actions in a dumbness and deafness like a thick rubber Halloween mask. I don't know who gave us breakfast; I ate it. I don't know what happened in school; I was there and managed to perform whatever was asked of me. I did my homework; it was correct. They told me I had a little sister; I didn't say anything. The women on the street asked me how my mother was; I said all right. This went on, the living in a cold, flat country, for several days, the guilt pushed down, out, away, and kept away. When my mother called to me from her bedroom to come and see the new baby, it was pretty, I called back, 'Tomorrow,' and ran to the street.

One of the days when my mother was still in her bed and we still fed by the neighbors, a monitor came into my classroom and handed a note to the teacher. We all sat up, eager for whatever news it might bring, an injunction from the principal about noise in the auditorium, an announcement of a shortened school day, possibly. My teacher called me to her and told me that I was wanted by my brother's teacher. All the kids stared as I walked awkwardly (was my skirt hitched up in back? my socks falling?) out of the room. When I reached his classroom, my brother was standing at her desk, looking shamefaced but not especially stricken. His teacher, Miss Sullivan, one of the smiling young ones, said she knew my mother had just had a baby but a big girl like myself could take care of a little brother almost as well as his mother could. But maybe I was too busy to notice that he didn't wash too well. Pulling his collar away from his neck, she showed me a broad band of dirt that began at a sharp edge just below his clean jaws. I had said every morning, 'Wash your face,' but forgot to mention his neck. Everything became hard and clear, as if it were cut out of metal, in that room, as deeply indelible as the painting of the boys listening to Sir Walter Raleigh's adventures in the auditorium: Miss Sullivan's blond lashes, her left eye a little bigger than the right, the spot of spit at the corner of her dry lips, the gray clouds of old chalk marks on the blackboard, the word cards, SENT, WENT, BENT, on the wall, the gluey tan wood of the windowsill, the pale afternoon sun streaking the floor, a red sweater and a brown sweater hanging crooked in the half-open wardrobe, the brown desks on iron legs, on each desk hands folded as for a somber occasion like a visit from the nurse, above each desk eyes staring at me.

I stood there leaden with shame until Miss Sullivan dismissed me with, 'See that he washes better,' and sent me back to my classroom. It was difficult to open the door and walk into those eyes that were going to stare at me and later, at three o'clock, come closer to ask what happened. I answered, 'Oh, nothing. Miss Sullivan wanted me to check my brother's homework; he's careless, she said.' I wanted to vomit, to stamp, to scream, to break, to kill: him, me, them, my mother, my father, everything, the whole world. But I had to walk him home. He searched my face as he ran across the playground toward me, hesitated, and attached

himself to Jimmy, walking near me, as he had to, but a safe distance
away, on the far side of Jimmy. As soon as he dropped his books
on the floor of our bedroom he ran into my mother's room, where
I heard them giggling together. She called to me, 'Don't you want
to come and see the baby?' I yelled back, 'Tomorrow,' still afraid
of what I might see, a baby with a ditch in its head, a mother all
rags of flesh, an exploded, splashed cartoon animal. All my fault.
My brother came back into the kitchen where I was trying to peel
an apple in one long coil, an especially delicate operation because
I was using a big breadknife. He pushed my arm, breaking the coil,
and ran toward the hallway, laughing. I threw the knife at him and
saw it quivering in the wall where his head had been a second
before. It fell from the wall. I picked it up and continued cutting
the apple as I listened to him screaming to my mother, 'She tried
to kill me! She threw the knife, the big knife, at me! She's crazy!
Send her away! Please, Mama, send her away! I'm afraid of her!' I
heard her slippers patter down the hall, closed my eyes tight shut,
and waited. She shook me. 'Open your eyes. Look at me.' I looked,
I would have to sometime, and saw her as she was most mornings,
in her thick brown bathrobe, her short hair not yet combed, her lips
pale. 'What's the matter with you? Do you know you could have
killed him? Do you know that he would be dead, forever dead?
Never talk again, never walk, never see, never hear? Do you know
that you would be locked away in an asylum for crazy people? And
spend the rest of your life, many, many years, with other crazies?'
I said nothing, tried not to be there. 'I've got to go back to bed now
and attend to the baby. This your father will hear about and I won't
get in his way. Whatever punishment you get you'll deserve.'

It rained that evening and my brother was granted the privilege,
usually mine, of carrying the umbrella to the El station. It was a
special pleasure, a special ceremony, to go out into the wet night
as if on an emergency mission – a nurse, a doctor – to rescue
our fathers. We clustered, at the bottom of the steep El stairs,
admiring the dark shine of the trolley tracks, the rain bubbling
the puddles like boiling black cereal, holding the handles tight as
the wind fought our umbrellas, listening to the rumble and roar of
the train, the screeching stop, the rush of feet down the stairs. For
many of us, the big smile as we yelled, 'Pa, here I am, here,' and
were recognized and patted on the arm or head was the only overt
affection we knew from our fathers. The umbrellas, now taller and
single, separated to walk on their two long legs and their two short

up Tremont Avenue, down to Bathgate, or shadowed themselves under the struts and tracks of Third Avenue.

By the time my brother and father got home and the wet umbrella placed in the bathtub, the story of the knife had been told, so serious a matter that it came before supper. Asked why I had thrown the knife, I answered – and it seemed a feeble reason – 'Because his neck was dirty and he made me ashamed in front of his whole class.' I couldn't say, 'Because I hate mothers and babies and screaming in the night and people being pulled out of bellies with instruments and brothers who jump around and play while I have to take care of them.' I couldn't find the words or shape the sentence because they were truly crazy things to say, worse than throwing knives. There was no preliminary lecture, cause and effect clear and simple. With a few words to my mother about the *gilgul*, the restless, evil spirit I must have in me – although he didn't really believe in such superstitious things – my father pushed me into the bathroom and, while he carefully pulled his belt out of the trouser loops, told me to lie across the covered toilet, pick up my skirt, and pull down my bloomers.

I had been slapped, on the face, on the behind, punched by boys and pinched by girls; my knees were often scraped, my fingers blistered and cut, but there was no preparation for the pain beyond pain of this first beating, the swish of the strap becoming a burning scream through my whole body, my arms shaking as they clung to the edge of the bathtub, my fingers scratching at the squealing porcelain, my ribs crushed against the toilet lid. I shrieked and begged, 'Papa, don't. Stop, please. Please stop. Please, Papa.' He stopped when he was out of breath, his face red, his brown eyes bulging. Replacing his belt, he walked out of the bathroom, closing the door. I stood there for a long while, then splashed cold water on my behind, fixed my clothing, and stood some more, not knowing where to go. In time I heard fumbling at the doorknob and my mother's voice telling my brother to get away, to let me be. A few minutes later she opened the door to tell me it was time to eat. I slipped out of the bathroom and into my bedroom, pushed the big chair against the door that had no lock, piled my books, my brother's books, the wooden sewing machine cover, and the heavy coats that were in the closet on the chair, and got into bed, pushing myself way, way down under the featherbed, stroking and rubbing myself until I fell asleep.

The next morning my brother banged on the door for his books.

As I pulled the heavy chair away so he could get in, I noticed his neck was clean. My mother was back in bed with the baby I had no intention of seeing. I grabbed a roll from the breadbox in the kitchen and ate it as I dressed, then left the house quickly, passing my brother, who stood on the third floor waiting at Jimmy's door. We avoided each other for the next day or two, he hanging on to Jimmy, I watching that they looked each way down the street before they crossed broad, busy 180th.

After my mother had spent her traditional ten days in bed, she put on the clothing she wore before the big belly and fixed us nice lunches: noodles, pot cheese, and raisins with cinnamon and sugar, radishes and cucumbers in sour cream, salami sandwiches. Ordinariness washed, day by day, over our lives except for the baby lying in my mother's lap in the kitchen. She looked unfinished and wandering, making strange faces, her eyes a milky blue and bobbling in her head, the tiny fingers reaching and curling toward everything, nothing. When her eyes turned to gold and steady, and some of the grimaces became smiles, I began to like her a little and let her pull at my fingers and hair.

8

Coney and Gypsies

Our baby sister was in a perverse way a great boon. She was frail, easily caught cold, had pinworms that had to be purged, which sometimes made her sicker, and was a troubled teether. With each tooth she had a fever and cried a lot. The first doctor we ever saw in our house – the obstetrician came and went behind our closed bedroom door; Dr. James was a fast-moving black shadow – was called in for the baby several times. It must have been an affluent time to afford doctors' visits, a time when my father brought home fairy-princess shoes to decorate. The extra piecework money he made was also spent for two summer weeks in Coney Island when my sister was nine or ten months old, teething and sickish all the time. Sea air was what the baby needed, my mother kept saying. After all, hadn't she cured us of whooping cough by spending days with us on the Staten Island ferry? And Coney island wasn't so expensive and my father could come out a couple of times a week maybe and have all day Sunday on the beach and the boardwalk.

It was arranged, and after royal farewells to our less fortunate friends, the rich consoling and soaring over their poor relatives, we dragged the baby's crib and our bundles to El Dorado, the house in Coney Island, a ramshackle wooden place with a big porch. The several vacationing families like us each had one room crammed with two or three beds and clothing hooks on the walls. There was one community toilet and one large kitchen in which all the women cooked, whether separately or together I never found out. (That sort of summer living, whether at the beach or in the legendary 'mountains', was known as a *kuch alein*, cook for yourself, the cheapest way to give one's children fresh air and escape for a week or two some of the exigencies of marriage.) The baby must have been quite sick because my usually careful mother let us loose on Coney Island every day for two weeks. After a breakfast of cold cereal with a couple of other children at one of the kitchen tables and a visit to the toilet, with two or three lunch nickels tied in a handkerchief knotted to a shoulder strap of my bathing suit, and instructions not to go too far into the water, not to buy candy with our lunch money, and to be back for supper at six, we were off.

We fought little or not at all during those weeks, too happy to want anything but what was: walking long streets staring at old people nodding on porches, at two kids with braces on their legs (the sea air was recommended for children with polio), who hopped up and down the stairs of one house like crooked birds, at the brilliant beach balls and shovels like derricks in shops on the boardwalk, at the machine in one shop that folded and kept folding skeins of taffy, at the fat plopping people and skinny stick people, at the white-skinned with red masks of sunburn, at the negro grasshopper children leaping and flying on their faraway street. It was a dazzling new world, like those in the movie travelogues that closed with, 'As the sun sinks slowly in the west . . .', and it was all ours. When it grew hot, we walked over to the sea and dared each other to go farther and farther out into the water. Both of us were several times dragged out in the undertow and grabbed by adults who demanded, 'Where's your mother? Why doesn't she watch you?' and thrust us back on shore. After daring and daring more, being thrown and twisted, blinded and deafened by the water, shouted at by frightened and annoyed strangers, we became more cautious by silent accord and spent more time making sand castles and burying each other 'up to the neck, keep away from my mouth and ears.' We were both eager to spend the lunch money as soon as we left our house, and did it the first day, but learned to be patient after hours of hunger pangs. Lunch was a five-cent hot dog at any of dozens of stands, loaded with sauerkraut and, if we had an extra nickel, an ear of corn out of a big steaming cauldron. Dividing it was difficult: it didn't always break into two just halves, a meticulously observed principle, so we tried other solutions; one of them meant counting the rows of kernels, and if they were even, he crunched two rows and I the next two, and so on. If that didn't work out justly, the loser sucked on the cob, or got to lick the paper of a melting Baby Ruth on those days we decided against corn. Popcorn should have been easier, but counting out kernels, one for you, one for me, was too time-consuming for something we didn't care that much about, so we let it go. The tacit goal was to live as peaceably as we could in this paradise, 'with liberty and justice for all', the Snake of Contention tied in his tree.

We found the Gypsies. They came through our Bronx streets from time to time, two or three women in big swinging skirts like colored winds, dusty long black hair, flashing gold teeth, and bold hands that demanded money, unlike the quivering old bums who bashfully begged. We were told to avoid them; they were filthy, they were thieves, and they kidnapped children. Our Coney Island Gypsies sat in a store behind a draped entrance, just off the boardwalk. The front of the shop was decorated with a naked head marked off in sections, probably for 'studying bumps,' which I had heard about from Helen Roth's big sister. Next to the cut-up head were a hand with lines on it and a watery picture of a glassy ball. over the entrance, FORTUNES TOLD. COME RIGHT IN. We spent a good deal of time examining the head, the hand, and the glassy ball, trying to figure out how they told fortunes. Did a bump on the front slice of the head mean rich or smart? Could the glass ball show you a picture of whom you would marry? The lines on the other hand, maybe they showed who would work hard, like the men who carried coal to the cellar, and who would have a soft job, like a teacher or librarian. All the fortune-telling we knew was a pick board crammed with little papers that, for a penny, could be poked out and unfolded to tell us, 'You will marry rich', 'You will be a success', 'You will travel' – dumb things, we said; not altogether incredible, we thought. But this was the real goods, arcane, high-class fortune-telling that required mysterious charts and globes and the strange wisdoms of women in long red and pink satin skirts.

As we stood one day, edging toward the side of the draped doorway, a young woman in a long skirt and earrings like chandeliers came out and said, in recognizable English, 'Hello. You're here again. Want some cake?' We were afraid and as usual much more afraid to confess fear. After hesitating, feeling shy, poking each other in and out of the doorway, we entered, looking for the cake. It was there, big and covered with chocolate icing, on a folding table, near it an older glittering Gypsy lady holding a knife. She gave us large chunks and cups of black tea with a lot of sugar. Was this the way they poisoned children to take them away, inert and senseless? Between small bites of the cake I waited for a numbed tongue, dizziness, pains in my stomach, anything ominous. I felt fine and my brother was doing well, babbling about our family and the sick baby and we had to take her here to the healthy air and we lived in the Bronx and he couldn't shut up. The young woman told the older one who had cut the cake what my brother was saying in her language – Romany, she explained – and invited me to sit down on a long low cushion if I wanted to. I sank to the purple and green flowers of the cushion, feeling as if I were floating, and accepted another piece of cake. While my brother continued entertaining the ladies, who smiled at him and each other broadly, I looked around. It was the most beautiful place I had ever been in. On the walls were intricately woven mazes of deep colors, little flowers and leaves caught in boxes of dark blue and red. Near these hangings were long spills of sky-blue satin. Other than the small table and two chairs there was no furniture, only cushions, heaps of them in brilliant colors and patterns. Near the back of the store, more and more like an Arab tent in the movies, there was an open cabinet of dark wood, carved as delicately as the shoes my father carved, on one of its shelves the glassy ball pictured outside. One lamp of metal with hundreds of little holes in it spread soft spots of light like stars. Sounds and smells of cooking came from behind a far curtain, but I never saw that room.

We didn't know when to leave, what the polite way of being with Gypsies was, so we stayed talking and staring, until the older woman said it was probably time to go home, our mother must be expecting us. Nothing was ever said about the Gypsies at home, though we went there frequent afternoons, always hanging around outside, near the skull and hand, waiting to be noticed and invited in. Sometimes we were offered sandwiches instead of cake, not too disappointing because we assumed that the strange meat in the sandwiches was ham or pork, of rarer value than cake. Sometimes the purple door drapes were folded together for a long time. That meant a customer and we tiptoed away, aching to peek through the folds to see Gypsy magic. We didn't dare risk the anger of the black-haired, black-eyed queens with the gold chains and earrings. They might yet hit us or poison us and sell us to other Gypsies.

The afternoon we said our last good-bye in Coney Island, the older woman, who had shown a great interest in the baby's teething and fevers, gave us a bone ring attached to a twisted, hornlike piece of coral, saying it was a teething ring, the coral attached for good luck. If our baby bit on it, she would feel much better and make nice strong teeth, too. I thanked her and thanked her again, nodding to be emphatic and to show I understood as she

put the ring into my hand. We said good-bye – no kissing, no
hugging, no handshaking, a great relief. As we walked home my
brother asked to see the ring and, turning it around and around,
decided it was old, used, and maybe full of germs. (It was old,
used, and probably an antique that I regret not having saved.) We
couldn't take it home, couldn't tell where we had gotten it. Even if
we said we had found it, my mother would have thrown it away. So
we dropped it into a sewer opening and forgot it.

The two weeks of freedom and being Gypsy children were not
as easily forgotten. There was still a month before school started
and we ran wild. The block wasn't enough anymore, even the empty
lot. We snooped in the Italian market, a hundred times bigger than
the local greenstores and butchers, hung with walls of salamis and
cheeses like big clubs tied with ropes, all the way up on 183rd Street
and Arthur Avenue. We skated far along Tremont to stare down on
the tracks below Park Avenue, peering far downtown as we waited
for trains that never seemed to run. But there was good garbage on
the tracks, the rare sight of dozens of whiskey bottles along with
the more familiar rotten oranges, old shoes, and mice rustling in
torn bags of bread crusts and chicken bones.

It didn't last; we knew it wouldn't. We burst in, disheveled and
streaked with dirty sweat, late one evening after our father had
arrived. He ordered us into the bathroom to wash and comb our
hair, declaring that we had become animals in Coney Island, it was
time we were better controlled. My mother said nothing, but after
that she took us and the baby, who was somewhat easier, to the park
every afternoon to play quietly within her vision. I didn't mind, I
read. But it was hard for my brother to live in circumscribed space,
although he tried after our mother shouted him back from a game
of Indians and Cowboys, himself both Indian and Cowboy, tracking
fast and far.

During the hottest days we took off for Orchard Beach after
an hour of scurrying preparation: Where are your bathing suits,
put them on; put the bananas into the big shopping bag; I wonder
if the eggs are hard-boiled yet; put your shirts and pants on over
your bathing suit; Katie, run down to the grocery and buy six rolls,
there's money on the table; don't put on those shoes, wear your old
sneakers; not that dress, wear the blue one; hold the baby while I
take the eggs out; take her bottle of milk out of the icebox and wrap
it in a diaper so it won't get too warm; wrap up the towels in the
old blanket and tie some string around it; leave the grapes alone,

we'll need them on the beach when we're thirsty; here, the eggs are ready, wrap them up with the farmer cheese. Are we ready? Everything in the shopping bag? Did you put in your shovel? Hold the baby while I close the fire-escape window and lock the door.

My mother carrying the baby, my brother with the rolled blanket, and I with the shopping bag went to Tremont Avenue to wait for the summer trolley, a chariot of the gods served by Mercury. It clanged, it swayed, it screeched, and when its delicate wand slipped the wires in the sky, it shot little lightnings. Mercury got down from his daring ledge that ran the length of the trolley and coaxed the capricious wand that bent and quivered back to its wire. When he wasn't mastering electricity (at times, I thought, like a young, graceful Ben Franklin, without the spectacles and the moral wisecracks), our hero swung from open row to row, collecting fares, tapping change from the coin-shaped tubes on his chest, ripping transfers off a pad, one foot on his narrow ledge, one swinging in the air behind him, like Mercury, like a bird taking off.

We transferred to another trolley and yet another, riding into a place that had lawns around the houses and trees to screen them from the trolley tracks. We got off where the tracks were gritty and pulled our feet through the hot sand toward the water. It was never as crowded as Coney Island nor as interesting. We couldn't go into the water over our heads, we didn't eat hot dogs, only wholesome everyday food, we couldn't throw sand at each other because it might get into the baby's face. The sailboats in the distance were pretty to watch, dipping and straightening like ice skaters, and we argued about cloud shapes, was it a giant or a rhinoceros (surprising to find the same discussion in *Hamlet*). We carefully sucked and picked the threads off peach pits, preparing them for endless rubbing on the sidewalk to wear them down until they could be worn as rings, theoretically. (It took so long to make a peach ring, demanding much more patience than any of us had, that although reports kept coming in about magnificent rings on Monterey and on Arthur, we on Lafontaine never accomplished even one.)

It was nice on Orchard Beach, with the trolley rides, the big bag of food to dip into, the sailboats, the clouds, the water and watching it flow into the canals we dug near the water's edge, but it wasn't Coney Island; nothing ever again was.

9
Battles and Celebrations

In the fall, shapes became brisk, as sharp as the folds on new book covers. The hat factory smoke gathered itself together like long horses to ride the wind. The pale, weak forearms of our summer fathers disappeared under stiff dark cloth. Buildings began again to look like precise cutouts. The leaves fell from my tree and dried and turned in the gutter, making sounds like funeral veils. The jingling wagon of the ices man and its colored bottles disappeared. The icebox iceman put on his wool beanie with the pompom. Mrs. Katz closed the front window of her candy store and one could no longer buy from the sidewalk or hang out there as if one were going to buy, any minute. The gardeners in Crotona Park pulled out the red spikey flowers and gave them to us in big bunches. The *goyish* butchers hung the gray stretched-out bodies of hares in their windows. The kosher butchers heaped mounds of chicken fat to be rendered for use in Rosh Hashanah meals that celebrated the Hebrew New Year. Warm-skinned fruits gave way to cool apples and round purple Concord grapes appeared in slatted baskets in every greenstore, and Jews and Italians on the block began to make wine. In a corner of every kitchen was a purple mess to which sugar was added and, I think, alcohol; it was watched and fed, attended to as if each family had a new baby. And, like a monstrous new baby, the wine stank up the street; it was a fleshy acrid smell, dark and dusty, and the end product that we sipped never seemed worth the trouble, the worried care. (Was I jealous of a small vat of spoiled grapes? Quite possibly. At times there seemed to be no limit to the greed for feeling jealous.)

Among the fall fashions that swept in on us from inventive Arthur Avenue, like making rings of dried peach pits, decorating the backs of our hands with cockamamies, soaking bubble gum in a glass of water overnight – as Joey's father did his false teeth – to make it hard and resistantly chewy the next morning, was that of embroidering, part of a *Little Women* phase, a time of maidenly dignity and refinement. We girls had small embroidery hoops, a few hanks of colored thread, and a stamped bit of cloth to work on. In for the sociability rather than the craft, a number of us settled for fast cross-stitching. When confronted with a leaf or flower, some would make a loop, catch it with a stitch at the end, and there it was, a petal. Those of us who, like myself, came from houses of dexterous, admired hands filled in the leaves and petals laboriously and with satisfaction as the spaces became shape and color, the cloth stippled with French knots and its edges tastefully tassled.

Ranged at the sides of the stoop stairs, six or eight of us sat like Old Country village women tatting or knitting in gossiping twilights. We let the gossiping go and sang and sang even when the light was too dim for sewing, outsinging the calls of our parents. We sang loudly at first, each voice outstriding the other. Shortly, an esthetic emerged; sad parts were sung heartbreakingly softly, jolly parts were sung jauntily but never coarsely shouted. We became divas, operatic actresses like Geraldine Farrar and Rosa Raisa, capable of melting the cement sidewalk with 'Because I love you, I've tried so hard but can't forget', with 'Not for just an hour, not for just a day, not for just a year, But Always.' We were seductive minxes, spit-curled soubrettes in 'Does your mother know you're out, Cecilia? Does she know that I'm about to steal ya', a felicity of rhyme matched only by Henry Wadsworth Longfellow. We were quivering, freezing, starving old ladies when we whimpered 'Over the hill, over the hill' on our way to the poorhouse. One of our most satisfying songs was a ballad that had wandered with pioneers and immigrants to settle, with small local variations, into many cities (one version, more recently heard as sung by Westchester girls, placed the action in Tarrytown; another *mise en scène* was Buffalo). Our version, sung with dreamy rue and gentle defiance, ran, as ballads do, to length. The truncated matter left by memory holds the bare bones of the story:

> *In Jersey City where I did dwell*
> *A butcher's boy I loved so well.*
> *He stole my heart away from me*
> *And sat another on his knee.*

He sat another on his knee
Because she had more gold than me.
Her Gold will fade, her silver fly
And then she'll be as poor as I.

We were, of course, repeating the joy of singing in the school auditorium and, more remotely, repeating traditions of which we had no conscious awareness, echoing the group singing on the evening streets of villages in Russia, in Poland, in Hungary, in Italy, to which we were still intimately linked.

The fights of autumn in Apartment 5B, 2029 Lafontaine, started with pencil boxes and rulers and went on to clothing for the New Year holidays. My brother didn't care; a new pair of pants meant staying clean and untorn, no marble shooting on his knees, no stickball and sliding to home base, a manhole cover in the middle of the horse-shit street. He would just as soon not, but he got them and suffered mildly. My growth was more erratic than his, all finished by the time I was eleven, a leaps-and-bounds development that left me bewildered and with clothing that never fit. To allow for lengthenings and broadenings like Alice in Wonderland, a new coat was bought two sizes too large, the sleeves covering my hands to the fingernails, the skirt almost to my ankles, and as poisonous as the cloak Medea sent her doomed rival Creusa. By the next year's holidays, the coat was tight across my back, the sleeves bared my wrists, the skirt was high above my knees, and the whole confection was as hideous as it had been the year before. I wore the coat when it was long, I wore it when it was short; I had no choice. But my mother and father had some sharp words on 'humiliating' a growing girl, and what the devil did she mean by 'humiliating'; wasn't the coat new or like new? Anyhow, she had no business indulging my '*pianovi chasto*' sensibilities. There were millions of children all over the world who didn't have a rag for their behinds, who were freezing in the streets of Russia or working, at my age, in the coal mines of Pennsylvania. They were off! And I took my misery to the fire escape, hoping I would catch double pneumonia in the wind and become as pale and thin as Bessie Love and almost die in a clean white hospital, my life saved by Wallace Reid, who told my father, straight out, not to be such a stingy louse and made him promise to reform. Otherwise, he, Wallace Reid, would go to the police and arrange to adopt me.

After the 'Ohlly Nohly' sung by our black neighbors on 98th Street came other religious experiences on Lafontaine, one on a Friday evening in November. The cookies baked that afternoon were in a covered dish on a high kitchen shelf beyond a child's reach, the kitchen smelled of gefilte fish and the rest of the house of lemon oil furniture polish, forever the smell of cleanliness. The wooden floors were slick and shining; there were freshly washed and starched curtains on the dining-living room windows. My mother had put two candlesticks on the big round dining table, lit them, and placed a white cloth on her head. She began to talk at them in the same singsong that Uncle David murmured when he bound his arm with black leather strips and swayed back and forth. It was talking to God, we had been told, and women did it only on Friday night, the only time God had for women. In the middle of a phrase my mother took off her headcloth, blew out the candles, and, turning to my astonished father, said – in Polish, which we still spoke sometimes – 'No more. I never believed it, I don't now. And I don't have to do it to please my mother, or anyone, here.' She never lit candles again, although Friday night kept its usual smells, shines, and crispness appropriate to the Eve of Wonderful Saturday the day of the movies, and later reenactment of our favorite bits, the girls snaking like vamps, the boys leaping up and down the stairs, thrusting and jabbing the air with sticks like the swords of Douglas Fairbanks.

Nor did our mother ever go to the synagogue on Arthur Avenue, except once or twice to hear my brother sing in the choir when she dragged me to join the women's section where the grandmothers held lemonlike fruits to their noses, meant to revive them should the Yom Kippur fast cause them faintness. It was insufferable to know that he earned two dollars for Passover and two dollars for the ten days of Rosh Hashanah-Yom Kippur. I could sing as true and loudly as he and could learn to make the Hebrew sounds as quickly, but they didn't – ever – take girls. It would be gratifying to suggest feminist passion in the resentment, but it dealt only with the stinker amassing two dollars and two dollars more, a fair advance toward a two-wheeler bike, while I earned nothing. Arithmetic, an abomination too, helped feed the angry fires: you could go to the movies twenty times for two dollars, or buy forty big five-cent ice-cream cones. I could be distracted now and then from my brother's pile of gold on Yom Kippur. I liked

Yom Kippur; there was something extreme, outrageous, about it, especially when the old men got angry with God. Passover was fun, seders with funny things on the table: baked bones, baked egg, a bitter mash, a sweet mash whose significance we were told and forgot in sipping wine and hunting for the hidden matzo. After we all sang 'Chad Gad Yoh', something about a little goat in one of those songs that got bigger and bigger (like 'Old MacDonald Had a Farm'), we were dumped on a pile of coats in the bedroom to lie in a nest, like birds, to sleep on warm clouds like Wynken, Blynken, and Nod. Passover meant bubeluch, plump matzo meal pancakes covered with sugar, and it meant, on rainy days when we took lunch to school, matzo smeared with chicken fat or, best of all, a cold scrambled egg between two slabs of buttered matzo. And then there was the great classic, matzo brei, pieces of matzo soaked in milk, squeezed into a delectable mess, and fried to golden curls and flakes – one of the dishes that evokes piercing darts of nostalgia in every Jewish breast and stories of childhood Passovers complete with lightly drunken uncles.

But with all its pleasures, Passover was only nice. Yom Kippur was weird, monumental. Imagine not eating for a whole day to prove something or other to God, or yelling at God in the synagogue as the bearded old men did in their white shawls, their heads thrown back, their Adam's apples tearing at their skinny throats. They made animal noises as their bodies whipped back and forth almost to the ground, their open mouths jerking their beards as they sang wildly of atonement and complaint. With a towel over my head, I practiced the urgent bending back and forth and making Hebrew sounds, but didn't get any feeling into it, or out of it, and no understanding. When I turned down oatmeal one Yom Kippur morning, announcing I was going to fast, my father said that in that case I shouldn't have had barley soup and boiled beef last night, the time to have started fasting. Anyhow, it doesn't count until you're thirteen and a boy, and anyhow, don't be crazy. Eat.

There was a certain enjoyable distinction and shame in being among the few Jews on the block who used the same utensil for both butter and meat dishes, blithely denying the Bible's injunction, as my father explained it, not to seethe lambs in the milk of their mothers. Why? He didn't know exactly. We never saw the forbidden shrimp and lobster; too expensive for anyone we knew, they presented no problem. Ham and pork were surrounded by trembling auras: the absolutely forbidden, made more repulsive by slabs of white lard like dead flesh and the smooth pink piglets like skinned babies grinning from the windows of butcher shops. Neither of my parents ate pork or bacon - my mother tried once when she was frying bacon for my sick sister and couldn't force the first bite into her mouth – simply because their upbringing and the millennia of ancestors, including Moses and the Prophets, thundered against the violation and paralyzed their mouths and throats.

Pretty, springy Miss Torrence asked me to buy a sandwich for her one rainy day; it was to be ham and cheese with lettuce and mayonnaise on white bread. I carried it back to school from the German delicatessen on 180th Street as if it were an explosive thing, away from my body, the bag held only by my thumb and forefinger, proud to have been given such a distinguished commission by one of the goddesses, heroic because I was risking God's displeasure. Carrying ham, its abominableness enhanced by being stuck to cheese, a milk dish, the forbidden esoterica folded together on elegant, neatly cut Tip-Top white bread, infinitely high-class compared to our thick slabs of rye or cornbread, made buying and delivering the sandwich just frightening enough, just forbidden enough, just confusing enough to be a glorious adventure.

While the fall and the Jewish New Year belonged to us, the winter belonged to the *goyim* and Christ, their closest relative, now only remotely ours because we had treated him so badly; stuck him on a pole with nails and cut open his side and made him drink vinegar. The customary American symbols of Christmas – the elaborately wrapped toys brought by Santa Claus and laid under a glittering tree, the green wreaths and red ribbons – were absent from the Italian houses. Instead of Christmas trees, the De Santises, the Silvestris, the Bianchis arranged little country scenes of farm animals and shepherds with crooks all looking up in admiration at the pretty blond lady with the new baby in her lap. The Bianchis also had beautiful little angels with long fingers like Good Fairies. They came all the way from Naples, Carla told me, brought by her silent grandmother, thin, austere, always dressed in black. No one, not even Carla, was allowed to touch them. The only house festivities, Maria Silvestri told me, was a lot of eating of fish on Christmas Eve and card playing and wine drinking when the men grabbed and pinched the women. Early in the morning, the women and the old men went to church to greet the newborn Christ, leaving the men and children who had come up from Mulberry Street sleeping all over the house, three and four in a bed.

Feeling a bit like a traitor and preening in my knowledge of a wider world, a witness to mysteries unknown to the other Jewish kids, I luxuriated in descriptions of what I had seen and been told of the Italian festivities. Given warm welcome in Italian houses mainly because my mother was available at all hours for emergency help and advice, my closest friends were Italian. I liked the shouting and laughter, the plants in backyards, the bossy, powerful grandparents, and the thrilling disrespect with which Italian mothers gave their kids wine with their lunchtime spaghetti so that they spent the afternoon school sessions sleeping, heads cushioned by arms folded on scratched wooden desks; fauns, children of Bacchus sleeping off Dionysian revels, my favorite anarchists.

Resenting my intimacy with Marias, Carlas, and Caterinas, the Ruthies, the Rosies, the Hannahs nibbled poisonously at me and my *krist* friends. They had additional ammunition in the obvious fact that our house was not kosher; my mother even gave our baby bacon, pig meat, *pheh*! How could I eat an Italian apple that lay in the icebox with pork? How could I play with dopes who thought the same baby was born year after year, maybe for as much as a hundred years, and decided he was God? And weren't they drunks (quoting the axiom that all Gentiles were drunkards, one of the feeble ripostes to anti-Semitism), sending their kids to school reeling, full of wine? What kind of Jew was I, anyhow? I didn't know. So I stopped displaying my ethnological enlightenments and compartmentalized my life, on one side of the street sort of Jewish, on the other sort of Italian, yet always trying to arrange a comfortable melding: Italians were really sort of Jewish, anyhow.

Besides the holiday, the tinsel like silver rain, in the five-and-ten, and the fat Santa Claus that bent and blinked like a moron from the window of the music store on Tremont Avenue, winter meant a constant struggle over warm underwear. My tall green-eyed goddess, Miriam Silverberg, the niece of the people next door, and rich enough to wear braces on her teeth, wore high knee socks all winter and no long underwear. When I pointed this out to my mother, she countered with Miriam's age, fourteen, and my miserably few years. Also, she wasn't Miriam's mother, nor was Miriam's mine, and I had to do what the mother with whom God had afflicted me said, and no more arguments. Tomorrow morning I was to put on long underwear, down to my ankles, and long stockings, pulled all the way up, attached to metal garters that hung from a cotton vest. For years, until I was old and strong enough to refuse to go to school so grotesquely dressed, I went through a stubborn ritual: out of the house in the morning, and into the cellar behind the furnace where I pulled down my stockings to become fat sausages twisted and rolled below my knees. Up went the underwear to make even fatter sausages about my thighs. Just before I got to school and snoopy teachers, as bad as mothers, the elaborate process was reversed. School out for lunch, down the stockings and up the underwear; around the corner from the house, down the underwear and up the stockings, and so on through eight changes each school day. Four fat rolls on baby-fat legs made awkward walking but I felt splendidly fashionable as the winds and winter rains froze my knees, and triumphant. *She* thought she had won, while, really, I had, my first experience of silent battles and silent victories.

I liked her much better late winter afternoons when we went to the butcher together and she smiled her small aristocratic Warsaw smile when the butchers made their coarse jokes aimed mainly at the country *yupkes* who came in bright-eyed and smirking. The men in broad, bloody aprons looked like giants, one with the bushy eyebrows of the huge cop in Charlie Chaplin films. The store was warm with light, with the glisten of entrails, of fat, of the big shining meat grinder and big hooks hung with livers and hearts that seemed still to be quivering, like live flesh, like the big bloody hands that cut and pulled and ripped carcasses apart. The warm, fatty air was full of the butchers' ringing voices: 'Come, my beauties of Israel, my Esthers, my Shebas, take what I've got – and have I got!' 'You want breast? Me, too, I want breast, *tsotskele* [cutie].' While he sawed up marrow bones (a delicacy, incidentally, that belonged to our father exclusively) or ground beef that came out like red worms, one of the men would tell the story of a butcher who suspected a woman of stealing a chicken and stuffing it into her blouse. The butcher quickly reached in to encounter an innocent featherless breast, and being a witty fellow, like all butchers, asked calmly, 'Already plucked?' The men roared, the women tittered.

Never quite sure of how much Yiddish we understood but

suspecting it was enough for dirty jokes (the reason our parents began to tell their jokes in Polish, which we children had mostly forgotten), my mother sent me out of the store to wait in the street as the spirits grew high and salacious. I didn't mind too much, if it was snowing. The street lamps were rippled like ballerinas' skirts and it was lovely to see the snowflakes come out of the dark sky, brighten along the ripples, glow for a second or two in the full light, float down to darkness and melt, a ballet to music too delicate to hear.

Visits to the butcher shop were only pauses, periods of détente, in the 'you'll catch a cold' battles. One constant battle concerned itself with wearing rubbers, which strangle, as throttled fury strangled me then. I wouldn't wear rubbers because they were ugly, a nuisance to take off and put on, and an impediment to the trials of endurance I was launched on. My father would complain that I was eating up his life by ruining my shoes, my mother would warn that I was inviting pneumonia and would have to go to the hospital where people died, but I had to try to endure the icy slush that seeped into my shoes, gathered in my stockings, and froze my feet blue and painful. As I had to climb the two-story rocks behind the hat factory (and made it a couple of times), egged on and sneered at by the practiced boys who flew ahead of me.

One solution to the rubbers controversy was to tear out of the house without them clattering down the stairs while my mother called after me to come back, reenacting a Tobie-Fannie Herman scene. My frenzied Tobie flight and my mother's suddenly shrill Fannie-voice always return when weather and reason, fighting passionate unwillingness, force me into a shop to try on overshoes or even sleek waterproof boots. They fit. Yet they strangle, as they did in childhood, and I give them away, self-doomed to dragging ruined shoes and blue feet through icy slush for the rest of my life.

10
Jimmy and Death

Jimmy Petrides, my brother's best friend from the time we moved to Lafontaine Avenue when both boys were about five, was lank and had a neat face, as if someone had made a careful drawing of it before he was born; the lines of his thin eyebrows and thin nose straight, the lower line of his eyes straight, and the arches above as complete and round as the pretty hollow at the back of his neck. Like all the other boys he leaped and bellowed in the street but he was quiet and shy when he came to our house on rainy or cold days to make trains of boxes or spools and to match baseball cards with my brother. Although they lived in our house, two stories below us, we knew very little of his family. His father was one of the many anonymous men in caps with paper bags under their arms who rushed to the El in the morning and came back more slowly at night. Jimmy had a younger sister whom he began to take to school when he was about eight, a dark-gold little girl who clutched his hand and wouldn't talk to anyone else. Once home from school, she stayed in her house; we rarely saw her on the street even as she grew older. Mrs. Petrides was also rarely visible and wonderful when she was, a silent solitary thing like a tree alone in a field. There may have been other Greek families on the block but not in our immediate houses, and she had very few English words to exchange with her neighbors. Nevertheless, families in immigrant neighborhoods being inevitably interdependent, for shopping advice, for medical information, for the care of each other's children and the exchange of kitchen delicacies, Mrs. Petrides was offered strudel by Mrs. Nagy, the *Ungarische dripke* who was the best baker on the block. Big, clumsy Mrs. Kaplan, the loudest behemoth of the house, took her a length of *kishka* (stuffed intestine), her specialty, which Jimmy told us they couldn't eat; all that rubbery stuff. My mother's contribution was to ask Jimmy if his mother would like to go to the English classes with her, explaining that they were held during afternoon school hours and she would be back before three o'clock. He said, 'She won't, she's too ashamed,' the word for embarrassed or shy. There must have been a number of women like Mrs. Petrides on the block, who had no one to speak with when the husband and children were away, no one to ask where she could buy feta cheese or Greek oil. Tall and slender, with Jimmy's long eyebrows and straight nose, her sandy hair in a long full knot at the back of her head, her high-arched eyes fixed straight ahead, she looked like a lady on the front of a storybook ship, as strong and as lonely.

My mother and the other women said that if Mrs. Petrides had taken them into her house to see Jimmy when he got sick – it didn't need words – or had asked the De Santis boys to take him to Fordham Hospital, Jimmy might not have died. We never found out the cause of his death; children were told about the deaths of the old but never of children, a knowledge too dreadful to speak. The first intimations of Jimmy's illness came from my brother, who was hanging around one rainy October day being mean and restless. He got in my mother's way as she was trying to boil diapers in the steaming cauldron on the stove; he woke our little sister, who had been sick and was napping; he hid my brand-new pencil with the removable cap eraser. My mother suggested he go down to play in Jimmy's house or ask him to come up. He said Jimmy was sick, he hadn't gone to school that day. The next day and the next when he was asked if Jimmy had been in school he again answered, 'No,' and although the weather had cleared, he refused to go down into the street. He pushed spools and boxes around for a while, read for a while, colored a picture with the baby for a while, but mostly he hung around, like a tired little old man.

The whole house was quiet. The women didn't talk much; only Tobie Herman clattered noisily up and down the stairs. My mother must have known that Jimmy was dying, but I knew nothing until my brother burst into the house crying as neither my father with his beatings nor I with my fierce teasing could make him cry. His face was broken, tears pouring down his sweater, his fists clenched and shaking as if he were fighting, his feet stamping. When we calmed him a little, though he still shuddered and wept, he told us that Mr. Petrides, home from the factory that day, came over to him and said that Jimmy was dead, that we would never see him again. 'What does he mean, *never*? That I won't ever see Jimmy again? What does he mean?' and his heels stamped the floor and his fist punched the air again and the terrible crying started again. I wanted to console him, not quite knowing what to say, saying something while my mother held him on her lap, a big boy of nine who allowed the indignity because he was in terrible trouble.

That evening when my father came home he was still shuddering, lying on our bed with the baby, who offered him her doll and conversation. He didn't respond, which made her cry. That night he didn't eat, and he slept deeply, shuddering every once in a while. Like the street, school was hushed the next morning. The news of Jimmy's death, carried in whispers through the auditorium, in the playground, on the stairs, in toilets, was a funerary garland that wrapped itself around the whole red brick building. Street life stopped: no ball, no marbles, no ropes lashing at the sidewalk, no stickball, no fights, no singing on the stoop. The day of the funeral must have been Saturday, there was no school. We returned books to the library and picked out others early and quickly, then went home to clean up and wait, not knowing quite what we were waiting for. We had seen funerals in the movies, in the news, but they were of grand and old people, not of a boy, not on our street. It was a cool sunny day, the big garbage cans and the metal roof of the De Santis garage shining bright and hard. As we sat on the stoop we heard stirrings on the inside stairs. The inner door opened and two men came down into the small hall where the letter boxes were, carrying a long black box. My brother gasped and I dragged him down the block, looking back to see what was happening. After the box came Mr. Petrides in a black coat and Mrs. Petrides with a black veil over her head and falling down her black coat. Behind them a few more people in black, one of the women holding by the hand the little Petrides girl whose head, too, was covered with a black scarf. The box was carried slowly down the stoop stairs, into the gutter, and then, followed by the family, headed toward 180th Street. Telling my brother that funerals were quiet so he shouldn't make noise, I ran ahead to look at Mrs. Petrides from the sidewalk. She wasn't crying; she had died, too, with only the clear drawing of her features left on dull white paper.

As the family walked slowly, following the black box, held high by the four black arms like burned tree branches, the children began to trail after, led off by the two youngest De Santis boys, both in their early teens, and then the other Italian children,

who seemed to know about funerals: Maria Silvestri and her brother
Louis, Caroline and Petey Santini, the Bianchi kids. My brother
ran into the gutter to join Petey, and I followed him, hesitating
for a moment, to walk with Caroline. Awkwardly, hesitantly, the
Jewish kids watching from the sidewalk began to walk with us,
some of them kids who might later be hit for joining a *goyish*
funeral. The two Ruthies came and Helen, Rachel, and Hannah,
Sidney and Milton, the Sammies, the Izzys. My brother began to
cry, quietly, and I went to him while Caroline took Petey, whose
face had begun to quiver. More crying around me, behind me,
growing louder and louder, coming out of twisted eyes, leaking
into open mouths. (Those weeping faces combine inextricably in
my memory with the image of the mourning cherubim of Giotto,
wailing as they hover over the body of Christ.)

I couldn't understand why they were all crying. My brother,
yes, Jimmy had always been his very best friend and he liked
him more than anyone else in the world, more than our mother.
The other boys had liked him too, an easy, gentle boy who yielded
to them rather than fight. But why were the girls crying over a
Greek boy they had hardly ever played with? What did they know
about death that I didn't? What were they seeing? What were they
feeling? Like them, I knew dead people were put in a hole in the
ground and covered with earth. Were they crying because the earth
might choke him, because he might open his eyes in the dark, alone,
screaming, and no one to hear him? Maybe then he would really,
truly die. Was that what they meant by 'Frightened to death'? As
a Christian boy he should become an angel. Was there a saw in the
coffin to cut through the black wood and a shovel to dig away the
dirt? And once out, how long would he have to stand in the dark
alone before God sent the blond lady with the naked baby down
through the windy night clouds to carry him back up with her?

Seeing sick Jimmy standing alone, waiting – for how long?
– to be rescued from the dark made me cry as fully, with my
whole body, as I couldn't on Third Avenue in the dark, when I was
five. Maybe my brother was crying the same memory: in a dark,
unknown place, lost, unprotected. We were crying for the same
reason that we hid our heads in the movies when a child wandered
alone, that we quickly skipped pages when a book threatened to
tell about an abandoned child. (Maybe we were also crying, like
the women who went to the movies 'to enjoy a good cry', for the
relief not too often permitted us.)

By the time we reached 180th Street, my mother had caught up with us. Taking us each by the hand, she said she didn't think they would let us into the Greek church and certainly not into the cemetery; come home, stop crying. We ate, we slept, we went to school, we asked no questions. One of the block chroniclers said the Petrides family had gone back to Greece, another said they moved downtown near cousins who had a stable. We were no longer interested in the family – the godlike child's gesture of quickly dissolving away anything that wasn't immediately attached to our ears, our eyes, our greeds, our envies. Our fears hung on for a while. No one mentioned Jimmy. His name was a black omen, a sign that children could die, and as fast as we could, we obliterated his name, too.

The Halloween after Jimmy's death was a brutal time. When the slashing dark rains of late fall came on Halloween, I was glad to stay at home. On clear nights I was impelled to go, curious, defying my reluctance and fear. The only children in costume – no witches, no gypsies, no pumpkin heads, no pirates – were small wandering foreign bands stumbling in their fathers' old pants, tottering on the crooked high heels of mothers' shoes. They did not invade houses to ask for 'trick or treat', expecting apples or candy. Their collections were made on the street, accosting adults with 'Got a penny, mister?' The pickings on Lafontaine were poor; this was begging, and begging was the ultimate disgrace, contemptible even for kids. Furthermore, there weren't too many spare pennies around, and those had to be saved for a stick of gum, a string of licorice for one's own kids. We were impressed and wary of their boldness, these invaders from Washington, Bathgate, and Third Avenue with their threatening, demanding hands, and when we saw them coming, moved step by step backward to the top of our stoops, ready to disappear into the inner halls.

It was an evening of mayhem for the bigger boys on our street, joined by a couple of their heroes from Arthur Avenue. They wheedled long black stockings, a color and shape of magic and malevolence, from mothers who were ignorant of their use that night and were too careless or busy to ask. The stockings were filled with flour or chalk carefully collected from schoolroom discards and pounded into white powder. They became whip sausages to beat legs, leaving white clouds on stockings and flesh. Nothing

serious, a mark of being with the daring on this night, a good
time for displaying agility in jumping, turning, running, avoiding
the whips. A more vicious invention, automatically blamed on the
Italian and Irish boys, was to fill the stocking with unbroken pieces
of chalk or, lacking enough of those, ash, coal, and small rocks. To
the game of hunter and prey was added the exciting element of real
injury, a young perverse version of Russian roulette: which whip
would only mark, which whip would bruise or crack a bone?

That especially violent night, the big bellowing boys twirling
the black whips over their heads like cowboys' lariats, like frenzied
dervishes, I decided to get out of the fun that was not fun and
turned my back to run up the stoop stairs and home. A sharp
blow hit my calf, throwing me on the top step. I looked at my leg.
Something completely impossible was happening to it: a thin spurt
of blood was coming through my stocking, straight as an arrow. I
knew blood dripping from a scraped knee, a cut finger, a bleeding
nose, but never in a thin fast burst like this, straight out into the
air. When it slowed, after moments when I saw my life leaving me
very quickly, to a dripping trickle, I went upstairs and into the
bathroom. My mother was reading yesterday's English paper in
the kitchen, and my father was busy with the piecework he had
set up in the dining-living room. No one asked any questions. I
washed the bloody stocking and my leg, given plenty of time for a
careful examination of my calf, which showed only a puncture like
a mosquito bite, by my brother's arrival. He was covered from head
to foot, a ghost boy, in layers of chalk and soot, ordered into the hall
to slap it off before he came into the house again. Then take a bath.
It wasn't bath time, he protested, it wasn't Saturday; he wasn't
dirty; he hated baths; it wasn't fair. My mother was implacable
and called to me to start running water into the tub, and then to
get ready for bed.

Alone in bed, I examined my calf again. There was only that
tiny hole, hardly visible, but because my blood had jumped out
of it in such a weird way, I knew I had a terrible blood disease.
And would soon die, like the children with rare diseases reported
by the Sunday *American*. My left calf became the focus of my life,
never forgotten for a moment. The bruise turned strange colors,
purplish streaked with a sick yellow like pus. It didn't hurt much,
but my leg felt heavy, draggy, beginning to reveal diagnostic signs
of the disease that would kill me. Some weeks before I had seen, in
the Sunday *American* magazine section that Mr. Haskell left with

the jokes, a drawing that filled most of a page: a woman carrying a little nude girl past a piece of sharp-edged furniture whose corner sent a chip of the child's buttock flying into the room. I read the article, mesmerized, memorizing each detail. First one affected area turned white and hard and then another. The child gradually turned to stone, as immobile as a statue: an actual statue, dead, when her lungs and heart became marble. That was my disease. I poked my arms and legs; they felt cold and stiff and the white mark made by my finger took an interminable time to turn pink again. My legs moved sluggishly, as if I were dragging stone shoes. My eyesight was becoming misty and I had to bend deeper into my book to see. I wasn't hearing too well, either. My mother said I wasn't listening, not paying attention, and I wasn't. It took great concentration to avoid the sharp corner of the piano, not to bump against a dresser or a classroom desk, not to cause a chip to fly off my arm, my back, a sign of the end. Death was surely coming, but I was not yet ready for conclusive signs.

At night, lying next to my brother, who thrashed around in fight dreams muttering the dirty words he was not allowed to say during the day, listening to the gurgles of my sister wrapped in her baby cocoon of sleep, I pushed and felt my heavy cold body and tested my eyes by trying to pierce the dark. Was I seeing the hook on the door and the knob on the closet, or only remembering, as people going blind must? Would I hear the clatter of the milkman's bottles or imagine them? What would my brother do when he found me motionless with white stony eyes one morning soon? What would my mother say? What would she do? Would everyone follow my box, crying, as when Jimmy died? Since I couldn't become an angel like Christian children, I would lie in the box, smelling myself rot, hearing the flesh fall off my bones, feeling my eyes roll out of my head and my hair creep down to my shoulder bones. At one moment during one of those dying nights the stoicisms I had been practicing, maybe to this end of suffering and dying without a murmur and alone, left me. I found myself running down the hall to my parents' bedroom. Their door was half open. I slipped through it and stood for a long time looking at them and listening to their breathing. They usually snored – a duet my brother and I imitated masterfully – but now there was no sound. I bent lower to listen to my mother's breathing, to watch her chest rise and fall. Nothing. My father's chest wasn't moving either, and there was not the faintest sound of breath. They had caught my

disease and turned to stone. They were dead. I had given them my
death.

I shrieked and both my parents sat up, sleepy-eyed and
bewildered, as if they had come a long way and didn't know
where they were. They asked me what had happened – was I
sick? Was the baby all right? And my brother? I said nothing, not
knowing how to think, what to say. On their repeated questioning
I said I had a terrible bellyache. My mother got out of bed and took
me to the bathroom for a large dose of the milk of magnesia that
was always in the medicine cabinet. I took it eagerly and stayed
home from school the next morning because I had to go to the
bathroom a lot. By lunchtime I was hungry and ate a large bowl
of rice boiled in milk, which was good for bellyaches, and went
off to school, hoping I hadn't missed yet another complication
of percentages, an impenetrable subject. By what means I made
a miraculous recovery, escaping imminent death, transferring my
death to my parents and their rejection of that death, the whole
terrible matter capable of being dispelled in a fake bellyache and
milk of magnesia, is difficult to explain. It was probably a swing
in the vagrant, impassioned imaginings of childhood that plummet
into black pits and fly into blossoming trees in dizzy alternations.
At any rate my flesh bounced back pinkly when I poked it, my
fingers became dexterous enough to weave a long string rope on
a spool with four nails hammered into it, and I outran Miltie,
something of a champ runner, in a race around the block.

11
Revelations

The spring I was ten and a half I was crazy with love: I was in love with Arthur, mostly because his name wasn't Sammy or Benny or Petey. He was so neat and tight, a clear, straight parting in his plastered hair, a starched collar fresh every day, clean neck, clean ears. An Arrow Collar boy. He sat at the desk in front of me, and as if my eyes were tongues, I lapped and lapped at his perfection, his goyishness. Although he lived on the block, he was never part of the Saturday morning hordes that skated down Tremont Avenue to change books at the library, nor was he ever in the Saturday afternoon crowd in the movies. He never played in the street, nor did he walk to school with us; his mother took him there, called for him at lunchtime, walked him back, and called for him again at three o'clock. Though we were in the same class, the same seats, for five months, I never spoke to him or he to me. At this long sour remove, it seems I should have resented his mother's protection against us, the flying kids with the falling socks, but at that time I considered her exquisite care a mark of his distinction, no more than a prince deserved.

I was in love with Mrs. Bender, the teacher who stroked her large smooth breasts as she read 'Hiawatha', her hand moving with the rhythm of 'By the shore of Gitche Gumee,/By the shining Big-Sea-Water.' I was in love with the 'Bacchanale' from *Samson and Delilah*, which we would put on the Victrola and whoop and holler and thump to while my mother laughed. I was in love with Mrs. Polanski's new poodle, white and round as a snowball, with a dirty ass. I was in love with the sadness of 'All Alone' and the tearful wit of the last line of 'Remember': 'But you *forgot* to remember'. I was in love with consumption, the artistic, graceful wasting that inspired Chopin. When my mother walked into the street in her new brown suit and beaver hat on the first day of Passover, she was so beautiful that I couldn't see her; her radiance blinded me. My brother, in spite of our steady urge to mutual mayhem, appeared all gold and dazzling as he played stickball in the street. And I was in love with me, grown suddenly taller and thinner, and I had, I was sure, what they called in poems a swan neck. I was as complete and smooth as a fresh pea pod.

Above all, I was in love with Helen Roth. She was bigger and older than I, broad-boned, fleshy, tough. She answered back to teachers, her mother, our mothers, who called her '*pisk*', Big Mouth. Awed by the fact that her mother sent her to the delicatessen – too expensive for most of us – to pick out whatever *she* wanted, I went there with her often to wonder at the profligacy with which she ordered and to be deeply moved by her talent for eating a whole hot red pepper without blinking or coughing. And she came equipped with an older brother, who went to high school and was distant and beautiful, and a big sister, who went to work, elegant, fancy, in shining high-heeled pointed shoes.

I adored Helen for having the monumental courage to be left back in school. My father would have killed me, beaten me to death. Or I would have run away to die in some distant cellar. Here *she* was, waving her dooming report card with an airy, untroubled gesture worthy of Gloria Swanson.

Helen's most admirable role, though, was that of friend and messenger to her neighbor, the skinny, trembling Mr. Ricciardi, the cellist with the thick glasses, for whom she organized secret little parties. Sunday mornings when his mother was in church, he sent Helen to gather three or four of her friends; no Italian girls, he said; they spoiled the fun, he said. I went once. She gathered us up with whispers and led us on, eager and excited, to the bakery on Tremont Avenue. There we bought rare gems of chocolate-mounded, pink-iced, custard-filled cakes that never quite came to two dollars Helen carried; Mr. Ricciardi had said she could keep the change, she told us. It was her honor to carry the pastry box, dangling it high and showily, to trouble the other kids not invited to the party. We walked quietly up the three flights of 2027, Helen first, as leader and to make sure her parents' door was closed, then we slipped into the Ricciardi apartment. It was close and dark as a cave. I could dimly make out religious pictures in the hallway, pink and blue saints, a Madonna in a white dress being lifted to Heaven by pretty angels, as our host led us into a

room of heavy, overstuffed chairs, a big deep couch, and a long
table. I wondered why there was so little light, why he didn't pull
up the window shades, but this was his party and adult oddities
were too many to think about one by one. Quick, jumpy, bending,
smiling, his thick glasses glistening above eyes like rolling marbles,
he served us the cakes on decorated plates, patting a shoulder, a
head, a cheek, as he placed each dish and fork. Since I had never
eaten cake with a fork, I paused, confused. But worldly Helen
knew how, she had done it before, and I followed her, the smooth
cut with the side of the fork, piercing the small piece, lifting it
daintily to the mouth. Mr. Ricciardi didn't eat. Patting, stroking,
urging more cakes and candy from a bowl on the middle of the
table, he moved constantly, his fingers trembling nervously. An
odd thing for someone who played the cello for a living, I thought,
but maybe it was just that trembling that made the cello sound like
sorrow.

While we were practicing the refined handling of unaccustomed
delicacies, Mr. Ricciardi sent Helen into the next room to bring The
Book. She came back with a notebook held in a rubber band. His
long shaking fingers pulled at the band, and having pulled it off, he
invited us to gather around him on the big sofa. As he turned the
blank pages, pictures slipped from between them to lie in his lap,
in ours. He was showing us something important and educational,
he said. The agitated face and fingers begged us to look, to learn.
Did we ever see a cock, maybe on our brothers or fathers? If not,
that's what a cock was, that thing, in the bush of black hair. See
the tits on that girl, they were not only for nursing babies, they
were for men to squeeze and pinch. Too bad her pussy was covered
with hair but we knew from our own what a pussy was like and how
nice to touch. Speaking faster and faster, his fingers pointing more
jumpily, he showed us naked men and women lying down close
together, sometimes head to feet, like kids who had to sleep three in
a narrow bed. One naked lady sat on a naked man's lap, but not on
his lap exactly. I didn't really care how they arranged themselves;
what horrified me were the bushes of hair. We would have them,
too, Mr. Ricciardi had assured us. I didn't want it, ever, and I didn't
want breasts. I wanted to stay a face, a stomach, a behind, arms and
legs, no more. Helen already had two big pimples on her chest and
he was stroking them while she sat there smiling plumply like Mrs.
Nagy when people praised her strudel.

I didn't want anything here, not more cake, not the candy,

no naked people, no bushes, no creepy, shaky hands. It was an enormous effort to get off the couch, to declare I was going, risking the accusation of being a scare-cat and spoiling the party, but I did. Helen ran after me down the hall. 'You dumb stupid, he'll give us some money soon.' 'I don't want it, he's scary.' 'OK, you'll be sorry.' Her voice changed, it wheedled. 'You won't tell my mother, will you? I'll give you some of the money if you don't.' It was a peculiar request, she knew that nobody told on anybody about such things. Tearing a school bag, yes, kicking in a sled, yes, stealing three cents off the newspaper stand, yes, but not these secret happenings, never. Any crack in this Pandora's box would open unimaginable disasters; heavy beatings and harsh separations that would leave us truly orphaned since we lived with one another more closely than we did with our families. So we never betrayed one another. And our antique wisdoms knew that it was better to appear united as a large bouquet of flowers, fresh, innocent, untouched, and a little stupid.

Helen's mother, Mrs. Roth, was a tall woman with the glamour of gray hair, which few of our mothers had. Her height and hair gave her an authority, a dignified composure that set her apart from the younger, frenetic mothers who argued with their children or shouted despairingly, like Fannie Herman, at their unheeding backs. Mrs. Roth simplified matters. When Helen was too loud or too long in refusing to go to the grocery, Mrs. Roth reached out her long heavy arm and slapped Helen hard, then turned back to her ironing board and continued the flowing hypnotic sweeps of the iron as if there had been no interruption at all. Mrs. Roth seemed to like me. (It became a minor source of shame in my adolescence to remember that most of the mothers liked me because I was that abominable thing, 'a good girl'.) The rare times I saw Helen's godlike brother he didn't see me at all, although Bessie, the working sister, sometimes spoke to me. The person I liked best in the family – my overwhelming crush on Helen was beyond mere liking – was the bent little father. Any time, all the time, he sat curved over a sewing machine, making seams in pants, steadily, rapidly, working from a tall pile of cloth on a bench next to him. He was always dressed in dark shapeless pants and a worn, limp jacket, a collarless shirt buttoned up to his bony Adam's apple, and a derby, shining with age, on his head. He looked like some of the poor old widowers who hung around the synagogue, nowhere else to go, and maybe a job now and then, like dusting or sweeping the synagogue floor. He looked like some of the poor rabbis who knocked on our doors for donations to East Side yeshivas, a few pennies, a nickel. Mr. Roth was religious, otherwise why would he wear his hat indoors? The household was kosher, I knew, because Helen boasted of the four sets of dishes they had as opposed to our meager all-purpose one. Yet I never saw Mr. Roth go to the synagogue, not even on the High Holy Days when the whole contingent of Lafontaine Jews, dressed in their stiff new clothing, marched on Arthur Avenue, even my nonkosher agnostic father. (Not to go was 'a shame for the *goyim*'. In spite of their palpable indifference to all religions, in the main, and a tolerance that grew of immigrant interdependence, *goyim* watched and judged Jews, according to our mentor, Mr. Kaplan. Therefore, a Jew must be self-respecting in all his ways, including his religion, and show the *goyim* how unassailably upright all Jews were.) Mr. Roth had no part in this stiff-necked wariness. I never saw him outside his house; I never saw him speak to anyone but his family, and that sparsely and almost timidly.

I couldn't place Mr. Roth, who sat there, constant, in the same posture, like a statue or a piece of furniture. He couldn't be connected with people in stories or the movies. At times, when Helen was knocking around on the street, I watched him, his thin white fingers, the claws of a delicate animal, directing the cloth toward the needle, pulling back lightly, guiding again. From time to time he would talk to me over the whirr of the machine. He knew a lot of strange things, like a rabbi, though he couldn't have been one. Maybe he was some kind of special Jewish priest. (Had I been of another time and place, I might have judged him a reader of the heavens, a sorcerer.) His head bent over the machine as if it were locked in just that space, in a voice as light and delicate as his fingers, he made astonishing, terrifying revelations. When a person died, God demanded all the hair he ever had and all his fingernails. How was I ever to collect, and where, the thickets of hair that fell in the barber shop and were swept up by Tony? I would spend centuries looking through stinking piles of garbage, sewers full of rats, all over the world, for the fingernails and toenails my mother cut and threw away. I couldn't do it and God would punish me in some unimaginable way, worse than prison, worse than the electric chair. After agonized days, I asked my mother if she knew about this rule and why hadn't she warned me. She laughed and said it was Old Country superstition and not to believe everything I heard. A bit reassured, I went back to sit near Mr. Roth's machine; besides his Doomsday messages there were other pieces of arcane knowledge I might pick up, and I did. He said there were rabbis who could answer all questions, in all languages, who could make birds sing and flowers bloom, who could, themselves, fly like great eagles. He told me that numbers weren't only for school and bookkeeping; every number meant something and combinations could be powerful things. Did I know that three really meant man's heart, head, and soul working together like the notes of music? Think of seven. Did I know that there were seven planets, big earths like ours, maybe bigger? And seven days of the week. Six was holy because there were six points in the Star of David. Too bad I was a girl and not learning Hebrew, or he would show me numbers that meant more than just numbers in the Holy Books, and where, in the Books, God ordered Moses not to tell the Jews everything but leave some mysteries for other Jews to puzzle out. That was called Kabala, he said. It meant translating the letters of words into numbers and arranging them and rearranging them, and if the proper combination of letter-numbers was hit on, the great secrets of the whole world, the earth, the oceans, the stars, would be revealed and the pure soul of the discoverer could then do anything, even fly directly to God. It was more difficult to follow than long division and I couldn't imagine a soul other than as a tiny angel. That was Christian and obviously wrong. I could, a little, make letters into numbers, matching their characters: 7 was an aristocrat like capital L; 4 was squat and rough like R; 6 looked like and might be C. How to combine them, though? What secret messages to look for? I couldn't ask Mr. Roth, he might think I was trying to learn the word-number patterns he puzzled as he sewed, maybe trying to steal his answer, like copying from someone else's paper during a test. It seemed hopeless, and after hours of devising triangles, circles, and rectangles of letters and numbers, I gave it up. I sat with Mr. Roth less and less, uncomfortable because I felt I had disappointed him. Maybe he had been grooming me, a *girl* (but a Jewish girl), to become a master of Kabala. He might have seen me – among the wonderful other things floating under his old derby – as a miracle *rebbitsin*, circling the earth with the magic rabbis. Or perhaps he had assigned me the role of breathing life into huge *golems* and inspiring them to fight for the Jews. I was sorry for him and for me, but I still loved him and his frail white fingers, his curved back, his derby, and his greatest mystery: how could such a pale, shadowy spirit become the father of big, tough, clanging Helen?

12

Newer Greeners

Probably through HIAS or some organization of 'landsmen' – the groupings of Old Country communities gathered for the comforts of the same dialects, for finding relatives, and for a wide variety of advice – my father dug up two antique, newly arrived immigrants who were our favorite caricatures. They were very distant relatives, but relatives nevertheless, and aged so that we had to call them Uncle Schlommke and Mimme (Aunt) Pessel, old-fashioned provincial names that enchanted my mother and, consequently, us. The Sunday visits were not frequent, but each was so superbly predictable that we children, on hearing of an impending visit, acted out every sentence of every phrase. (Mimicry of neighbors, of Rosa Ponselle, of Caruso, of liturgical chant, of the iceman's Italian accent, of the janitor's Polish accent, of Mary Sugar Bum's list and wobble, was an important sport in our house.) Pessel wore a reddish wig as deeply and rigidly waved as a bronze pillar. Around her neck hung a limp fur whose beady-eyed pointed face bit its own thin tail. Under the fur, which she never removed, layers of shawls and scarves protected her delicate throat. Her long yellow face was discontented, dyspeptic; she looked as if she had a terrible taste in her mouth. Uncle Schlommke's face was round and pink-cheeked; his body was round and I imagined his behind to be pink-cheeked, too. He wore a tight black derby and a long overcoat that my much taller father had given him, but when he took it off and stood in his tight suit, his belly straining the seams and buttons, he looked cute, like Tweedledee or Tweedledum.

They lived on the Lower East Side and had to take the El to visit us. Without fail Mimme Pessel arrived in a high state of agitation. A chair, please, and would someone get her a glass of water; she felt dreadful. A black man (once in a while it was an Italian) in the

El had stared and stared at her and had put a curse on her, stirred up her entrails, and feel how fast her heart was beating. There was no safety from these black demons and, almost as bad, the Irishers and the 'Taliener' and whoever else she could name between gasps. My mother went into the kitchen, followed by Uncle Schlommke, who liked to pat her plump arm as he examined with glistening brown eyes the food she was arranging on platters. My father, in the meantime, nodded in sympathy over Mimme Pessel while we flanked her, our heads bent like mourning angels on a Victorian tomb.

My mother carefully folded the dining room tablecloth, always with the roses tucked inside to protect them, and put on the white tablecloth on which she usually spread and stretched the immense sheet of noodle dough to be dried, then sliced with lightning speed in uncannily even slices. On the white cloth appeared the traditional Sunday night company meal: slices of salami and corned beef, a mound of rye bread, pickles sliced lengthwise, and the mild mustard the delicatessen dripped into slender paper cones from a huge bottle, gratis with each order. The drinks were celery tonic or cream soda, nectars we were allowed only on state occasions, in small glasses. Uncle Schlommke ate like a squirrel, sitting upright in his chair, his sandwich held in both hands close to his mouth, his eyes happy and searching the table as he nibbled rapidly, his red cheeks swelling, his derby rocking with each swallow. Mimme Pessel languished, sloping in her chair, one hand frequently stroking her distressed middle, and between sighs and ladylike groans made impressive amounts of meat and bread disappear, without mustard or pickle since they gave her wind. When the corned beef, of which we were given small bits because it was expensive and for company, was gone and only three or four slices of salami left and one wedge of pickle, we waited gleefully for the next development. It came from Uncle Schlommke, suddenly a wistful boy, Oliver Twist, with a thin, appealing voice. 'Maybe you have a little frankfurter?' The Sunday morning shopping discussion usually included a plea for frankfurters, not only for Uncle Schlommke, who was too poor to buy them, but for us as well, who ate them almost as rarely as he. The decision was always clear and final. Frankfurters were full of unwholesome things, my father said, and he wasn't spending his money on skinsful of garbage. Uncle Schlommke's plea was given a similar answer: they were not good for the digestion and a waste of money. Embarrassed for our father and for the old man, we watched the red cheeks droop and the baby mouth pucker, appalled that he might cry, hoping he would.

It never quite happened. On the signal of the 'little frankfurter', my mother began to pour tea into glasses, heaped the little cementlike cheese cakes she made on Friday and hid from us and rushed them to the table. His eyes and cheeks shone again as he stirred four lumps of sugar into his glass, tipped the tea into his saucer, and drank it in long slurps, each slurp a sigh of contentment. She was more refined, sipping more quietly out of her saucer through a lump of sugar wedged between her front teeth, 'na zukerkie' or something like that it was called in Polish.

After tea they left, carrying a brown paper bag in which my mother had put the remaining salami and bread and cakes. We didn't think it odd that they never addressed us children, not even to ask boring questions about school or exclaim over how much we had grown. We didn't like them, we didn't dislike them; they were cartoons, displaying themselves for our amusement, like Krazy Kat. Before we realized they were people, odd, old, very poor people, they disappeared, and in the fast spinning of our worlds, we never stopped to ask why or how.

Almost everyone had newly arrived immigrants, their coming as freshening as Passover or the last day of school. The big importers were the Santinis, patiently building themselves, starting with the old settler Pete, into the Seven Brothers. Giuseppe, red-cheeked and curly haired, quickly acquired intimacy with the family truck, calling it a sonomabeech when it wouldn't start; that, and a kick, often seemed to work. He learned numbers, one-a, two-a, three-a, and got himself a girl friend from Bari who worked in the Italian market on 183rd Street. She rode with him on her time off, for love and to teach him Bronx street names. The Santinis bought another secondhand truck, a real covered moving van this time, on which we – Caroline, Petey, my brother, and I – were not permitted to play, although we still had the freedom of the first truck. It was time for another brother to arrive from Naples. Sandro wasn't as rosy and juicy-looking as Giuseppe, more long and lean like Pete, shy, and a small smiler because his teeth were rotten. One look and we didn't expect much of him and didn't get much, turning our interest to the next arrival. Mr. Kaplan had said, in one park bench conversation, that they must be paying a lot of money to get the relatives over so fast; Italians had those big family clubs that cut through 'red tape' – I saw an immense red cobweb with shabby immigrants hanging on its threads like trapped flies – not like punctilious, slow-moving HIAS; the Jews always got the worst of things. We hoped the next Santini would be an actual gangster with a slanted hat, like a villain. But Ezio turned out to be big, blondish, young, a dancer and a singer who twirled us around as he sang, and he sang all the time, hopping dance songs and long-lined, sad songs that felt dark blue and lonely.

While the Santinis were filling their ramshackle attic with brothers, the Hermans were preparing for the arrival of his youngest sister, Shprinzel. She was even better than Ezio, a living replica of the 'Greene Cousine'. Like the Greene in the song, she didn't speak, she sang; she didn't walk, she sprang. She was as restless as Fannie, her restlessness, though, that of a bright windup toy, responsive to any touch. Everything amused her: my mother's Warsaw accent, which occasionally slipped out though she was working at tempering its broad tones; my brother's attempts to communicate with her in stumbling, no-tense Yiddish; a stove that was lit with a match set to a stinking little tube; the white and black of the piano keyboard, which she liked to slap with her big red hands to bring forth thunderous and shrill discords. She had never been to the movies, never been in a car, experiences she met first with explosive shrieks of terror and soon long hoots of joyous laughter. After a few rollicking weeks, she was given a husband, a quiet young man who worked in Mr. Herman's poultry market – no Valentino, everyone said, but steady; not 'overpointed', but not really stupid, either. Fannie, like everyone else, loved Shprinzel, who was so free of her own traps of anguish and terror, and insisted that Mr. Herman spend a lot of money on his little sister's wedding. She sent her to a lady's hairdresser recommended by Mrs. Haskell, way over near the Concourse, where rich women lived, and she returned beaming between two full, thick 'castle clips' on each side of her lovely, foolish face. Mr. Herman drove her down to Grand Street, where they hired a long white dress and a white veil, and to Orchard Street, where they bought a pair of black patent leather shoes, too short and pointed for her big feet. She didn't care if she had to hobble to the *chuppa*; they were beautiful, she was happy. Hobbling, burbling, waving the veil around her, chirping, laughing, down the stairs to the wedding ceremony and out of our lives. Never mind Noel Coward; 'blithe spirit' means Shprinzel, her shrieks of delight and her castle clips.

We had our own two immigrants, quite unlike the radiant Shprinzel. After innumerable visits to HIAS and consultations with Workmen's Circle friends, my father arranged passage for a nephew, the grown son of one of his numerous elder sisters. My mother wasn't especially eager to welcome him; when she had suggested that one of *her* unmarried sisters be brought from Warsaw, my father had said he was spending *his* money on *his* family, not hers. She went into one of her silent, glowering times. Cousin Yankel (addressed occasionally by my father, never my mother, as Yankele, the affectionate diminutive of his name) was nineteen or twenty, lanky and awkward, with a big Adam's apple that I liked to watch riding his throat. He had a long thin nose, cheeks scored with pits and pimples, and the shortest stubble of hair on his head when he arrived. A number of immigrants arrived with shaved heads, we were told, to get rid of head lice and the trouble they might cause if immigration officials found them. Other than his Adam's apple, I liked the fact that he was double-jointed, as he demonstrated in one light moment by pushing his thumb down to touch his forearm. We thought it might be a family trait, like curly hair, and when we couldn't do it, we felt disinherited. Yankel was bedded down on an old army cot my father found in a Third Avenue junk store and placed under the window in the dining-living room, an arrangement my mother didn't like because a country cousin, a young man, would probably not be careful of her china closet, her stone birds, her rose-covered tablecloth, the ugly sullen rubber plant she loved and wiped with castor oil to keep it shiningly healthy, and he might even in his carelessness kick the piano. Clearly, she had it in for him, and we might automatically have taken his side, shown him some favor, if he hadn't been so indifferent to us. He had other fish to fry. He immediately registered in a night-school English class and was gone after supper most evenings. The remaining evenings he spent with my father to make the rounds of acquaintances with marriageable daughters. Yankel expressed dissatisfaction with them all; a spoiled bastard who had been brought up in a crooning nest of women, as my father had been, he found none of the girls pretty enough for him or, judging from their houses and dress, rich enough. He wanted a good-looking girl with prosperous parents, as promised him by rich America.

Of the young women he saw on the block, he mentioned a couple of beauties. From one description we identified kitten-faced Concetta of the family from Posilipo. She was Italian, he was told, and the subject was immediately dismissed. The second girl turned out to be Helen Roth's big sister, the tall laughing girl with a shining rope of golden-brown hair who had a job in an office downtown and often ate at the Chinks, like the rich. Was she Jewish, maybe? Yes. Could he maybe take her for a walk after my mother introduced them? My mother hooted vengefully. That girl was American born, she said, a high-school graduate who would soon be taking college night courses. She had a very responsible, well-paying job, and who knows what high position she might ultimately be given? She had suitors who were going to be lawyers and doctors (we knew our mother was probably lying but silently cheered her on as we listened) and what in the world would she want with a greenhorn? Yankel stopped mentioning local girls and went back to the search for an heiress among the landsmen. A job was an easier matter; my father was then foreman of his section in a large shoe factory and could put Yankel to work as a paid apprentice first and move him quickly to a better job.

My mother's irritation with Yankel fed and battened on his inconsiderate habits: his dirty socks on the polished piano, his night-school books pressing the breath out of the embroidered roses on her tablecloth, his habit of carefully squeezing pimples before the bathroom mirror while my brother was twisting his legs trying to hold in his pee. He wouldn't eat lung or liver, and she couldn't tell him he had to, as she did us. He ate all the farmer cheese meant for morning breakfast during his night raids on the icebox. The *klops*, a huge hamburger stewed in onion, Polish style, disappeared in one sitting, leaving nothing for the next day's lunch sandwiches. And pausing between heaping spoonfuls of *kasha*, he described the delicious things his mother, a good mother and a wonderful cook, made for him. My mother listened sourly.

There were other night raids that my mother knew nothing about. Deep in the night, Yankel would appear in his underwear at our bedroom door. He stood looking at the bed and my sister's crib for a moment, like a careful Indian scout. He came in, gently nudged my sleeping brother to the far side of our bed, nearer the wall, and waited to make sure he was still asleep. One knee on the bed, he nudged me for space. When I clung to the edge of the bed to keep him out, he stretched one long leg, and then the other, across me and settled in the middle between my brother and myself. Unlike Mr. Ricciardi, Yankel didn't care much for stroking. Fiercely whispering at me not to make any noise, he pulled off my underpants and got on top of me. He pushed his big thing, pulsating like a machine, as near as he could to my opening but never went in. Near, on top, to the side, he pressed and rose, pressed and rose, and then stayed while warm gluey stuff spilled down my thighs. He got up, said nothing, and tiptoed down the hall to his dining room cot. Once, when a noise came from the baby's crib, he ran on tiptoe to the bathroom to make it appear, I suppose, that he had just gotten up to pee.

After several nights of this – I can't remember how or if they were spaced – I decided that this was bad and dangerous. There were adult phrases around the street and on park benches about the girl who died because Fatty Arbuckle had torn her. I seemed also in danger of being torn. When my brother and sister were fast asleep, I took the extra blanket hanging over the end of the bed, wrapped myself in it, and sat down in the chair on which we had draped our clothing, determined to spend that night, and all others if necessary, sitting up. He came in, stared, groped in the bed, and turned to find me sitting. He began to plead with me to go back to bed. He wouldn't touch me, never again. What would my mother think if she found me that way? Please go back to bed. Please don't say anything. He could be arrested and sent back to Poland if I said anything. He'd give me a beautiful present, a gold ring, if I went back to bed. Please. Please. I stared at him and said nothing. He looked at me out of his pimpled face for a while – waiting for what? – and then tiptoed down the hall.

Since my mother didn't like him and my brother was totally indifferent to him, the fact that I stopped talking to him at all made no conspicuous change in our lives. Not too long after I felt it safe to sleep in my bed again he said he had found a man from his province with whom he was going to share a room as a boarder, nearer the factory. I knew he was lying but only stared at him as insolently as Helen Roth did at her Italian cellist neighbor. The next day, when I came home from school, he was gone and my mother was practicing her mandolin in her dining room, with the red tablecloth roses fluffed, the birds pecking in their white stone bowl, the rubber plant gleaming with castor oil.

Our next greenhorn was my father's niece, Beile, another sister's child, an even more avid go-getter than skinny Yankel and his spills of semen. She insisted, after her first week in night school, that her name was Beth and kept on insisting until my father told her it was a Christian name and Bessie would be better. Bessie it was. She was older than Yankel, in her mid-twenties, and, as the neighbors said, no 'greene'. She was already remarkably sharpened for survival. It didn't matter to her that my brother and I needed a child's full sleep; since she shared our bed, she had a right to keep us awake to hear her lessons in grammar and spelling. At first I didn't mind. She was novel, she learned fast, she had hair like mine, a thatch of all flaxen and blond colors. And I could play teacher without contradictions or fights. My brother slept through most of those long, thorough lessons as she went over and over each word until she made not one mistake. I began to hate her but said nothing until my mother asked me why I was dragging myself around like a sleepwalker. When I told her about Bessie's keeping me awake to study with her, she had a short discussion with my father behind closed doors and it stopped.

Not altogether. Bessie decided I was good for other things besides spelling. I would wake up during the night to find her legs tightly wrapped around my thigh as she rubbed herself against it with mounting vigor and speed, moaning little sighs of pleasure and shaking; stopping and starting again. She was as greedy for pleasure as for learning English. Of course I knew what she was doing, but I had never known it to be on someone else's thigh; a pillow, a towel, a hand, but a thigh? Maybe that was the way they did it in Poland and I wondered who her partners had been. This didn't happen too frequently, nor did it last very long, and since I always made believe I was asleep and felt more curious than menaced, I didn't worry about it. Although my brother was a dedicated sleeper – each night a hibernation rather than the drop and lift of the shallow river of sleep in which I swam – he must have been occasionally aware of what went on in his bed with Yankel, with Bessie. He never mentioned it; he knew the code. Don't tell on anyone, don't rock any boats; save the troubles for something with fairly predictable results, like nagging for a bicycle or going on the rides in Coney Island.

There were advantages to having Bessie around; she now went on those long evening walks with my father, much more eager than I had ever been. They were dreaming a business career for her, I suspected. I heard many years later that she made a lot of money for herself and some for my father, too. He took her, as he had Yankel, on a round of visits among Workmen's Circle friends, among union mates, again with matrimony in mind. She may have then been his mistress (almost certainly later), but it was important to have her married. No raving beauty, she wore glasses, weak-eyed like several in my father's family. She was blond, blue-eyed, and spirited, though, and eager to follow whatever Uncle told her she must do. He found her a husband quickly, a fellow worker named Moe, who was small and thin with soft flat brown hair and glasses. (When they kissed, would their glasses clash?) He rarely said anything when he came to the house, always appearing with a Whitman's Sampler box of chocolates for her and a couple of Baby Ruths for us. Then he sat, drinking tea, for which he thanked my mother in a low voice, listening to Bessie, listening to my father, awed by the speed and number of their words. We didn't have to be polite with Moe and hang around as if he were company; we could disappear with our candy and no one cared.

When it was established that they were engaged (my mother said, and she might have been right or just enjoying herself, that my father took Moe to a jeweler of his acquaintance on Canal Street, himself picked out the engagement ring, and himself bargained the price down while Moe stood silently by), my father became their duenna, accompanying them to the movies and the Chinks on Tremont Avenue and visits to distant cousins. The evenings without them were lovely gifts. We could talk and even fight lightly; our mother taught us to dance the mazurka and the krakowiak, and she sang to her mandolin. We dressed up our little sister as 'Sandy Claws' by tying pillows and a red cloth around her; we made her one of the Seven Dwarfs with an absorbent cotton beard; we made her a bride with one of the curtains my mother had just washed. She was still afraid of our size and noise, examining us guardedly with her big golden eyes, but, invited to shelter on our mother's lap during intermissions she slowly came around, trying to dance and sing with us. We were happy enough, my brother and I, to tell her how well she danced and sang, and she did, considering that she was all eyes, fat baby legs, and fat baby belly. Once in a while I had one fleeting regret: that I wasn't out with Moe, Bessie, and my father at the Chinks. It certainly wasn't their company I missed. I wanted to pour brown-red sauce made of Chinaman's blood on pork ribs, which I had never tasted, and maybe I would drop dead and get into all the papers. And I hoped to find a Chinese pinkie, chopped off by a sword, among the pieces of Chinese chicken. When I once mentioned ruefully to my mother that I wished they had taken me to the Chinks, she dismissed me, once again, as one of those creatures who wanted to dance at all weddings; nosy, restless, discontented.

It took a long, exasperating time for Bessie to marry her Moe. In the meantime, she got a job in a corset factory and babbled English shockingly well, making few of the mistakes my mother did. In the English classes at the public library they apparently made an unforgettable point of the fact that a plural noun was signaled by a final 's': 'girl, girls', 'pot, pots'. Thereafter, until the day of her death, and after the acquisition of polished written Yiddish, decent English, perfect Polish, and fluent conversational Italian, my mother avoided 'lettuce' for one head, pronouncing it, carefully, 'lettu', a chic Frenchy sound, we thought; the icebox was always the 'icebock'. We enjoyed 'lettu' and 'icebock' too much to correct her, something we were ordinarily not reluctant to do.

Back to the golden girl, Bessie. My father began to bring home samples, exquisite handmade shoes, in size four and a half, narrow, Cinderella shoes my mother couldn't wear; she was a wide six. They fit Bessie, always showing off her dainty feet and hands, and I looked on in misery as she pranced around in silky suede carved in tiny flowers on graceful heels. There was some conversation behind the closed bedroom door, and shortly after, my father brought home two pairs, one for me. They fit tightly but they fit, the color and smoothness of a faun, a rosette of suede at the instep. I was beside myself and even kissed him in thanks. Another conversation behind closed doors the next day. My father emerged to say that he had made a mistake, those shoes should not have been taken out of the factory, but he would buy me another pair, soon. I knew what kind they would be: strong, well made, good for school, and flat-heeled. Worse still, we would have to go through *that* conversation with the salesman once again: my father expansively the expert sample-maker, the salesman listening respectfully, his silly head to one side, an admiring little smile on his face. It was going to be deeply embarrassing, trying not to listen, staring down at my shoeless, vulnerable feet. After time had stopped dead still, the choice would be made, not mine, but the pair with thick shit-colored laces, then the blood-covered money paid out. Mourning at my assiduously accumulated graveyard mound of broken promises and disappointments, I retreated into my tower of

silence. We'll buy shoes after the movies on Saturday. I shook my
head, no. You need shoes. No. Denying them access to the usual
weapons, I practiced the piano seriously, a whole half-hour for
scales, each piece meticulously allotted its time so my father of the
hundred ears wouldn't call out, 'What about that new nocturne, the
one for the recital?' The baby was walked around and around the
block for her full dose of fresh air, and I didn't forget to buy the
gluey farina on our way home. My mother couldn't say 'Where's
your head?' or warn that I was growing up to be a '*luftmensh*', a
floater on clouds. That silence was a powerful place: my brother
kept out of my way, my mother's face looked as if it were shut in
a dark closet; my father yelled, once again, that my mother was
breeding a white silent snake and slammed the door as he went
out in his new hat and coat to a Workmen's Circle meeting.

It is curious that though I remember the Hermans' Shprinzel
so vividly and happily as a bride, I cannot remember Bessie's
marriage and departure at all; obviously I was glad to have her
erased. The rare times that Yankel and Bessie come to mind,
they appear with a chapter title: 'The Wet Seasons', the steamy
jungle time of semen and coiling female moistures; the rest, the
shrewd intelligence, the variety of greeds and ambitions, remain
as thin abstractions. That Bessie was, finally, married came at us
tangentially. My father's outings diminished, he was around more.
We heard by the usual eavesdropping on the kitchen conversations
during homework time in the dining room that the '*chommer*' (dope)
Moe frequently complained about Bessie during the factory lunch
break. She spent his money faster than he could earn it; she didn't
want to buy on Orchard or Division Street but found her way to
the uptown stores, not even afraid of Altman's on Fifth Avenue.
Fifth Avenue, mind you. She didn't want to stop working and have
children – he loved children – not at least until he helped her
buy a corset shop. When he came home tired from the factory, she
slapped any old thing on the table and told him to eat fast, they
were going to the movies or Maurice Schwartz's theater on Second
Avenue, hurry up, for God's sake. Sometimes she didn't come home
until nine or ten, working overtime, while he ate a roll and butter
for supper; there was nothing in the icebox. My father laughed and
my mother laughed. They were disgusting; what had skinny little
Moe ever done to them that they should laugh like spiders watching
a fly struggle in their web? True, my mother hadn't enmeshed Moe
– my father had – but to be so indifferent, so amused, so

un-noble, so unlike the gentle, generous women in books; she was truly disgusting.

Still cocooned in my silences, I practiced demonically for the borough piano contest, the same contest in which I had won a bronze medal the year before. Every kind of nervousness assailed me as I prepared. I anticipated falling on the stage steps, wrong notes in pieces I knew perfectly well, my foot frozen on the pedal, making howling noises when I should be tapping gently, my bowels churning and running as they did with Friday morning arithmetic tests. As I walked up the stairs of the school auditorium toward the piano, I did what I had to for getting through and surviving. The frightened, trembling, bellyached person was pushed far away. The other person, bowing, sitting, striking the notes, and pushing the pedals, was cool, indifferent. It didn't matter if she forgot a passage or her fingers jumbled in a fast run, or she slipped off the piano bench or dirtied her pants; all that might happen in the distant place of the scared, shaking one and had nothing to do with here.

It went well, silver-medal well, and I went home carrying my medal with a harp on one side and stately words on the other in my wet, quivering hand. The school had also presented me with a small bouquet, of which I remember only the tremulous baby's breath that seemed to be tiny people echoing my excitement as I strode through the dark streets ahead of my family and a few neighbors. We had store-bought fancy cake and were allowed to stay up extra-late even for a Friday night. Too excited, too tired, worried whether this triumph would revive my father's dream of me as a concert pianist, I couldn't talk much, but the icy silence had to begin melting.

13

Brothers and Fathers

My brother stamped and twisted as my mother tried to tie a woolen scarf around his neck, making him look like a sissy, he growled. 'Sissy' was the worst a boy could be, a boy who now went to school and adventured only with a knights' circle that severely abjured females according to holy rules. Never touch a girl's library book no matter how attractive its pictures; hiss 'Mush' in concert when the Sheik folds his pale captive in his warrior-banded arms and beams his dark eyes on her trembling mouth; never listen to an older sister but always report her street iniquities; refer to a younger sister as 'that dopey kid'. Interfering with the idiotic female pleasures of bouncing balls and jumping ropes was a constant duty of the knighthood, as triumphant an accomplishment as finding the Holy Grail. Their Camelot was a thicket on the Monterey lot, their sacred festival something they spoke of in whispers as 'King of the Hill'. (It was called 'House on Fire' on less romantic streets.) This mysterious ritual held us girls in awe; we tried to spy but guards ran us away, the more dedicated with handfuls of pebbles and sticks. Before these holy rites took place the boys baked stolen potatoes, 'mickies' (after the Irish word for potato, 'mick') lifted from grocery bins and green-stores while the proprietor was busy elsewhere, although the men probably knew what was happening. One's own kid might at this very moment be robbing a competitor, and one potato, what the hell; there was a rough justice in the arrangement and the boys sensed it. Lifting a mickie was playing at stealing, while swiping a couple of nigger babies from the candy store was real theft and thrillingly fearsome with potential for beatings and arrest by the implacable blue mountains of cops. (The girls, trying for masculine freedoms, did a little of this stealing, as well. I tried it twice, one nickel and four pennies off a newsstand, a yellow pencil from the five-and-ten, and then gave it up because I suffered inordinately. Some book said that the eyes were the windows of the soul, whatever important thing that was, and I couldn't raise them to my mother or teacher, who would see through my eyes the black stain on my soul. I was accused and punished by every unexpected sound, by every small misfortune like breaking a dish, by a mistake in arithmetic. I walked for days in stomach pain and black mists and thus became a reasonably honest person.)

After the feasting on burnt mickies – on an exchange deal I made with my brother, he brought me a cold piece, ashes outside, raw inside, and inedible – at their Round Table, the 'King of the Hill' ritual took place in their lot chapel. One afternoon Minnie Rosen and I went up to her roof, in the middle of the block, and looking down, saw an astonishing, disappointing, profoundly enlightening sight. The mickie fire was being fed more sticks and twigs, and when it reached a high, bright magnificence, the boys unbuttoned their pants and put the fire out with their piss. And that was it. It was always fun to catch a glimpse of a boy's thing if one could, and here there were eight or ten, more to be imagined than seen at that distance, but unmistakably there and streaming in those enviable arches. Minnie, the toy and victim of older brothers who cuffed her and bought her candy, and a cynic, said, 'I could have told you it was nothing, just a dumb game.' My responses were more complicated; the first impulse was to run to my mother to tell her about the dirty thing my brother was doing. I didn't. My brother had just been beaten after yet another graphic, detailed description of the rats, the bread and water in the airless, lightless solitude of the prison that would enfold his life, and while he was shouting and peeing like a happy savage around the fire, I still stung from his terror and pain. Something else was happening, too, a letdown I had to think about, a different view of the male world. I felt as I walked down from the roof that their secrets were not so impenetrable or even worth penetrating. If it was a 'man's world', as the women kept saying, it wasn't all that remarkable. The actuality of the 'King of the Hill', the masterful name for a feeble power that was an accident of birth – being able to pee standing up – was my first primitive experience of feminism, enhanced by my father's irrational furies and my brother's wails. I might try myself against that world of paper strengths.

The experiment of a jump from the highest rock, a sheer

tall cliff in Crotona Park, exclusively the terrain of boys, had mixed but unexpectedly rewarding results. I was afraid to jump and, as usual, more afraid not to, and I slipped off the edge, to land cross-kneed and incapable of getting up. There must have been pain but I remember only the incredulous fact of my legs being useless, as my brother's had been long ago. Some sort of vengeance? I believed in vengeance as a world force, like the sun rising every day and the change of seasons. Somewhere there was a vast hall, an auditorium where there were scrolls of happenings that had to be paid for, sins waiting for the 'Vengeance of God', who kept careful records like truant officers.

By falling rather than jumping, I lost my chance to be a 'tomboy' semirespected by the real boys. Instead I entered a time of joyous queenliness. The baby was taken out of her go-cart and given to my father to carry, and I put into it, my mother, finally, finally, pushing *me* in a carriage while my brother, who also enjoyed all irregular situations, pushed along with her. On the way out of the park, the benches full of Sunday grown-ups, the girls making buttercup chains, the boys skimming rocks in the pond, the babies crawling in the grass, everyone asked, 'What happened?' and were told in full, lingering detail as they stared at *me*. The gardeners scraping the flower beds asked what happened, and Mrs. Katz came out of her candy store to be told, holding a hand to her cheek, shaking her head in worried disbelief. Some of the kids hanging around the store followed my carriage. It was a progress worthy of Elizabeth I, leisured and regal, which continued through most of that Sunday afternoon. As we neared our house, my mother ran across to the De Santis garage, and the eldest boy, Federico, one of the beloved incandescences too beautiful to look at, came back with her and carried me in his arms, like Agnes Ayres, to his car and drove me to Fordham Hospital. Some slight disappointment there: no thick casts, no steel braces, no surgical armor of leather and straps as I had seen in the Sunday *American*; no pathos of crutches, not even bandages. The doctor said I was to stay in bed for a week. He insulted me, so special and frail, by saying I was a healthy youngster and a week in bed would fix my pulled muscles fine. Federico carried me out to the car and drove us home, and my father carried me up the five flights of stairs as he had done when I was a very little girl and fell asleep among the coats on Uncle David's bed when we went there for Passover.

The week was a dream of omnipotence. My food was brought

to me in bed, and extra Lorna Doones and Fig Newtons with my
afternoon milk. The baby's crib was taken out of our room and
put into our parents' bedroom. My brother slept on two chairs in
the living room to avoid kicking my delicate legs. He was told he
might play with me but any rough stuff and he would be banished
from my royal presence. Ruthie and Minnie came every afternoon
to bring me my homework assignments and a note printed – like
a book – with GET WELL SOON from our teacher, Miss Monahan.
I greeted them languidly, spoke to them in a thin voice, asked them
please not to shake the bed, and generally, as my mother began
to complain after a few days, acted like a *kimpeturen*, a woman
in childbed to whom these languors rightfully belonged. Like all
halcyon glories, this, too, waned, and after a brief rekindling of
interest when I returned to school, vanished altogether.

The trials of strength weren't over, though. Walking with
my eyes shut, feeling my way along the walls and furniture,
tried me in the world of the blind. Limping lightly or deeply,
hobbling, sliding, twisting my feet far inward, walking on one
ankle, proved I could be a successful cripple. Holding my hands
over my ears made a silence that was insupportable; I couldn't
make it in the world of the deaf. When my mother caught me
playing blind or crippled, she was, I thought, excessively disturbed.
She said I was odd, peculiar (a stamp as indelible as a concentration
camp number), and ordered me to stop being Susie Bren (Burn), a
caricature of a fiery actress. If my father caught me, he said I was
crazy, and then she leaped, she thought, to my defense, countering
once again with my resemblance to *his* sister, the one who had died
in a madhouse. A plague on both their houses; I'd show them not
how odd but how distinguished I was and as accomplished as any
boy. In our repertoire of heroes were the older boys on skates who
grabbed at the backs of passing trucks, and, holding on to a chain,
a rope, anything, flew with them as far as Southern Boulevard, as
far as the Grand Concourse, as far as West Farms. It was dangerous,
a sudden stop or turn might throw a boy hard enough to break
his head or smash him under the wheels of another car. And
absolutely forbidden, the repeated prohibition embroidered with
horror stories of the Irish boy from Arthur Avenue whose neck
was broken and who would probably be paralyzed all his life; the
Italian boy on Third Avenue who died, a bundle of broken bones,
in Fordham Hospital. There were no Jewish boys among the
examples; they were too obedient to play such suicidal games was

the implication. As eager to try the big boys' world as I, my brother joined me in hitching on the backs of trucks, an important act of complicity that required a coordination of lies. We still informed on each other, we still fought – often in itself an act of complicity, designed to annoy *them* – but we had honed fine the antennae that sensed out the times for mutual protection. We were both fast, skilful skaters, and although our few breathless words during these flights were my powerful, motherly 'Hold on tight' and his 'Shut up', some respect for each other's capacities moved subtly, always mutely, between us. I found myself thinking, He's only a little boy, for God's sake – as he might have been thinking, She's only a girl, for God's sake.

His opportunities were much greater than mine. After six months of practice that ruined the kitchen clock, which he kept on the piano to push ahead so that his practice hour might be completed in twenty minutes, my parents decided his lessons were a waste of money. I continued to practice, never betraying that I sometimes enjoyed it; a stream of grumbling and sullen lurching was the required way to approach practice. His role with our baby was to kootchy-koo her as he dashed in from school and down to the street while I thumped the carriage down the five flights, up and down again with the pillows and blankets, up and down again with the baby. While he, the grasshopper, sang and danced, I, the ant, sat demurely rocking the carriage. He was in the full sun, I in shade; he was young, I was old. When I caught sight of him hitching on a truck on one of the cross streets – never on our informer block – my fury was fire in my limbs. By telling my mother the baby had coughed and sneezed a lot on the street, she was surely getting a cold; by swearing I had sprained my hand in school and couldn't possibly practice, I made time to latch on to trucks, too. Often, finding the sky darkening and the street names altogether unfamiliar – Prospect, Intervale, Westchester, Burnside – I pulled us both away and started the journey home, slipping again into the irresistible role, burdensome and magnificent, of telling him not to worry, I knew our way home. I did know it, having observed the outward journey, a deeply embedded habit planted in many places, now rooted in Crotona Park, where lingering over a bright insect in the grass, or splashing in a puddle, or picking up a dusty lost marble evoked from my father the 'teach him a lesson' act. He would push us all behind a big tree, to watch my brother suddenly look around, his face half-speaking, breaking into bewilderment, then tears. Sometimes my mother ran back to him; usually it was I.

It was at about this time of strengthening to disobedience and daring that a chivalric battle took place at Lafontaine, in front of the hat factory. It was a warm spring afternoon and five or six of us were playing potsy on the broader sidewalk there; no interfering house stoops and the ugly humpbacked watchman had not yet arrived to yell at us for chalking up his street ('I brek you henk 'n feet ven I see you'). Suddenly, from Arthur Avenue, a gang of boys, big boys, came loping down 179th Street and surrounded us. Taunting, foulmouthed, saying things we didn't understand but knew were dirty, they began to lift our skirts and poke at our chests. Hearing the yells of 'Get-outa-here' and 'Maaa', a group of boys sprawled over a game of marbles down the street leaped up and some of them began to run towards us; the rest remained fixed on the marbles, afraid of this formidable gang. One of the few who came running was my brother, who jumped at the boy trying to grope under my skirt and began to tear at him, trying to pull his arm away. The tall gang boy shouted, 'I'll shoot your sister full of scum, shrimpy', and met a small, whirling fury, pummeling, scratching, kicking. A couple of men, coming out of the factory for a smoke, sent Arthur Avenue about its business with a show of clenched fists. My brother's shirt was torn and his lip swelling, but he sauntered back to the marbles game as cool and expressionless as Elmo Lincoln. That night I was, as usual, blamed for the shirt and the lip. Instead of battling the injustice of my situation, as was expected, I explained that he got into a fight with an Arthur Avenue boy who was bothering me. He said, 'Yeah.' My mother asked what the boy had done, and I said, 'Oh, nothing. He was just pushing and trying to make me fall while I was playing potsy.' I knew what she really wanted to know, whether my skirt was lifted and my place touched. I wasn't about to tell her; as long as she kept her secrets, I would keep mine. I wished I had the nerve to ask my brother exactly what 'shooting full of scum' meant; it wasn't fair that he knew things I didn't. Still, as often in such vague and momentous matters, I knew enough to put the phrase in its proper category, dim and wide as that was: the place of shut bedroom doors, of people squirming on hot roofs, of dogs stuck together, of how babies were seeded or peed or stuffed into bellies.

Of course I never thanked my brother or praised him, but I

must have been impressed, and in spite of my parents' infuriatingly boring injunctions that I take care of him, watch him, don't let him get dirty, and, and, and, and, I began to release him more and more to himself. Furthermore, I had become chummy with some older girls who *knew everything*. I intended to concentrate on 'shooting scum' and related matters with them and was determined to brook no distractions. We ten- and eleven-year-olds hinted and giggled at each other over key words: 'things', 'breasts', 'love', but we were still lost, though we tried for slant-eyed looks of wisdom, like Anna May Wong.

One of the older girls, twelve, was new on the block. Her name was Deborah May, but she liked to be called Debby, like one of the blond paper dolls she claimed to scorn, baby stuff. She said her mother had a permanent that cost five dollars and a lipstick that she let Debby use sometimes. We younger girls granted her wonder and admiration as we recognized our own lies. No use in accusing her of lying, of antagonizing her. She had things to tell us, and for that, we could accept her garbage. She was the teacher of menstruation, the 'monthlies' that all women got and had to use rags for. Each month, Debby informed us, the thighs separate from the lower belly, held only by a thin thread of skin. From these immense gashes, which I saw as the deep wide cuts made by a butcher's cleaver as he severed a leg from the rest of carcass, flowed blood, rivers of blood, for days and days. She told it coolly, clinically, but it disturbed my sleep for days and weeks; the thighs hanging by a skin thread appeared on my geography page, the twin rivers of blood on the sheets of the Mozart sonata I was practicing. Alternating with my periods of crippled limping and stumbling blindness, I tried to walk as if I had a mound of bloody rags between my legs. How come I never saw a woman walk that way? I thought that Debby might be wrong on another score, too – anyone so hideously butchered must surely die after one monthly – but I had to trust her because she knew and told, which no one else would. (Her nightmare picture remained so convincingly vivid that when I actually began to menstruate and found some drops of blood on my bloomers I had no idea of what was happening, made no connection with Debby's enlightenments.)

The next set of lessons, by big, bosomy Italian Rosa, left with the Bianchis while her parents went back to Caltanisetta to find a bride for her eldest brother, was less gloom, more fun and variety. Her specialty was the most important one, 'shooting scum', who does it, how it's done, and other unbelievable things, including the fact that scum makes babies. Her approach was juicily conspiratorial. She would teach only on the foreign territory of Monterey, her pupils a select few sworn to secrecy: big Helen, who knew a lot about bushy hair from the pictures in her neighbor's house but needed filling in on other details; Ruthie Meilman, with lank brown hair and a sharp little nose like a mouse, a showoff who liked to masturbate on a pillow near her kitchen window so everyone in the courtyard could see; Minnie Rosen, who stammered; by courtesy, Carlotta Bianchi, Rosa's cousin and really too dumb to care; and myself. Rosa was a good teacher, a skilled raconteur who supplied specific identities, a cousin, an uncle, an aunt, to make her lessons vivid, immediate. Apparently she spent a good deal of her time prowling, peeping into keyholes or gaps in warped doors. (She was too graphic to be only a voyeur, we suspected, she must have been a participant too; all the better, more real.) First, the vocabulary lesson. A man's thing was a prick or a cock, a woman's hole a twat. If a lady stroked a man's prick, it would become big and fat and he would ram it in her twat and keep ramming until they both had a shivering pain that made them yell and then they stopped. Sometimes the lady rode the man's thing like a horse until the shivering came and she fell on him. Sometimes he turned her over, pulled her ass up, and rode her like a big dog until he shook and collapsed. Afterward they looked sweaty and the bed smelled of the man's scum. And there was apocrypha too difficult to believe, about pinching and slapping and tasting and sucking, and a story about her uncle Sandro who got stuck inside her aunt Assunta; they had to be pulled apart by her uncles Tullio and Gino. I didn't think the story was funny, people stuck like dogs, and some of the rest was beyond acceptance, but accept it I must have, since I fought it all so bitterly. The swelling and pushing, the sweating like the hot shine of the butcher shop, the smell like singed chickens, the contortions like the roof people – that's not how I was born or our cute baby who blew milk bubbbles. This couldn't be what they meant by 'So they lived happily ever after' when Cinderella and the Prince got married, when Beauty married the beautiful Beast, when Assunta Paterno in a long white veil kissed Sandro Bondi in their church, all this crazy stuff mixed up with places for peeing and shitting. No and no and no.

The lighter contributions Rosa brought from Carmine Street were much more acceptable. In our long ball-bouncing and rope-jumping careers, we had progressed from the limpid dopiness of

> *One, two, three a-lairy (right leg over ball in midair)*
> *I spy Mrs. Sairy (leg over)*
> *Sitting on a Bumbleairy (ditto)*
> *Just like a chocolate fairy (ditto)*

and

> *Teddy Bear, Teddy Bear, turn around*
> *Teddy Bear, Teddy Bear, touch the ground*
> *Teddy Bear, Teddy Bear, show your shoe*
> *Teddy Bear, Teddy Bear, please skiddoo*
> *Teddy Bear, Teddy Bear, go upstairs*
> *Teddy Bear, Teddy Bear, say your prayers*

to chants that recognized school life, family life, marriage, careers, and death:

> *Ding, dong, ding, dong, ding, dick*
> *Here comes the teacher with the big fat stick*
> *Now get ready for arithmetic*
> *One and one are two*
> *Two and two are four*
> *Now get ready for spelling –*
> *C-a-t, cat; r-a-t, rat*

> *Bouncy, bouncy, ballee*
> *I let the baby fallee*
> *My mother came out*
> *And slapped my mouth*
> *Bouncy, bouncy, ballee*

> *Johnny on the ocean, Johnny on the sea*
> *Johnny broke the sugar bowl*
> *And blamed it all on me*
> *I told Ma, Ma told Pa*
> *Johnny got a licking*
> *Ha! Ha! Ha!*

A long-lasting chant, a specialty of practiced jumpers, was a trip through the alphabet:

> *A, my name is Alice*
> *My husband's name is Al*
> *We live in Albany*
> *And we sell apples.*

> *B, my name is Bessie*
> *And my husband's name is Ben*
> *We live in Boston*
> *And we sell balloons.*

And so on.

Several songs ended in rapid counting when both rope and jumper took on a frantic pace:

> *Fudge, fudge, tell the Judge*
> *Mama's got a baby*
> *Not a boy, not a girl*
> *Just a little lady*
> *Wrap her up in tissue paper*
> *Send her to the elevator*
> *How many pounds does she weigh?*
> *Ten, twenty, thirty, forty, fifty, etc.*

> *Mother, mother, I am sick*
> *Send for the doctor quick, quick, quick*
> *Doctor, doctor, will I die*
> *Yes, my daughter, by and by*
> *How many hours will it take?*
> *Ten, twenty, thirty, forty –*

Rosa added new spice to our games with:

> *My sister had a baby, his name was Sonny Jim*
> *She put him in a pisspot, to teach him how to swim*
> *He swam to the bottom, he swam to the top*
> *My sister got excited and pulled him by the—*

Uncontrollable giggling here. I liked better the piquant imagery of:

> *Old Mr. Kelly had a pimple on his belly*
> *His wife bit it off and it tasted like jelly.*

We didn't have the essential meaning of this one but the salacious aura was pleasurably there.

After the active grapevine of Lafontaine mothers and brothers had delivered some lurid details, we were forbidden to talk with Debby and Rosa. Their remembered voices, their excited faces, their troubling information helped make a rocky voyage of my eleventh to twelfth year.

I fought more with my disgusting mother and braved louder disobedience to my disgusting father, and while I fought, I tried to shape the breasts under her housedress and pierce the front buttons of his pants. As I walked to school, to the movies, to the library, I looked for the shape of breasts – titties, Rosa had called them – and 'things', not yet ready for 'prick'. I began to examine myself carefully, to search my armpits for hairs and my breasts for signs of swelling. My friends were proud to report a body hair or two and boasted of soon needing 'bassiers'. I tore out the hairs I found in my armpits with my fingernails. When my breasts began to swell with horrifying rapidity, I searched the sewing machine drawers for cloths and ribbons to tie around them, to stop them. My mother had brought from Warsaw wide pink and blue silk ribbons that she had used in her shop and, when I let her, had put in my hair. I lifted one of these, a blue one, out of the machine and took it to the bathroom, undressed, and tied it tight, tight, around my chest, and dressed again. The ribbon was never tight enough, never stopped the ghastly swelling. I pulled it tighter and still tighter until it dug long cuts under my arms, the blood staining the ribbon. Still I pulled. Still I swelled.

My mother never saw the cuts or the bloodied ribbon; by now I was insisting on, shrieking for, intense privacy during the weekly bath, and on dressing and undressing in the bathroom instead of the room I shared with my brother and the baby. The baby didn't matter, but my normally sleepy, indifferent brother might just open his eyes at the wrong time, look, and ruin my life once again by commenting on my cuts in his clear choirboy voice. My mother would ask questions, scold me for the scars that might give me blood poison and for the dirty, dried-blood ribbon, once so lovely, all the way from Warsaw. There were other matters involved, dimly reasoned, strongly felt. The ribbons were another test of strength, of stoicism, and a denial of sexuality, of being filthily conceived, the need for privacy an evolutionary step in the gathering of myself as me, solely me, a separation from the strangling claustrophobia of four people continuing too long to be one.

If I didn't want to talk, I wouldn't. I was good in school, except in arithmetic, could play Chopin's 'Fantasie Impromptu' fast with all the notes clear and the slow part sweet, sad, and deep; under my care the baby carriage turned over only once, the baby unhurt, smiling as she slid out with her pillows; my brother hadn't been run over while I jumped rope, a standard prophecy. Miss Torrence let me walk a few blocks with her after school, asking me what I thought about 'Chickie' in the Sunday *American*, and I answered freely and wisely. After we had a geography lesson on Italy and I wrote a composition about Venice, she asked me when I had been there, it sounded as if I had. Miss Califano, who let me erase the blackboard once, said I was pretty. My skin still crawled with shame when I remembered stupid things I had said, cruel things I had done, lies I had told, but I could no longer be convinced – in spite of my father – that I was the worst girl in the world and the ugliest. For his own interesting reasons, my father called me 'Luna Park' when I smiled, the reference to the huge-mouthed, moon-faced advertisement for the Coney Island amusement park. I stopped smiling or tried to, tying my face into a grotesque knot to show only my top front teeth. Whereupon my brother said I looked like a big rabbit, so I had to practice making my mouth smaller, biting my upper lip while I tightened the lower, pouting like Mae Murray, studying the shapes other people's mouths made and imitating them as I lay in bed before I fell asleep. But I was not the ugliest girl in the world.

At the corner grocery where I went for prunes, a constant of our icebox that my father considered a major lifeline to health, and that we (in the innumerable little acts of feeble vengeance that were *our* lifeline) never ate, I found the usual gaggle of women talking with more than their usual animation, their voices hopping over one another. They were discussing a contest announced by a Jewish newspaper, soliciting pictures of candidates for the prettiest Jewish girl in New York. She would be named Queen Esther, get gorgeous presents, be given a big party by the editors, and have her picture printed in the paper. Two of the women turned to me and said, 'Why doesn't your mother send *your* picture in? Mrs. Halpern is sending in her Miriam and Mrs. Katz her Hannah. You're prettier, much prettier than they.' I didn't say anything and didn't know what to do with my face; to smile would appear show-offy, not to smile was to be '*mudne*' (odd). I ran out of the store stuffed with rainbows, down the street and up the stairs to our apartment, calling 'Ma!' as I pushed the door open, shouting as I ran down the hallway asking if she knew about the Queen Esther contest and wouldn't she send my picture in. She knew about it and wouldn't send my picture in. I was too young, you had to be at least thirteen, and anyhow my father would never permit it. But I was big enough to pass for thirteen – people often said that – and wouldn't she please, please, try to persuade my father. She shrugged doubtfully and sent me back to get the prunes for which the water was already boiling.

That night nothing was said at supper and nothing afterward while I did my homework and listened. Nothing. My mother read a letter from Warsaw of which I now understood only the salutation, something like 'kochana shustra', Dear Sister, and then she boiled the diapers while he read the paper. The next night and the next, nothing. I was as good as gold, practiced and practiced and didn't slam doors. It wasn't possible though, it never was, for me to sit with the rest at Sunday breakfast in spite of the big fresh rolls and farmer cheese on the table. On Sunday mornings there lay on the table a fatty *matjes* herring with oily accusing eyes and an oily, dead tail. It was left to my father's enthusiastic connoisseurship, as lively and contentious as I later found in martini connoisseurs, to make the purchase in the delicatessen on 178th Street, the only food purchase he ever made. Come flu epidemics, teething, postabortion pains, chicken pox, mumps, measles, a man should never carry grocery packages. How could he carry this one, a monstrosity in stinking, fat-stained Jewish newspaper that made me want to vomit? It was after several struggles during which I sat heaving, threatening to vomit, that I was permitted to have Sunday breakfast, corn flakes and milk, very early and alone, another concession to my oddness. That special Sunday, inspired by the vision of myself in the long golden dress and jeweled crown of Queen Esther, I made restitution for not sitting with them and the herring by drawing a picture of the baby's profile, a little fruit bowl of curves and pouts. They liked it, even my brother. This might be the right climate for asking about the contest, and I did, choosing my words carefully, not allowing the spill of enthusiasm that would result in the absolute final dismissal of 'Nonsense! Don't be crazy.' My mother said nothing, the stage was my father's. I was too young, that was for sure, he said, and didn't I know that beauty contest winners didn't become movie actresses, as I hoped to become, but street girls, too spoiled to go to school to learn typing and stenography and become secretaries for good salaries? We were, I knew, approaching white slavery gangs and the vicious brothels of Buenos Aires and my bitterness was threatening to become visible tears. He mustn't think he could make me cry. I ran to my refuge, the locked bathroom, where I stood and held myself together, literally, as if my bones had been broken and I must knit them up again.

When I came out, my mother asked if I didn't want to take the picture of the baby to school to show my teacher, it was very nice. No, she could do with it as she liked. I sat down to practice my four Sunday hours, interruptible only by one drink of water and one visit to the toilet, looking forward in misery to the pupil concerts my father would find that afternoon as he did many Sunday afternoons. These were free showcases in school auditoriums of neighborhood piano teachers who had their best pupils perform, something I had begun to do, too. And my father wanted me, unremittingly, to see how it was done by others, better than I. Once I had accepted that no part of those Sundays, the day of the father, was to be designed by me, I resigned myself to the concerts as well as the long practice session.

I couldn't say I didn't like music. Unless we were fighting or sick, we all sang, even my father, who would yodel 'Vesti la Giubba' with Caruso as he paced the long hall. Music appreciation was a happy hour in school where we sang together with records, 'This is the symphony-y-y-y-y that Schubert wrote and never fini-i-i-ished, This is the key of C that' and we dropped it waiting to shout 'Italian, Italian!', celebrating Mendelssohn. The names were dazzlingly esoteric: Mendelssohn (my father said he was Jewish, but my father said all important people were somewhere in their ancestry Jews), Saint-Saëns, Massenet, Tchaikovsky, and frowning Beethoven who wrote the thunderous 'Da da da daaaaa, Da da da Daaaaa', like the voice of God.

We sang a great deal in school, which made most of us very happy, and I one of the lucky few who were aware, at that moment, of being perfectly happy. We sang 'Santa Lucia', which later paced my first gondola ride and became the twin of Schubert's 'Auf dem Wasser zu Singen', a curious duet that I would not for anything sever. 'Funiculi, Funicula' was skating downhill fast, roaring past houses on the El, the pretty jingling and hooting of merry-go-round music. The words of some of the songs moved me inordinately and I sang them pipingly, gently, in tremolos, as their meaning dictated: 'As the sun-flower turns on her god, when he sets, The same look which she turn'ed when he rose' became an ideal, rarely achieved, in my life with the boys. 'I sent thee late a rosy wreath, Not so much honoring thee as in the hope that by thy side it might not witheréd be. But thou thereon didst only breathe and sendst it back to me. Since when it lives and breathes, I swear it, not of itself but thee.' Jonson's slightly altered song cast a long, golden light over all my life, gracing what I came to know of courtly love, of madrigals and cavalier poets, of Shakespeare's sonnets. (One of the remnants of my early musical life is the music that was played during the film of Disraeli's life, starring George Arliss; any English garden can restore it almost intact.)

In spite of some necessary and a few unnecessary bestialities, it was a fine school, P.S. 58 on Bathgate Avenue and 182nd Street, and I still miss it, which is to say I miss being the full-throated thrush, the throbbing nightingale I was there.

To return to the Sunday afternoon concerts: I knew some of the music and could sit in a mixture of contentment and embarrassment listening to the clinkers a nervous kid on the stage was striking. Some of them had demonic techniques, some of them could make really singing sounds. There were a few things I wanted to play because they were so tuneful, like the Arensky waltz and something called, with deep respect, Bach, which sounded difficult and important. When the music was boring, I could examine the girls' hair and wonder at the patience of both mother and daughter that produced cascades of curls. The white dress with lace was too much like a communion dress, the pink more appropriate. And I fervently wished I had a ring to take off my fingers and put down, with a languid gesture, at the end of the keyboard before I began to play.

Much more than the concerts I hated the long walks and talk afterward. I was told, and accepted as accusations, that Marilyn, who had played that difficult Chopin étude, and Martin, who had played three Bach inventions, and Amy of that fast cross-hands piece – what's its name? – didn't go to school anymore, just stayed home and practiced six and eight hours a day, not like me who practiced only two every day, even Saturday when I had no school, and only four on Sunday. If I stopped going to school – all I had to do was announce to my teachers that I wasn't coming back – and practiced all day, he and I would, someday, travel around the world giving concerts. Striding in the evening winds, his coat open and flapping like an old-fashioned cape, he looked wild, carried away, like Mr. Rochester in *Jane Eyre*, like Heathcliff. He talked of concerts in Paris and London where all I had to do was play the piano on a stage – the pupil concerts in which I now performed were important preparation – and he would take care of getting the halls and collecting the money. We would be rich and travel all over the world, have beautiful clothing, and be admired by important people. I saw it all at first like becoming a princess, a young Queen Victoria gesturing daintily in lacy white gloves to the multitudes. After a good number of these Sunday evening walks into a make-believe that I enjoyed less and less, I began to grow distinctly uneasy, wanting to tear away from him. The message across my head – the same ticker tape that told me that my father liked to walk alone, several paces in front of the baby carriage my mother was pushing, my brother and I at either side, in order to be seen by passersby as a young unmarried man – reappeared to insist that this, too, was wrong. Never was there any mention of a mother, a brother, a baby sister to share the wealth and fame; they were erased, they didn't exist.

For him, but not for me. Often disgruntled, often resentful, often aching to be free of them, I wouldn't have them disappear, not for being as rich and famous as Mary Pickford. Had someone suggested that I 'loved' them, I would have spat. They were my landscape, my geography, and what, who, would I be without them? I listened as he elaborated on his glorious theme, repainting his warm colors as the darker reality of a life controlled into infinity by him alone: being called 'Luna Park' when I smiled; told not to be crazy when I wanted to do something, anything, of which he didn't approve; practicing eight hours a day; burning bowels and diarrhea before each concert; having no street to run to or my mother to argue for me. How would I know whether my brother grew up with two stumpy front teeth, broken when he cracked down on the steering rod of his sled, belly-whopping on the icy hill of 179th Street? Would my sister ever grow out of sitting hunched in a corner, her eyes tight shut as she covered her ears while my

brother and I screamed at each other? She was a smart little
kid, and I wasn't going to give up my ambition to teach her
to read, to make her the wonder child of the block who would
dazzle the librarians when they gave her the first library-card test.
I had to finish a stuffed doll I was making for her in school and
finish hemstitching a camisole; I would never wear it, I didn't know
what it was for, but the orderly stitches becoming a pretty row had
become as satisfying as drawing. I certainly didn't want to miss the
backyard of P.S. 58 when it was a summer vegetable garden where
I could watch my kohlrabi and lettuce grow and carry them home
in both hands stretched before me as if they were boxes of precious
jewels for my mother, the queen. No, he couldn't really have me; I
had another kind of life to lead, whatever it would be.

His distressing fantasy took on tangents that I felt were
connected to his ambitious dream, though I couldn't clearly see or
understand them. Although the games boys and girls played were
usually distinctly masculine or feminine, there were some games
we played together, 'ring-a-levio', stoopball, hide-and-seek, races
on foot or skates around the block. Seeing my grinning, sweaty
face coming around the corner neck and neck with a boy one early
fall evening on his return from work, my father told me to come
upstairs right away. The supper lecture that night was directed at
me; I was getting too old to run around like an unleashed thing
with the boys, that's what street girls did. If he caught me ever
again playing with the boys, I would not be permitted to go into
the street after supper, not even to sit on the stoop embroidering
my dish towel and singing 'Cecilia' and 'All Alone' with the other
girls. I promised while I began quickly to figure times safe and
unsafe for the forbidden games.

One of those same early evenings, a Friday, no school tomorrow,
the Paradise of Saturday promising and three cents for the weekly
ice-cream cone in our hands, we ran right after supper to Mrs.
Katz's candy store. We were several, including tough Helen. As
we approached the store we saw an unusual crowd, much larger
than the usual Friday night clusters.They were gathered around
a tall, elderly gentleman with smooth pale hair, as well dressed
as the De Santises' gangster uncle. With wide gestures and in
a German accent we recognized from vaudeville skits, he was
inviting everyone in sight to take candy, order ice cream,
cigarettes, anything. He was paying. And he did, putting down
ten- and twenty-dollar bills that Mrs. Katz quickly hid. I watched

him, I watched her, and realized that she was taking much too much money from him, claiming that a handful of Tootsie Rolls and a few fistfuls of Hershey bars had exhausted ten dollars and she needed more. He gave her more from a thick roll of bills, thicker than I had ever seen, while the kids and a few adults pushed one another and roared for chunks of halvah, five-cent ice-cream cones, packs of cigars and cigarettes, handfuls of gum. I couldn't understand what the stranger was doing or why. Was he drunk? But I had never seen a drunk other than Mary Sugar Bum, and maybe she was only crazy, old. I was afraid of what he was doing; it was craziness, like the wild talk and rolling eyes of Mrs. Silverberg the night they took her away, and I hated what Mrs. Katz was doing to him. I started pulling away, back toward our house, calling to Helen, who had made her way into the middle of the crowd, to come back with me. On hearing her name, he paused and, peering at me, said, '*Ach, die schoene Helene.* I know that face; there's music in that face,' and continued to stare at me. Such extraordinary praise I had seen only in poems, and it didn't belong to me. I stayed, though, and watched the noisy, crowding grabbing as he stripped more bills off the plump pack, looking over at me now and then, calling, '*Die schoene Helene.*' Suddenly my father, who usually kept himself aristocratically away from street life, appeared, dragged me off by the arm, hurried me through the street and up the stairs. I had done nothing, absolutely nothing, but stand with the other kids; I hadn't even taken a stick of gum for free. I tried to tell him so as he flung me into a kitchen chair, but he wouldn't let me. It poured out of his black mouth: I was not to go out of the house for a week, not to the street, to no friend's house, not to the Hermans or the Haskells or the Roths or the Santinis, not even to school, he shrieked, his pale face sharpened like a murderer's. No library, no movies that Saturday; no concert on Sunday.

On Monday, after my brother had gone to school, I asked my mother what I had done. She didn't think I had done anything wrong; my father was in one of his nervous fits, unusually long this time. Don't worry. I did; we were learning fractions and percentages and I was having trouble with them. By next week they would be learning something else and I would never catch up. In spite of my mother's assurance that I had done nothing, I didn't believe her. I must have done something to be punished so severely that I couldn't even go to school, but what it was I couldn't imagine. I went over every detail of that evening, over and over again, and understood little except that it was bad and I was central to the badness, having disturbed my father's dream in some way. Our suppers were altogether silent that week, no one spoke in the evenings, not even my brother, who had taken one timid piece of candy at Mrs. Katz's and was afraid that he, too, might be discovered and put under house arrest.

The return to school was not triumphant. I had been deeply shamed by being yanked around publicly, like a bad baby about to be spanked and ashamed of the terrible thing I had done, something everyone but me could see on my face. I handed our teacher the note my mother gave to say I had been sick – another lie – and slid into my seat, my eyes down so I wouldn't see *their* eyes looking at me.

14
Tony and Company

The end of that term, the end of the sixth grade, was a decisive one. Some of us would go on to 7A and two years at P.S. 57 on 181st at Crotona Avenue, the smart ones would go to 'rapid advance', a junior high school where three years were accomplished in two. I hoped and prayed to the bearded God, making him extravagant promises of eternal goodness, no more lies, no more fights, total perfection, because I was afraid arithmetic would do me in. It did. I had to submit to the spotty sympathy of friends who had made it, to the 'we don't care, do we' of friends who hadn't, to the compassionate murmurs addressed to my disappointed mother. Miss Torrence was some consolation. As we walked down the street from school the day the 'rapid advance' selections were made, she said that judging a person's capacity to learn from a few mistakes in arithmetic was very foolish. Why didn't they take into account the fact that I knew more books and poems than anyone else in the school and wrote the best compositions? A few teachers disagreed with the selections; they thought I should have been on the 'fast' list, as she did, and were annoyed because Gracie Makerios hadn't made it either, just because she had a slight Greek accent. Why hadn't they taken into account how much she had accomplished in only four years in school?

My father's reaction was monumental, even for him. Although he was eager to pull me out of school, this was a searing wound to his vanity. He said I was inattentive in school; not true, I always got A for attention. He said I didn't try; not true, I always got A for effort. Maybe I was more stupid than he thought, maybe there was something wrong with a head that couldn't cope with simple numbers. Or maybe – he paused – I did all this to spite him, contrived to flunk whatever tests or standards so that he would be humiliated in the eyes of the neighbors, in the eyes of the men in his shop whom he had told I was going into rapid advance classes. It was an absorbing, titillating new idea, worth considering in a future context, but here so absurd that my mother called to him from the kitchen not to make such a fool of himself and we'd had enough of the whole matter. That went for my brother, too, in case he should be thinking of taunting me.

I marched with my fellow discards a new route, altogether free of my brother, who remained in P.S. 58. The walk was now past my tree on 179th Street, up Arthur Avenue, past the synagogue to 180th Street, east on 180th and the big Italian fruit and vegetable store, its bins burbling with shapes and shining colors. Near Belmont the wallpaper store with pictures, the same one over and over again of blue birds in bamboo cages, and then the red brick building with a big yard, P.S. 57, at Crotona. We picked up a few people from other sixth-grade schools along the way, not too many girls. But maybe I only noticed the boys. One of them was Marty Green, who looked like Huckleberry Finn, like the boys on the *Saturday Evening Post* covers with spiky hair, freckles, and one knicker leg falling to his ankles. A jabberer, a joker, a jumpy walker like a marionette; cute. And distinctly not my type, which was sleek and sloe-eyed like Ramon Navarro, or like thin-faced Chopin in a sad, soft cloud of hair. Worst of all, Marty had no dignity. He jumped around me, made dumb loud jokes in my direction, and, most odd, began to follow me, silently and at a discreet distance, home from school. Flattered and preening, trying to walk with my feet pointed forward, not to walk like Charlie Chaplin as my father said I did, I found the situation distinctly worrisome. Knowing something of hopeless yearnings for one word from Federico De Santis, for a glance from Helen's ravishing high-school brother, I was sorry for him. And afraid. Even if I decided to acknowledge interest in him, what would I say? What must I do as his girl friend? Would I have to wind myself around him like the couples we spied on in the park, necking and petting, playing gidgee, even? Could I kiss him as I did my little sister, or would I have to kiss him as they did in the movies, mouth to mouth and breathing hard? This being followed at a distance, which I liked, I also disliked because it was a little like being spied on by my brother, who had decided with my father that I was boy-crazy and becoming a flapper and had to be watched. Somewhere in the confusion there was a sense also of waiting for a more challenging adventure; much as I hated them,

I did have breasts, inappropriate for a freckled boy of eleven or twelve. The Love of My Life had to be at least fifteen, suave and slick, surrounded by gaggles of girls over whom I would triumph brilliantly, like Gloria Swanson. (I found him, or invented him, but that's a later story.)

In the meantime more damned trouble, more and more, with being 'felt up'. Every once in a while my recalcitrant stormy hair had to be cut professionally and I was sent to my father's barber, Tony (they were all Tony, as all Mexican gardeners are Jesus), on Tremont Avenue and Washington, usually after a Saturday morning visit to the library nearby, a pleasure spoiled in anticipated dread. Tony was short and smiled like a villain, calling me a nice pretty girl he would make even prettier, as he spread a huge, imprisoning cloth over me. He was extraordinarily dexterous, combing and snipping with one hand while his other explored under the sheet, slowly, carefully, with gentle pinches and soft circles around my imprisoned breasts. When I squirmed to pull myself away from his hand, he laughingly warned me that if I didn't sit still he might cut my ear. So I sat still, irritated with time that now moved so slowly when at other times it moved so fast; trying to concentrate on his accent and in my mind mimic it; staring at the bottles of barber tonic on the mirror ledge; staring into the mirror to see if it would betray his creeping hand. No, the sheet was spread too wide and taut. There was nothing to be said; he was my elder and mustn't be rebuked. Anyhow, how did I know that this wasn't the way all girls got haircuts? It was a doubtful thing, but the doubtful, weird, ununderstandable, and erratic were everywhere I looked and touched; almost every experience carried its shadow of madness except the library and the movies.

After the interminable infuriating session at the barber shop, I wouldn't eat lunch. My mother wasn't, of course, to be told what had happened, but I was furious with her for sending me to Tony, and it would worry her if I didn't eat, an extraordinary occurrence, especially when she had cooked a pot of barley soup with lima beans and dried mushrooms, one of my favorites. She said I couldn't go to the movies if I didn't eat, upon which my brother threw down his spoon and began to yell at both of us because he couldn't go to the movies without me. My mother relented about the movies but said we couldn't have a nickel for candy, half for him, half for me. So he kicked and kept kicking me during the news, which didn't interest him at all, and managed to

be especially offensive during the day's love scenes when he hissed
into my ear, 'Mush! Mush! Icky mush!' while I was melting into the
screen.

It was a surprise but no longer a shock to find other men,
men I knew as fathers, capable of acting like Tony. Mr. Silverberg,
whose wife was still institutionalized, often came to visit his cousins
next door, the Goodmans, and visited us as well. One early Friday
evening, he asked my mother if he could take me to the movies, the
expensive movie that also had vaudeville. To forestall a refusal, I
quickly babbled out that I had practiced my whole two hours and
I didn't have to get up early to go to school the next day and I had
lots of time for homework. Please. Please. She said I could go; wash
my face, comb my hair, change my dress. I hurried, afraid my
father would come home to stop me and Mr. Silverberg. We were
lucky and got to Loew's without meeting him. Mr. Silverberg was
one of those men who looked like an old baby, with the infantile
features and worried looks of a Child Jesus who knew there was
trouble in store for him; he was round and soft, like a grandmother,
but I liked his brown suit and the tan tie attached to his very white
Arrow collar. It seemed as if he had dressed up for me and I was
glad I had on my concert dress. At the box office the immense
dignity of having a special ticket bought for me, rather than the
childish Saturday scramble of proffered dimes and the 'Take us in,
mister, please' to one of the few adults who dared the matinee mob
of kids. Mr. Silverberg bought me a Hershey bar, a whole Hershey
bar for myself, and asked me where I'd like to sit. I suggested
the orchestra, timidly, since I had rarely been anywhere but the
balcony, where kids were required to sit in the Belmont Theater.He
helped me off with my coat, asked me if I was comfortable and
could I see all right. I muttered something out of my overwhelmed
face and then the vaudeville show came on, unfortunate because
I hadn't had time to prepare for one of the *mudne* moods that
vaudeville plunged me into. I adored, was ready to give my life
to, the clowns and jugglers and the young people who sang and
danced snappily in curly costumes and glistening slippers. When
the old men in baggy pants came on to make lame jokes that no
one laughed at and the too-jolly women in pink tight dresses, like
swollen frankfurters, sang in harsh, flat sounds, I would – were
I with my mother – hide my face not to be part of their shame.
But I was not with my mother, who had, in any case, vowed never
to go to the movies with me after I hid from half the vaudeville acts

and cried all through *The Gold Rush*. With my grown-up escort I sat
and smiled straight ahead of me, applauding as he did, laughing
when I thought I should, being as little odd as possible, although it
still hurt to hear the dead jokes, the hectic rough singing, and feel
all the frantic trying.

The movie was with Nita Naldi, my favorite vamp, black hair,
black eyes, black veils, black beads, a glorious creature who moved
like a big snake, who didn't talk much but just looked out of her
long, smoky eyes and withered all but the strongest heroes, who
managed through riveting hours to resist her sorcery and survive
to marry the blond heroine. Sitting with Nita Naldi, my chest heavy
with her beads and magical amulets, on a broad throne, one hand
covered with rings dropping languidly over a chair arm carved like
a lion's head, I felt a touch on my thigh, the hand of Mr. Silverberg.
I hoped it was some sort of accident and waited. The hand crept up,
tried to get into my bloomers, but the elastic was too tight. It tried
to get into my bloomers from above but my dress belt, pulled to
make my waist small, got in his way, too. He unbuttoned the back
of my dress, put his arm and hand in, and began to finger the one
breast he could reach, flattened under the ribbon, which he tried to
peel away; it was held firmly by two big diaper pins. He went back
to my bloomers, stroking on the cloth. I crossed my legs tightly,
which gave him one buttock to work on. His other hand seemed
to be busy in his pants. I couldn't turn to see but I could sense the
familiar trembling.

When the movie was over, he helped me on with my coat
and in the course of the walk home made grown-up conversation:
Wasn't that a good movie? He always enjoyed Nita Naldi, didn't I?
Wasn't that clown with the electric-bulb nose funny? I answered in
monosyllables, wondering once more at the perfidy of adults who
could do such dirty things in the dark and then talk as if nothing
had happened. He didn't ask me not to tell my parents, he knew I
wouldn't. When we reached 2029, I asked him to go up without me,
please to tell my parents I would be right up. The stairs were dark
and I wanted no more groping, no more trying to squeeze myself
into a tight ball, no more of his bland voice or his sharp-edged
collar; no more. I stood for a minute or two in front of the street
lamp. It had begun to snow and watching the snow flakes dance
on their golden stage of light helped erase Mr. Silverberg. When
I got upstairs I could say to my parents, yes, it was a good show
and a good picture; yes, I had enjoyed myself, very much; yes, I

had thanked him; yes, Mr. Silverberg was very nice to take me.

The sequence is unclear but within a few months Frankie Polanski, then about seventeen, was arrested and jailed and his sister Carola, a year younger, disappeared for a couple of days, reappeared, and left again. The Polanskis, our janitors, lived in a basement flat near the coal cellar and the mammoth stoves that made the hot water and steam heat, their one visible window below the level of the street at the side of the stoop. They had a bad-tempered curly white dog and three children, Frankie, Carola, and Stella, the youngest, who was somewhat ahead of me in school and a good girl who did her homework and ran errands for her mother. Neither Mr. Polanski, almost invisible in his cellar life, nor Mrs. Polanski spoke English except for a few barely recognizable warnings and curses when she found chalk marks on the stoop or a broken ball discarded in the hallway. She was tiny and had thin light-brown Polish hair, like my mother, like the gaggles of cleaning women who now board the city's buses, chattering in Polish, at eleven o'clock at night. She walked quickly, bent forward, propelled by a ferocity of purpose. When she scrubbed the stairs, all five flights, on her knees and skated on rags in her bare feet to polish the landings, we didn't dare pass her, didn't dare make a mark on her pristine stairs, no matter what the urgency, hunger or toilet. That went for adults, too, who humbly apologized as the discontented wrinkles twisted into 'Sonnamabeech! *Pshakref*!'

Since my mother was her only Polish tenant, we had fair doses of Mrs. Polanski when her children were in trouble. Both Frankie and Carola were practiced truants, and when the truant officer came around, ununderstandable, terrifying, Mrs. Polanski rang our bell as if it were a fire alarm and then ran into the courtyard to shout my mother down. We were never permitted to go with her, it was none of our business; anyhow, we knew they were truants and what happened to truants. Hanging around the basement window, we often heard beating and shouting, Stella rushing up her stairs to cry on the stoop. No effect on Frankie and Carola; they continued to pursue their secret, free-roaming lives.

We hadn't seen Frankie at all for some time when the boys' admiring grapevine reported that he had been arrested along with a couple of his gang for stealing – what, where, we didn't know – and was in prison. Those days Mrs. Polanski sat in our kitchen – only after the stairs had been cleaned and the landings shined

– crying and questioning, all in Polish. Nor was the report to our father when he came home helpful, also recounted in Polish. We gathered slowly, bit by bit, that my mother had told Mrs. P. to go downtown on the El to where many Polish people lived, on First and Second avenues, around 7th and 8th streets, and to ask them to take her to the Polish immigrant center. There she would find advice and maybe a lawyer.Mrs. Polanski had never, once she came to Lafontaine, been more than two blocks from her house and was sure she would get lost on the El and the downtown streets. She didn't go and Mr. Polanski was reported to have said when his wife suggested he make the trip, 'Let him rot in prison.' My mother continued to be concerned about Frankie but my father was soon bored with them and announced, 'Enough, enough already, about those ignorant barbarians and the criminals they breed.'

Carola's sporadic returns to the street were movie scenes from pictures about bad girls in France. They always took place in the afternoon when many of us were out to watch the poised, graceful progress of the tall girl with slender hips and full breasts. No practical Buster Brown haircut for Carol, as she now called herself. Her light hair was waved in deep curves, spitcurls pasted on her forehead and around her face, almost into her long green eyes and pointing up her high cheekbones. She always had something remarkable to show: a new red patent-leather pocketbook, shining high-heeled shoes, and real money, dollars. When we asked where she had gotten the splendors, she gestured languidly. 'Oh, I have a lot of friends, rich friends, who give me presents.' We had no idea how such friends could be acquired, but I got some inkling from my father and his indignation when he caught a glimpse of her one Sunday afternoon, strolling vampishly, eyeing the bench sitters in the park. He didn't bother with the tact of Polish, his Yiddish fury obviously was meant for me to understand, to take warning. See, he was right. Carola had started as a 'street girl', a girl who didn't go to school, who could hardly read and write, who stayed out late and hung around with boys, and now, as he knew she would, had turned into a full-fledged *nafka*. At sixteen, with beauty-parlor hair, silk stockings, and her cheap, vulgar pocketbook (his expertise extended to bags as well as shoes), what was she looking forward to? A good job? A decent husband and children? No, of course not. But in a few years she wouldn't be pretty, she would have to go into a house of *nafkas* and serve men who would beat her. And then would come the diseases and the hospitals like Bellevue where the crazy people were kept also, and finally out in the street, wrinkled and ugly, to beg at thirty.

He may have gone on, but I had stopped listening. All that stuff about disease didn't matter; he was always talking about disease, in frankfurters, in ices, in a life without prunes. Although I was vague about some of the essential details in spite of my education by Rosa and Debby, Carol's seemed an alluring life, free and rich. I decided to start practicing to be a street girl, as usual not ready but eager for the difficulties that might entail. As my first practice piece I chose Miltie of the third floor, a good runner but otherwise something of a sissy who always listened to his mother, who had forbidden him to play marbles because it made his knickers dirty, to steal or roast mickies because it was dishonest and dangerous, or ever to remove his glasses (thus he could never fight). He was measured and joyless. I picked him also because he was always standing in my way; he must like me. When the weather grew cold and there was no more singing on the stoop, we crowded into the inner letterbox hall for talk and horseplay. Watching him staring at me through his watery glasses, I said suddenly, 'You wanna wrestle?' He continued to stare, not a word. 'You wanna wrestle? Take off your glasses', tough, like boys beginning a fight. As if he were a puppet I was pulling, he rose from the steps, one leg up, then the other, and slowly approached me. Our audience of four or five boys, my brother among them, moved the rubber mat into the precise middle of the floor and gathered at one side of the small hall. Still a toughie, I put my hands forward, ready for grabbing, got his shoulder, and twisted him around. He lost his balance, fell, shot up in a fury of humiliation, whipped his glasses off to hand to the nearest boy, put a foot between mine, and tripped me. I fell on the stairs, sat up, put my arms around his knees, pulled, and felled him again. I jumped on top of him and we pushed, grabbed, rolled, pulled each other's hair, elbowed each other's bellies, I in my sweaty efforts noting just what it was I was pounding and how it felt. Our audience, who might ordinarily be yelling instruction and criticisms, was silent; it was an awesome event, this match with a girl, and beyond comment. When someone yelled 'chickie!' because Mr. Haskell was mounting the stoop, we leaped up, brushed our disheveled clothing, wiped our wet faces, and tried to look conversational. Fortunately Mr. Haskell was child-proof, never saw, never gave a damn, indifferent to our disordered clothing and our boiling faces. As we walked up the inner stairs to our apartment I told my brother that if he mentioned the wrestling I would tell that he had called Manny a fuck. OK. He didn't and I didn't.

The wrestling went on through a number of sessions, Miltie no longer reluctant, no longer waiting to be challenged. We made appointments. 'Tomorrow, five o'clock.' 'No, I can't. I got Hebrew school tomorrow.' 'OK, Wednesday.' We met and wrestled vigorously, Miltie improving mightily as we punched, shoved, and explored each other's anatomy. Until someone forgot to yell 'Chickie!' before Mr. Kaplan, our morals committee, walked in on us to stare, without comment, at the octopus of flailing boy and girl limbs. He gave me a look of burning contempt, not Miltie, stepped by us and into the house to report immediately, we all knew, to my father.

As we had learned to say, we girls of almost thirteen, old enough for monthlies and 'bassiers', 'then the shit hit the electric fan'. My father bellowed, he stamped like the bull in *Blood and Sand*, he shook with outrage and ordered me into the bathroom for a beating. My mother yelled 'No!' Folk wisdom forbade the beating of a nubile girl on her bare buttocks; it suspected a scent of pleasure. He slapped me instead, thrusting me like a top from one wall of the narrow hallway to the other with each ringing blow. When my sister ran out of the kitchen crying and tried to get between us, he stopped. My mother held on to her disapproving assistant-principal face as I went by her to my bedroom and didn't say a word when my father accused her of encouraging me to become another Carola Polanski.

The wrestling stopped and Miltie stayed away from that part of the street on which I talked or played, no longer hung around me in the school yard. It didn't matter much, I still had my other puppet, Marty, and had begun to fix my eyes and imagination on Sal Venturi, the Man of P.S. 57. He roused storms of feeling in me, a full sun of elation when I saw him alone, a sack of despair when he talked to other girls. I whirled in dreams of living with him in enchanted castles, a life of pure white satin, or, scorned, trailing after him for the rest of my dragging, boneless life. Sal had blond hair and blue eyes, an exquisite phenomenon in an Italian; he was tall, the champion of the swimming team, of the basketball team, a man of legend. He was masterful with the teachers, looking at them with a twisted smile and insolent eyes when they rebuked him for not having done his homework. The younger teachers spoke to him with the same smile and bold eyes, as if they were sharing a secret. His name was dragged into countless girl conversations, the subject of luxuriant gossip. He had, they said, several girl friends, big girls who used lipstick, with whom he played gidgee, the real thing, the big act beyond petting and muzzling. He never did his homework, they said; he flunked tests and skipped school and didn't care because he knew how to twist the teachers around his little finger. He paid no attention to the girls in P.S. 57; his was stronger game. When I tried to speak to him, after much deliberation and gathering together my fraying courage, something inane came out, like 'You think you're great, don't you? Well, I don't.' He didn't seem to hear and I could have torn my tongue out. Since there was to be no conversation, I began to follow him to find out where he lived, to have a picture of his street and house, to give him a landscape. I was sly, wary, staying well behind at first until I realized that he and his gang, shoving each other into the gutter, pummeling each other's arms, wouldn't know who I was even if it occurred to them to look back.

He lived near the Italian market a few blocks north of school in a house with a glassed-in porch (must be rich), and here I stationed myself frequent evenings, sometimes across the street, sometimes behind a nearby tree, to catch a glimpse of him and his sophisticated girl friends, to see what they did. I got to know his fat father and an uncle or a friend who played dominoes for hours on end. I learned that his mother used a wooden egg for darning socks and wished my mother had one. His plump blond sister buffed her nails as she talked with her mother. It was like looking at paintings, out of the dark street into the bright, framed light of the porch. It became evident that the porch was Sal's on weekends only so I limited my spying to Friday and Saturday nights. The high-heeled girls, undoubtedly wearing brassieres under their tight-waisted flouncy dresses, bounced around on the couches, allowing a boy's arm to rest on their shoulders for a moment before quickly shrugging it away. Mostly they laughed and ate crackers and candy and danced the Charleston. I suspected the other things would happen later with the lights turned off but I couldn't stay. It was painful, the bright liveliness; it made me an outcast, cut off from all pleasures forever and ever. I spent the rest of those evenings, and others, and much of those days, in dark caves of self-pity and gnawing jealousy.

The evenings of spying on my love resulted in heavy muttering at home. My excuse for coming in late was that I had taken a long walk and hadn't noticed the time. It was an unfortunate excuse, the long walk. Why didn't we take them together, as we used to, suggested my father. Since I had presented myself rather suddenly as an enthusiast of long walks, there was nothing I could do but let him play impresario again. Again, I was to tell my teachers that I had to quit school (they would tell the principal, nothing to it) so I could practice the piano all day. I was the best piano player on the block, he said, and the best of Mr. Stone's pupils; a respected teacher wouldn't trust just anyone to play Chopin's 'Fantasie Impromptu' at his student recital, would he? And listen to this, listen. He would get rid of the old secondhand piano that the blind piano tuner said couldn't be fixed anymore without spending a lot of money and put that money down on a new piano, a real Hardman-Peck, almost as good as a Steinway. How would I like that? I said that would be very nice, telling myself it wouldn't happen. Promises held OK among kids but not among adults. They were temporary bribes, a mechanism for 'get off my back' or 'do what I say'. What if he should actually buy a new piano, though? I would be in serious trouble: leave the school, the street, my friends, my tree, my mother, my brother, sister, the library, the movies, Crotona Park, and be his exclusively the rest of my life. The new piano became a larger and larger presence during these forced marches. He described a piano he had looked at, its size and high, new shine, the carved music rack and the big golden letters on the lid. Sounds like clear bells and no stuck notes, no buzzing lower notes. Of course, later on when I had become a concert artist we would have a huge Steinway whose top could be lifted to become a great wing. And with it would come a plush-cushioned seat that a pianist could adjust for reaching the notes and the pedals perfectly.

The piano actually, shockingly, came, wrapped in felt cloths and ropes and lifted carefully by four men with swollen muscles up the five flights of stairs, every door open to watch its progress. The dollar my mother paid the moving men, the noble size of the piano, and its luster, which emblazoned the room, were things to boast of, to show off to special friends. The glowing pedals could be touched subtly, to make soft rainbows of sound. The keys were shining white and obeyed every touch of my fingers; they made me feel like a pianist, not just a kid practicing. This piano was for Beethoven sonatas, not the 'Rustle of Spring', and still the Great Threat, the Terrible Enemy. When my father came home that night, he examined the piano minutely, asking that I admire it with him, mentioning several times the unbelievable price – hundreds of dollars – and asking if I wasn't pleased and grateful. I admired, wondered at the price, and said I was very pleased to have it. Now was the time to settle down to real practicing, he said, to prepare for my career. And no more reading in bed half the night and fooling around with my stupid friends; practice would need my full strength and concentration.

The prison gates were yawning open. Each evening I was asked whether I had told my teachers I was quitting. Each evening I lied: my teacher was sick and we had a substitute who didn't know anything; the principal was off at a school conference; Miss Bender had told me my father would have to come to school himself, lose a day's work. He scorned my stories and information. I was a coward, a big mouth at home and incapable of making a simple request in school. I lied about practicing; yes I was now practicing two and a half hours a day rather than the usual two; neither my brother nor my mother informed against me; like myself, they sensed threatening developments and chose to remain silent observers. They knew my father would keep urging that I leave school. They knew I wouldn't. They watched and waited.

I was running out of lies and my father out of patience when we received a letter from Yankel. He was living in Toledo, working as a bookkeeper, and was coming to New York to see a girl he had met earlier in an English class; her father owned a big store on Grand Street. Could he stay with his dear family a couple of nights? It wasn't the skinny, pimpled boy who walked through the door. This one wore a stickpin in his tie and a ruby pinkie ring. His suit hung neatly on his full shoulders and he had stopped biting his nails. He walked through the hall, past the kitchen, and sat himself confidently at the dining room table, placing a box of chocolates in its center. No one opened the box. My mother was reluctant to accept a gift from Yankel; it was not my father's business to open boxes of candy; we didn't dare. It sat there growing taller and wider under our anxious eyes, and we finally left it as unattainable as he went on and on describing his New York girl's father's store, big with two salesmen who measured out hundreds of yards of velvets, satins from Italy, and lace imported from France, no kitchen curtain stuff, mind you, and in a busy, choice location. How was business in Toledo, my father asked. Was Yankel going to get his citizenship papers soon? Did he think he could get his

mother over this year; my father's landsmen would of course help
out. It grew late, the conversation dwindled. The tea glasses were
washed and put back into the kitchen cabinet, the lights went out,
and then the long night silence, dotted by my parents' snorts and
whistles.

The folding cot had been taken out of the closet and arranged
for Yankel under the rubber plant that, by now, almost touched
the ceiling. As usual, my brother was asleep as soon as his head
fell to the pillow, my sister was already long asleep. I took my
shoes off but not my dress. Yankel had made a fuss about how big
and pretty I'd become, almost a woman, and I'd better watch out
for the boys. I knew that kind of praise from the watchman of the
factory next door, from a Bianchi relative who owned a bakery on
Catherine Street and courted us girls with Italian almond cookies,
and I knew Yankel. And I waited. My brother, a talkative dreamer,
muttered a conflict about 'immies', the choicest of marbles; my
sister smacked her lips as if she were sucking a lollipop. From
the farthest room came the muffled duet of my mother's high
rattle and my father's deeper, calmer snores. The wind shook the
window shade now and then. Nothing else. I was beginning to fall
asleep, still fully dressed, when I heard a light sound at the door,
the loose doorknob stuttering as it turned, the door creaking open
slowly. There was Yankel, his short American underwear clear and
white in the dark. Before he could approach the bed I jumped up
and ran at him, hissing, 'Get out! Get the hell out of here!' One
startled look and he disappeared. I pushed the chair against the
door just to make sure, although I doubted he would try again, got
undressed and under the covers, but I didn't sleep, hot with hatred
of Yankel and my father. My father, like myself, slept lightly; he
must have known what Yankel was doing and had done before, and
Bessie, too. He permitted it because they were Family on whom
he had spent considerable effort and money, eager to get them
to New York: Yankel, Bessie, and later numerous sisters in black
and brown sateen stretched over broad horizons of bosom, and
the unforgettable Sarita. (The stringent tightening of immigration
laws kept Sarita, the last, for a longish period in Cuba, before her
importation to New York. She was a bandy-legged, pitted thing,
adroit and assiduous in her flattery of Uncle and his son, who
suddenly found himself with a generous allowance to take Sarita,
a good number of years older than himself, to the movies and
ice-cream parlors. My brother hated 'old' Sarita, whose presence

was interfering with his growing reputation as the Don Juan of the
block. To escape her, and to parallel my later freedom, he signed on
as cabin boy with a Caribbean freighter. She hung on, encouraged
by Uncle, who was hinting at an ultimate marriage as soon as my
brother could earn a good living – he was fifteen at the time. My
mother loathed her as ugly and a hypocrite and my few encounters
with her revealed a stupid, transparent conniver. We were all saved
from her when she had an agonizing attack of abdominal pain.
One of my friends, an intern at Beth Israel, drove us there in his
father's car. It didn't take long to determine that she was suffering
a flare-up of a well-ensconced case of gonorrhea. She couldn't stay
there; Belevue was the hospital for venereal diseases. Get her out
of here and up there. Now. Quick. Shocked but undiscouraged, my
father found her a room and a job after months of treatment, and
since his son would absolutely, definitely, not have anything to do
with her, searched out a lonely, elderly *shlemiel* for her to marry.)

There are several variations of a story in which a dying Jew
is making out his will with the help of a friend. 'But,' the friend
protests, 'if you leave the store to your brother Ben, your money in
the bank to your brother Sol, and your house to your sister Rosie,
what's left for your wife and children, your family?' 'What family?
What are you talking about? Rosie, Sol, Ben, that's my family.'

This was my father and his Family, who obviously had the
additional privilege of using me. It was he who was making
me a 'street girl' for anyone in the Family, a thing that had
no feelings, no thoughts, no choices. There I was to lie, a
slice of fresh cornbread, a chicken leg, a snack before sleep.
Triumphant over Yankel and furious with them all – why
didn't my sharp mother suspect something and protect me? –
I began to put my hands on my hips when I answered back, like
Carol Polanski. Asked where I was going, I began with 'Out', and
built up to 'None of your business'. I refused to take walks with
him, vengeful and dead scared with the new piano shining at me,
of his wild imaginings. When I caught him following me to the
Italian market section to be nearer Sal, I changed direction to a
distant library that was open in the evening. Though I could not
take books out, I was allowed to sit and read, catching glimpses of
him pacing back and forth at the entrance in the brisk night. He
managed to stay a block or two behind me as we walked, but he
knew that I knew he was there. When my mother protested that
our walks were growing too long and late, he said I was getting fat

and lazy and didn't so much need sleep as exercise. The practicing diminished, my mother a weekday witness to the fact. All she said was 'What a shame. So much that piano cost. What a shame.' Much of the nonpracticing time was spent across from the corner candy store that was Sal's hangout, adoring the way a lit cigarette dangled from his lower lip, adoring and hating the way he stepped in front of a neighborhood girl, standing straight and close, staring down at her until she moved away with a small smile on her face.

Imagining, planning, rehearsing, practicing stances of courage, I announced one Sunday morning, not directly to my father but rather into the air around him, that I was not going to the student concert that afternoon, nor was I, anymore, going to practice four hours on Sunday morning, with time out for one toilet trip and one drink of water. Riding on the wind I had churned up in myself, I continued: Two hours was enough for any day; I wasn't going to be a concert pianist and maybe not even play in Mr. Stone's next concert. My brother and sister slipped out the door and down the stairs; my mother began to rattle pots and dishes in the kitchen. The big battle between us was joined, very much as I had imagined it would be. It was he who decided such important matters, not I. What did a thirteen-year-old flapper (he liked to be up to date in his English), a girl who had a head only for boys, know about great rich careers open to talents like mine? Carnegie Hall was full of people every night paying to listen to children younger than myself who made hundreds of dollars for each performance. I answered that I didn't have that much talent, I knew it and so should he. Came the expected roar: What did I know about talent and how it could be developed with enough practice? I was not, not, not going to leave school to practice and he could do what he liked about it. Anyhow, he had lied to me; I had found out that it wasn't easy to remove a pupil from school without getting into trouble with truant officers. I had a right to stay in school and I was going to stay, maybe even finish high school. High school? Sure, one year of commercial high school to learn typing and stenography, and then, if that was the kind of life I wanted, find a job to support myself and pay back the cost of the new piano, the big tombstone that would stand there to remind me of the hundreds of dollars, saved carefully over the years, the family deprived of many things, only to be wasted by me. Dumped like potato peelings into a garbage can, spilled like muddy rain into a sewer. I didn't answer and walked out.

The ticker tape in my head busily clicking observations about

power and vanity, theirs and mine, and yet knowing nothing, I went
on the day of my graduation from elementary school to change my
child's library card for one that permitted me to use the downstairs
room for adults. Some writer there would tell me what Louisa
May Alcott couldn't, nor Dickens nor the children's biographies
of Mozart and Beethoven. Where the titles came from I don't know
but I had ready a mental list of books to take from the adult shelves
and found them: Knut Hamsun's *Hunger*, Hugo's *Les Misérables*,
Nietzsche's *Thus Spake Zarathustra*, the plays of Chekhov. Armed
with these mighty weapons, I would know, I would understand. The
clotted brambles would melt away from the secret door and I would
be in the adult garden of clean colors and shapes where everything
had its own unchanging name; white-petaled truth always truth, the
slender trees with silvery bark always promises kept, the mazes of
love and sex clearly marked, brilliantly illustrated and immutable.
Anyhow, it was a proud thing to be turning the pages of such
great thoughts and emotions, and although they didn't teach me
enough – just what was it Zarathustra was preaching? Why
were all those people mooning and yearning for Moscow? –
they were pushing me, little by little, I hoped, toward that garden
of crystal clarity. The books grew heavier, some not helpful at all
– Dostoevski's brothers Karamazov were as irrational as the
people around me – some, like Chekhov's stories, confirming
in whispers things I almost half knew about people.

As I was reading Chekhov's 'The Darling' one morning, envying
her fullness of devotion, contemptuous of her dopiness, I felt as if
I were losing urine, without the usual warning sensations except a
heaviness in my lower belly. When I took off my bloomers in the
bathroom, I saw a few red drops of blood on them and on my
thigh. I called to my mother, astonished and frightened; maybe
this, not going blind or crazy, was the result of masturbating. She
said, smiling, that it was my monthlies and slapped me hard on the
face. She had not been particularly friendly since my practicing on
the new piano had diminished, but she hadn't seethed or boiled
like my father. So why hit me now, what had I done? Was this
some sort of punishment? For not practicing enough? For reading
instead of going to the grocery store? For not watching my little
sister carefully enough? For running after Sal? Why? I was back,
slapped back from the growing confidence of being over thirteen
to the bewilderments of eight and nine. It was months later, after
I had learned to use and wash, reuse and rewash the strips of torn

sheet she gave me, that she explained the slap; it was to restore a girl's circulation and all mothers did it in the Old Country. I was relieved but unforgiving; she could have told me sooner, and what was this Old Country junk in a woman who scorned so many of its practices?

It was a day in May. I had achieved my first menstrual period, my white wedding dress tree on 179th Street had covered its sky with blossoms. In the library that Saturday morning were my two favorite librarians, the young woman with long blond hair twisted in a satiny band around her head who spoke English as Miss Bender did, as I was determined to, even though my friends called me a 'show-off' and 'teacher's pet'; the word 'affected' was not in their vocabulary. The other favorite librarian was a short woman who always wore a brown dress with a lace collar and brown shoes. She had puffs of brown hair and round brown eyes and I thought of her as one of the plump brown birds I saw in Crotona Park. She spoke with a slight accent, nothing like the cadences I heard on Lafontaine, not marked enough to mimic. She was intensely interested in what I was selecting, what I had chosen to take home. *War and Peace?* She looked doubtful, but said to try it anyway. *The Great God Brown*, maybe not, but it, too, was worth trying. She never said absolutely no; a good pedagogue, she let me glean what I could out of any choice I made. She must have sensed, as well, how proud I was to be carrying these ponderous works by masters through the street, not on skates anymore, but on foot, like the college student I meant to be mistaken for.

Just before lunch and the movies, my mother asked me to try on the dress she had been making for me, a surprise. It *was* a surprise, no loose, shapeless pongee dress with a sailor collar, the usual summer dress-up dress. This was of thin voile printed in irregular boxes of blue and lemon yellow, no collar, peter pan or sailor, just narrow ties at the open neck.It was shaped, pinched in under my breasts, narrowing down to a waist, billowing out in a gathered skirt, covering my knees. It was a woman's dress. I wore it when we went walking in the park the next afternoon, refusing to put on a sweater. I heard little and saw less; aware only of the tucks on my ribs, the sloping seams at the sides, the swing of the skirt as it brushed my knees. I held my naked, collarless neck stiff and high, placed my feet straight before me, step after step, careful to avoid the Charlie Chaplin turned-out foot-slap my father derided.

My waist was a golden ring, my sides as I stroked them had the curved perfection of antelope's horns. My arms below the puffed sleeves were cream-colored velvet. I approved of the taste of all the strokers and pinchers. I understood what they felt, felt it myself as I continued to stroke my superb sides. I saw Sal Venturi at the stoop of 2029, waiting adoringly, humbly, his eyes rolled up like a saint waiting to be pulled up to Heaven. After a slow while I would emerge, gazing at him quizzically, mockingly, one eyebrow raised above a crooked little smile. Or – there was a boundless world of choices opening around me – take his arm and walk with him into a pink twilight. The next time Mr. Silverberg offered to take me to the movies I would suggest that we go to the Chinks first, like a real date, and push his hand away firmly when it began to crawl. Or let it crawl while I laughed at him. I might let Tony play his finger games under the sheet or punch his round belly. I might say 'Son of a bitch' or even 'You fucking bastard' to the humpbacked watchman if he tried to pinch my ass as I passed the factory, or dance around him, my skirt swirling flirtatiously, as he lumbered toward me. The next time I went to Helen Roth's house, her high-school brother would kneel and lay at my feet a sheaf of long-stemmed red roses. Federico De Santis and his brother Berto would stick daggers into each other for rivalrous love of me.

I was ready for all of them and for Rudolph Valentino; to play, to tease, to amorously accept, to confidently reject. Lolita, my twin, was born decades later, yet a twin of the thirteen-and-a-half-year-old striding through Crotona Park, passing the spiky red flowers toward a kingdom of mesmerized men – young, old, skinny, fat, good-looking, ugly, well dressed, shabby, bachelors, fathers – all her subjects. As desirable as Gloria Swanson, as steely as Nita Naldi, as winsome as Marion Davies, she was, like them, invincible and immortal.

PORTRAITS
IN AN ADOLESCENCE

For Miriam and Jeremy

The author, having finished the first part of her autobiography with a description of the onset of puberty – and all the feelings and emotions that go with it – opens the second part with an account of her desire to break away from the Bronx into new exploration and adventure. In her introduction she writes:

In time, I abandoned my infantile rule of the country of Lafontaine. Its subjects had become less mysterious and engaging, they had no more information about sex and birthing to give me and my adroit eavesdropping. My boundaries of school, library, movies, and home had become too tight, like outgrown shoes. I needed new shoes, maybe with shining high heels, and new streets to try them out on: frightening, alluring streets paced by exotic strangers who would have many things to teach me. Packing a bundle of fear, courage, and practiced stubbornness, I was readying for exploration. Not just yet; there would be forests to wander in and tall walls to climb, as in most brave stories; but the need and the right time would meet, I knew, and I could wait, ripening with them.

15
James Monroe H.S.

I am thirteen and a half, graduating from elementary school and hoping to go to high school. It was a rite of passage that would call for light rejoicing, especially in the houses of immigrants, to whom eight years in elementary school meant a long and broad education. In our house, my mother expressed her approbation by buying me a rose, my brother treated me with a modicum of respect on that day, my five-year-old sister beamed at me, so smart and big and the cause of an extra ice-cream cone. For my father it was a day of silent rage, staring at me, staring at the new piano.

If I insisted on going on to high school, he said at supper, it would be only for one more year, a year in which I would study typing and stenography to prepare me for the job that would wipe out – and it would take years – my enormous debt, the piano. Cocooned in guilt from the earliest time, the time when I could walk and my rachitic brother couldn't, I had taken on accretions of additional guilts, like huge warts. You have to respect and love your father; I didn't. You must never lie; I did. You mustn't play doctor; I had. And here stood the greatest glistening, most expensive, most accusing thing in the house. Because I knew how much the money meant to him, and the glory and future riches it symbolized if only I were a good daughter and used my talents profitably, the piano became a dry, sharp pain in my throat, as if I were being punished with laryngitis because I had silenced the piano.

Here I stand, hobbled in a sack of doom, determined to tear out of it, knowing that I will. There is no clear direction to follow in the welter of impractical ideas that storm my naive mind; nothing but rocklike determination, chiseled and honed to serve as armor and weapon. I keep hoping and looking for clarity in a world that heaps complexity on confusions. The paths opening to clear light under the bowers of bewilderments remain sparse and evanescent. Much, much is sensed, almost learned, but what does it mean, how does it mesh together, if at all?

My voice returned, that of the piano did not, while I struggled with new puzzles in a country entirely foreign to me. Although I had begged to be allowed to go to a general high school, where they taught biology, history, and writing book reports, my father insisted I enter a commercial high school, where the concentration was on office subjects, with classes in English and one foreign language. This with the constant reminder that I would leave at the end of my first year. I didn't know whether he could legally yank me out of school at fourteen and I didn't care after a short while. Nothing could be more depressing than these classes in which I was mud-stupid. My fears of numbers reduced me to idiocy in the bookkeeping class, the finger dexterity the piano had taught me confused my typing. Anger and resistance helped make an utter idiot of me, except in English. I was the best in the class and not too bad in German, my accent sharp mimicry, my vocabulary often reshaped Yiddish.

As the school year was approaching its end, the warnings to look for a job accelerated. How did one get a job at fourteen, and with no skill? I could probably handle a job at the five-and-ten, but most of the employees there were grown women. Where does one begin? Whom to ask? How? If I was asked questions, could I answer? Would I be struck dumb? Would I fall off the edge of the world? Maybe it would be easier to leave home and make money, like pretty, painted, and high-heeled Carola Polanski. But too frightened to apply for a job, how could I hang around street corners and make friends with strange men?

Came an extraordinary event, a miracle worked by exalted personages. My father received a letter signed by my English and German teachers and the principal. It said politely and firmly that I was in the wrong school, that a girl of my interests and capabilities should be offered the broader education of a general high school which might prepare her for college. No one could deny the authority of a high school principal and my father agreed that I be transferred to James Monroe, a new school with an unusually permissive curriculum.

My father's reminders at the end of each semester that I say good-bye to friends and teachers – that was enough school, get a job – helped shape an erratic program for which I have been forever grateful. Since the ordinary stream of studies that answered college requirements were not for me (although I was determined to stay, no matter the cost in effort and quarrels), my courses, other than those absolutely required, were a set of improvisations. First off, no math was demanded, none at all, the school's most bountiful gesture for one blinded by the simplest combination of numbers. Instead, a music course, where I first heard 'This is the symphony that Schubert wrote but never finished' – the very short version of elementary school – in its truncated entirety, and a lovely piece of weaving that was a Brahms quartet. An essay on the differences among the Beethoven symphonies earned me a startling compliment from the teacher, a swift little woman who swooped close to the phonograph like a plump hawk when a particular phrase or combination of instruments possessed her and, impelled by her passion, possessed us. She suggested, after having read the Beethoven essay, that I become a music critic. I was pleased but not impressed, since I seemed to be able to knock off an essay on almost any subject easily and fairly well. At any rate, being a music critic was too remote for a girl who had it dinned into her that Jewish goals had to be modest and those of a Jewish woman more modest still.

The English Department, small, talkative, dedicated, maternal, held me in its collective eye, particularly after I had, as a midterm essay, done a small (and, they said, original and pioneer) work on the street cries, the ballads, the game songs of the Bronx, a work I was urged to continue by the head of the department, Mr. Brandon. Any work sustained and slow was, however, too much like practicing the piano to master a late Beethoven sonata. I had no time for step-by-step projects; the urgent need was for swift voyages, with short stops at many ports of call.

James Monroe was the first stage on which I created of myself a distinctive, conspicuous character. My ears had been pierced by my grandmother in Poland when I was a few months old – to preserve my vision, she said. The little turquoise earrings disappeared in America – I suspect my mother's hand. By poking at my earlobes with pins and toothpicks, I opened the old punctures, and with the money I earned teaching six- and seven-year-olds to play the piano, at twenty-five cents a lesson, I bought a pair of Spanish hoops, to become the only girl in school who then had pierced ears, and the fitting Gypsy earrings. The Bergsons, for whom I

had become mother's helper during my fourteenth summer, and
later on baby-sitter, offered me discarded clothing, my favorites a
long dark-gray raincoat and an ancient dark-gold Borsalino hat, the
hat of actors and writers. To complement the dark coat and the hat
like Renaissance velvet, I bought, out of earnings from teaching old
foreign ladies English, two pairs of black cotton stockings and black
sneakers. In my earrings, my romantic hat, my slightly sinister coat
and black stockings, I could not be mistaken for anyone else in the
world. Nor was there any other girl who acted Hedda Gabler in
a drama class, twisting a long string of borrowed wooden beads
very symbolically and smoking cigarettes, nervously, expertly,
throughout the performance, spoken in a voice of sinuous evil.

The indulgent English Department loved all of its promising
children with a springtime faith, to the point of freeing them
from ordinary curriculum rigidities. Thus some of us were excused
from the routine English classes and permitted to gather as poetry
groups, as drama classes, as classes in Shakespeare, and I had
permission to attend them all. Mr. Brandon, whom I loved as I
should have liked to love my father, also invited us to after-school
lectures on several subjects. I remember still a lecture on Oriental
rugs, illustrated by examples from his own collection, describing
their provenances, their variety of weaving techniques, and the
meanings in their patterns. He remains one of my immortals, my
Marco Polo in Samarkand and Istanbul, the guide to whom I owe
the first radiance of Shakespeare sonnets, the flight into Keats's
'Eve of St. Agnes', Wilde's dazzle of words and of countless designs
and colors that made my eye happy.

The rest of the teaching staff, other than the music and English
departments, remain blanks, except for two German teachers and a
redheaded vixen in the French Department. One German teacher,
Dr. Mankiewicz (an ancestor, I believe, of the movie eminences of
that name), was the prototype of the well-padded, easy, philosophic
German. When the repetitions of *aus, ausser, bei, mitt, nach, zeit,
von, zu* (I think) grew unbearable, I would take a library book out
of my bundle and, placing it on my lap, read and read. Once he
caught the cast-down eyes in my entranced face and called me
and the book to the front of the room. I wasn't afraid, no one
was; the atmosphere was of a kindly tolerance just this side of
indifference. He asked me what I was reading with such rapture.
It was a Knut Hamsun novel; as Dickens and Chekhov had been
earlier, Hamsun was my then current bible. Dr. Mankiewicz said

my taste wasn't bad, but couldn't I try to learn a little German grammar between the Hamsun paragraphs, as an act of politeness, if nothing else? The other German teacher, Dr. Huebner, who became one of the heads of language studies in the city's schools later on, was beautiful, as precisely featured as a Gothic carving, but unlike those dour knights and saints, he smiled a lot, teaching us a good deal of German by way of songs and simpleminded jokes. So we sang and laughed and earned high Regents' Exam scores for Dr. Huebner.

Miss Ricco lived in a room hung with a huge map of France and a tricolored chart of its cheeses and wines. During the first session she made me take off my distinguished hat and romantic cloak, and continued to gaze at me with suspicion in her raisin eyes. Like the music teacher she was a swooper, not out of enthusiasm but through dislike and boredom. A spinster in her later forties, she had probably been teaching elementary French grammar for too many years, and although sympathy for adults, unless they were run over, or murdered, or something conspicuously bloody like that, was not yet an active ingredient of my adolescence, I was a bit sorry, when I bothered to think about it, that her life was so repetitious and angry. She disliked us all, and any misstep in the mazes of irregular verbs elicited a small, frowning shriek which blew all the verb forms out of our heads, leaving us dumb and empty until the bark of '*Asseyez-vous*' returned us to momentary safety. Between verbs and practice in the placing of slippery little *en*, we read the fables of La Fontaine and were required to memorize and recite one. Mine turned out to be '*La Cigale et la Fourmi*'. The recital, from the front of the room to thirty or so students, was impressive. My charlatan vocal cords and mouth, which could shape many sorts of sounds, produced a most elegant accent. Anyone who could play Hedda Gabler had no trouble with the pathos in the voice of the improvident grasshopper: '*Se trouva fort dépourvue / Quand la bise fut venue*', and the harsh, puritanical command, arm extended like a Calvinist reformer: '*Vous chantiez?. . . Dansez maintenant!*' It was a splendid performance and even Miss Ricco seemed satisfied; it was so splendid, in fact, that I scorned all other work in French and flunked the course, a shocking injustice. How could one humiliate Sarah Bernhardt because she stumbled occasionally on the stupid pebbles of the *plus-que-parfait*? Fortunately, I no longer had to present report cards for parental signatures, and in any case, I was rarely at home and not talking much to anyone there, certainly not about flunking a course, no great matter since I had no interest in accumulating grades for college admission – not for me.

Home was now a workers' cooperative in which my father had invested his savings, on the edge of the upper reaches of Bronx Park, cornering Allerton Avenue, a burgeoning area in the northeast Bronx. Between Lafontaine and Allerton there had been a short stop in an apartment near West Farms, of which I remember only two things: it seemed dark everywhere, even close to a sunny window; and one Saturday afternoon a nice, shy fat boy came to call for me to go to the movies and was so thoroughly questioned by my father about which movie were we going to? when would he bring me home? did he go out with girls much? what did his father do for a living? what were his expectations for a job when he graduated from high school? that the boy suddenly rose, said 'Excuse me,' and left. It had probably become too late for afternoon prices and the boy was not ready by many years for paternal inquisitions. I left shortly after, scorning my father's 'Where are you going? To meet him outside, I suppose,' and walked for hours, making sure not to return until ten o'clock, avoiding a spate of questions by locking myself in the bathroom.

For a time I enjoyed the 'coops', as the new houses were called. Our apartment was light and fresh and the atmosphere as impassioned in its own way as that of Lafontaine Avenue, my childhood street. This was to be Utopia, a workers' Utopia, run justly and lovingly, truly democratically. It was culturally avid, education of all sorts organized before the last toilets were placed in the bathrooms. There were dance classes, classes in Russian, in English, in political science, in crafts. There was a cafeteria that served huge Jewish-kitchen portions with generous slabs of bread and side orders of pickles and beet salad. There was a large food shop, run cooperatively, to which I refused to go after a comrade clerk laughed at me when I asked for Oscar Wilde sardines. I should have asked for King Oscar but hated him for correcting me, although my error proved the superior quality of my thoughts. In time the food store failed, partially as a result of excessive democracy: a committee of cutters, bookkeepers, and Yiddish journalists, in spite of – or because of – their lengthy discussions, failed to catch the freshest crates of spinach at the most advantageous prices, were bilked by capitalist canned soup suppliers, and blamed each other for costly errors. The cafeteria closed; too many disputes among the cooking comrades, the serving comrades, the cleaning-up comrades, and prices didn't stay idealistically low.

In spite of difficulties and disappointments, spirits stayed high and hot. Rent strikes in the neighborhood were signaled by a banging on apartment doors. 'Come! Out! Run! Leave everything, the cossacks [cops] are here!' Whether they wanted to or not, many ran, not always sure they knew where or why, especially the unenlightened housewives caught elbow-deep in washtubs or frying the delicate, perishable crepes of blintzes. Others, always at the ready, dashed with revolutionary fervor. My mother never responded. She said the women who did were '*mishigoyim*' looking for excitement, anything to get away from their sinks and kids. She might have been somewhat right. The children of the most vigorous rent-strike militants, the most insistent shouters and bangers on doors, were the shabbiest, most neglected children, free of bourgeois traits like socks that matched and regular meals. They were often renamed, to their bewilderment, from Solly, Benny, Davy, to Lenin, Marx, Trotsky, which, with the addition of the inescapable diminutive, became Leninel, Marxele, Trotskele. Their mothers, married to the same passive hubands for twenty years, redesigned their lives as well; now members of a new world, they discarded the word 'husband' and spoke of their bland men as 'mein comrade' – a stormer of barricades, the bearer of the reddest banner.

Observing this noisy, optimistic, unreal life was entertaining and touching, but other than playing the piano for a dance class once, I was not part of it. Life was elsewhere: On the East Side subway to West Farms, picking up a discarded copy of the *World* and living with its savants and wits. The news was of minimal interest, but the shining icicle sentences of Alexander Woollcott, balanced by Heywood Broun's good-natured twisting of humanity's ear, F.P.A.'s rhymed, witty gems, and Frank Sullivan's sweet cockeyed world, made me feel, as Erasmus said of his time, that I was living in a golden age. Then off the subway at West Farms and a long walk through wide, empty grounds, spiked with brambles, in my mind the place where Eustacia Vye met the reddleman. Then a still, scummy canal leading to unambitious Starlight Amusement Park, yearningly lonely early in the day. Here and there, a tattered Gypsy tent with a hand-lettered sign that signaled MIND READER. Was it a promised blossoming, this conglomeration of dull earth and water and tacky bits of brightness, or was it dying, or both? I never could decide, was never there in the night blooming of the amusement park, if blooming there was. It was a curious, stimulating walk; threatening, pleasing, and with its brooding Hardy atmosphere, not yet gone from my mind.

After school, when we didn't have jobs to go to, a few of us hung around in the cellar of Harry's house, meant to be a fashionable 'playroom', actually a zoo of bulky old things Harry's mother couldn't bear to discard: a fat misshapen couch burbling stuffing, a porch chair with a sagging cotton bottom like a full diaper. This was our Florentine academy, our sitting room in Oxford, our Montparnasse café where Zola met his painter friends – the place for our discussions of Life and related matters. Religion *was* a drug, we agreed with the savants who said so. The Pre-Raphaelites painted pictures suitable to school auditoriums, but the pink, nude frankness of Renoir – that was real, pertinent. Trotsky really should have succeeded Lenin; it was his right as proponent of World Revolution. Was John Dos Passos more class conscious than Upton Sinclair? And what about Dreiser and Sinclair Lewis? Hell, they were social critics but not devoted to the suffering poor like the great Dostoevski. 'Dostoevski? A religious zealot and arch conservative.' 'You're crazy.' We spoke, of course, much of love and sex, gleaning most of our wisdom from Havelock Ellis, from dirty jokes, from a rare page of pornography, from someone's elder brother's medical books, and from Krafft-Ebing's confusing revelations about people who were wildly, sexually in love with shoes. Virgin and eager as we three or four were, we were afraid of sex and there were few gestures among us, except when I happened to be alone with robust, direct Harry, who, on the principle that no red-blooded man alone with a female would pass up a pass, did a bit of poking and embracing. I didn't entice him enough to persist when I said, 'Cut it out.' He did. Fred, stork-legged and bound in significant silences, was dedicated to poetry and reviled 'the double-backed beast' (he was always finding the sharpest phrases in Shakespeare, like 'the astonished flesh' to go with a bleeding knuckle) that crazed man's bestial mind. He as school poet and I as master of prose were linked by our friends and our romantic English teachers. He was frightened by my vigorous 130 pounds of blond flesh, or simply disliked me, and I was frightened by the mysterious cynical thoughts behind his Byronic frown, so we avoided each other when we could and looked abstractedly high-minded when we couldn't.

During one semester, a sophisticated, elderly stranger, maybe eighteen, began to visit the cellar on Harry's invitation. Ralph was extraordinarily handsome, with keen, shining, narrow eyes in a dark, sharp face, like a jeweled scimitar. He made contemptuous judgments about our writing – he was writing too, but wouldn't say what, except that it had nothing to do with dumb class essays and school-magazine poems – and our naïveté about sex; virgins, masturbators, all of us. To hell with pouncing Harry and anaemic Fred, this *man* was for me. He was a prize catch who certainly must be a better guide to sex than our abominable boarder, my would-be rapist of some years before. In the breathless competition for Ralph, the man of the world, my advantages were few but significant. There were infinitely better-looking girls in school and girls with more experience, accumulating a harried something of a sex life on family couches when their parents were out. But not one of them had a room of her own, as I frequently did. The Bergsons, for whom I baby-sat, would take off for occasional amorous weekends of their own, to be undisturbed by the night calls of their two children. I had a room, two rooms, plenty of rooms, when they went away, and I let it be known: 'Dammit, rattling around alone again in that big apartment in Greenwich Village' – the absolutely irresistible name, the place of Art and occult adult magics – 'with only two sleeping kids for company.' It took, as it had to. At ten o'clock one night, after the children had been fed and read to, and had sipped their innumerable delaying drinks of water, Ralph tapped at the door. I let him in. Neither of us knew what to say except 'Hello.' Neither of us knew what else to say, my Persian prince dwindled to skinny young, I, Village denizen, to shy dope. I hung up his coat, asked him if he wanted something to eat, had he ever eaten French goat cheese? there was some in the icebox. He wasn't hungry, thanks. Like a hired guide, I walked him systematically through the library and pointed out its many volumes in French and German. I took him through the salon to point out the paintings, modern, original. I showed him the two large,shining bathrooms with separate shower stalls. I pointed out the copper molds in the kitchen and explained the Chinese woks. My voice grew flatter and flatter as I showed him Dr. Bergson's initialed silver hairbrushes and his silver shoehorn and the delicate old Kangra painting on the wall.

When the tour was over we stood at the door of the living room, each searching for a helpful phrase. I could summon nothing; he supplied the expected 'Wonderful place'. Nothing else to do, he grabbed and kissed me, hard, like a stamping machine, and began to pull me away from the living room, not quite sure which direction he wanted. I hadn't imagined that he would sweep me up in his arms while I trailed a long silken scarf, like Gilbert taking Garbo, but I had hoped for some grace and suavity, maybe subtle gestures and slow fire. It was obviously up to me, so I led him, with my limp attempt at grace and suavity, into my bedroom and there we stood, I hoping for melting words, tender nibblings, impassioned embraces or facsimiles. Instead, we seemed to be actors who had forgotten their lines. Teasingly, coquettishly, I thought, I undid the many buttons of the long Oriental silk gown I had borrowed from Laura Bergson's closet. Ralph undressed bumpily, his belt buckle clanging on the bedpost, the buttons on his pants nervously eluding his fingers. We didn't undress altogether, blatant visible nudity beyond our daring. We hastily leaped under the covers in our underclothes. For protection from each other? In the hopes that we would not have to try the awkward act we had ordered of each other? As required, we twisted, stroked, turned, thrusted and folded, slid and kissed, and before I knew what was happening his breath grew hot and gasping and I could feel a warm stream on my belly, long inches from where it should have been.

There was still a long night to go, but we didn't know what to do with it, he stricken by his early ejaculation and in an embarrassed torpor, and virgin I wondering what I had done wrong. Lying flat like two tomb figures, disappointed and worried, we knew nothing to say to each other until, mumbling, 'I'm sorry', he dressed quickly, asked which way was out, and was gone. It seemed, I thought, that Ralph didn't know more about techniques than Harry, in spite of his big-shot boasting. Or was there something wrong with me? I wasn't dirty; I had bathed before he arrived and even washed my hair. I didn't stink. Or maybe I did? Maybe I was too fat? Maybe he didn't like the cigarette taste on my mouth. Maybe I had no sex appeal and no one but furtive subway gropers would ever touch me. Maybe I didn't respond properly or enough, maybe I was really a lesbian without knowing it. How did nuns live? Maybe I ought to learn; not convert or enter a nunnery, just find out more about them and their freedom from all this sex trouble.

It was a thick, heavy night and I was relieved to be bothered at dawn by the kids, always difficult when their parents were away overnight. The little girl slapped her spoon spitefully into her cereal, splashing it all over the table and the floor, the little boy hid his potty and, although carefully toilet trained, decided to soil his pants after breakfast. I didn't mind the soiled pants, the floor splotched with cereal, the stomping and shouting of the children. They helped make living more ordinary, more endurable, farther and farther away from the grotesqueries of Ralph and Kate was Antony and Cleopatra.

Ralph stopped coming to our club and shortly left school altogether. Harry's father, who had been threatening for a long time to clean up his cellar and get those damn kids out, finally did. Harry took a job as grocery-delivery boy after school. No more discussions, no more groping, no more club.

16

The Men

Ralph gone, Fred floating, Harry and his den preempted, it was essential to find another clubhouse. That was a dark ice-cream parlor in the shadow of the elevated subway tracks on Westchester Avenue, hardly a distinguished place, but it served for the afternoons I was free to meet with a new circle, a very small one. Comparatively well-heeled at the time, I treated to Cokes, although black coffee and a string of cigarettes better suited my more decadent persona. One of us three regulars was lissome, white-skinned Bernie, who liked to wear bright flying scarves and asked that we call him 'Bernarr', in the French manner. He and I frequently went downtown on Saturdays to search out cheap matinee tickets at Gray's. These had to be serious, possibly classical, preferably foreign plays. We found everything we saw entrancing, though it was required that we express light scorn of the costumes, or the sets, or the acting, and unless it was Shakespeare, Ibsen, or Chekhov, of the writing. We were laboriously witty and high-flown; we never talked simply with each other, yet were close friends, essential to each other as actor and audience. He was sixteen and I fifteen and, like many adolescents, inhabited an exaggerated Mannerist world of overlarge, shocking volutes alternating with deep niches. We were also tearing away from the restraints of who we thought we were to the freedoms of who we thought we wanted to be, trying on a succession of identities. We were palimpsests of masks, the earliest one, of open-mouthed bewilderment, covered by a questioning, frowning mask and, at the current level,a thin screen of fake sophistication, uncertainly attached, slipping as it tried to hold to a semblance of imperturbability, of confidence. (Many years will pass, amorphous adolescence supposedly long faded, yet shades of the masks will cling, even into the folds of the shroud. James Joyce: 'We walk through ourselves, meeting robbers, ghosts, giants, old men, wives, widows . . .' And Jorge Luis Borges says it as: 'among the forms in my dreams are you – Shakespeare – who like myself are many and no one.')

A third member of our circle, a portly wearer of fancy waistcoats and a big, old-fashioned watchchain, was not of the school and our only explanation for his persistent presence was that he had seen Bernie in the neighborhood and was courting him. Derek enhanced the possibilities of homosexual interest in Bernie by being awesomely, lengthily encyclopaedic about Hadrian and Antinoüs, about the Spartan warriors and their devoted young companions, about Alexander, about Leonardo. In his languid and vaguely British speech, he would recite long sections of 'Reading Gaol' and the brightest conversational thrusts attributed to Wilde. An odder now and then member of the club wore a mannish suit and a porkpie hat over a boy's haircut. She carried a slim volume of verse with always a fresh rose to mark one poem we were never allowed to see and which she wouldn't identify. The rose and the poem were an immortal dedication to one love and muse, she said, a melding of Sappho, Isadora Duncan, and Colette. She had originally come to search me out because a mutual friend had told her I wore a golden Borsalino and black stockings and was in other ways rebellious and attractive.

At some point I grew tired of the three. The girl reminded me of John Held, Jr., cartoons of slick-haired, vapid young men, her appreciation of me became uninteresting, her paeans to the fair unknown, ultimately boring. She soon returned to her private isle of Lesbos or wherever she had come from. Derek left us shortly after, perhaps for more worldly companions who might be closer to the imagined witty green rooms of London theaters where someone like Bosie might be sitting, maybe waiting for him. Bernie-Bernarr and I continued to hunt out bargain tickets and remained friends, without clinging to each other as before.

A curious 'Through the Looking Glass' scrim fell over my life. As the porkpie hat and one perfect rose, as the rosy plump finger on the watch chain, as the flying scarves faded, I was steadily assaulted by shocking, hallucinated smells: of the thick fattiness of entrails on the butcher's block, of the singed chicken feathers in a neighbor's kitchen, of hot roof tar, of the heady metallic odor of menstrual blood, of acrid semen – the smells of sex. Brilliant dreams were the paintings of the smells. The setting of one dream was in the laundry in which I ticketed bundles of wash, surrounded by fellow workers who cheered me on as I sat hatching a large egg which would soon produce my baby. They were playful, I was playful; there were no labor pains, no instruments, no swelling, no convulsions, words and images that had filled my childhood with guilt and horror. Though I had several versions of the dream, I never hatched the baby. I sat and talked and was admired and encouraged and there the amusing dream floated away. A less forthright, slyer dream had me walking through sun-dappled birch (birth?) trees wearing a fox around my shoulders, the proud ornament of lower-middle-class women. My fox was handsome, full-bodied, and alive (had I read the Lawrence story?), feeding at my breast. Though he drew a trickle of blood, his gnawing and nibbling didn't hurt at all; it was rather pleasing to have him there, burrowing into my chest. That dream was also very entertaining and still is: the economy of a symbol that suggested so much – nursing, the breaking of the hymen, its trickle of blood. The masterstroke was, I thought, 'fox', for 'fuck', a word I couldn't get myself to say until much later (it was thoroughly the property of men and boys), and here I made so adroit a pun on the word without having to say it.

Another set of dreams was a total denial of sly foxes and hatching babies; they were romantic and lyrical. I was being softly kissed and gently caressed by a shadowy phantom lover. Always the place was lovely – a meadow of flowers like millefleur tapestry, the edge of a dimpled lake, bowers of fruit trees – and always the same denouement: the shadowy lover became flesh. When his ardor began to agitate the delicate languors and the fairy-tale landscape, I would sit up, reach for an apple from the branch curving over my head, and crunch into it vigorously and loudly, or admire extravagantly the strong, rapid head of a woodpecker nearby. The disconcerted lover disappeared and I was left contentedly alone, a pure white blossom not yet plucked, and reluctant, it seemed, to be.

The fox, the birthing, the smells, the dreams preoccupied so openly with sex as yes, sex as no, may have led in some subterranean way to the night of the cat.

While I was foraging in literature and music, biology was becoming interesting as well. The smell of formaldehyde became yet another of my especial odors; the frog splayed out and pinned, his efficient, neatly arranged inner geography suggesting more mysteries to be explored. The boy with whom I shared a dead frog in a shallow baking tin was rather like an early P.S. 58 admirer, shaggy, fetching, and freckled, like a *Saturday Evening Post* boy. The resemblance ended there. Barry was utterly indifferent to me and, seemingly, had no interest in anyone else. He was alone most of the time, a mediocre student except in biology, where he was a wonder. He rarely spoke to me until, under his muttered warnings and imprecations, I had become a fairly skillful dissector. One day he asked me to meet him in the lunchroom, I couldn't imagine why. He offered a troublesome proposal. Since the laundry in which I worked wasn't too far away, and he lived around the corner, why didn't I meet him in the evening, after work, to chase down a cat – there were lots of strays in the neighborhood – which we would chloroform and dissect in his cellar laboratory. Because I liked and respected cats, because I didn't want to kill anything but wanted to know if I could, because I was sure we would be caught by the police and imprisoned for years, because my chest and head pounded '*No!*' I said, laconically, 'OK'.

We met one evening at about eight o'clock in front of the school and walked into the long spread of my Thomas Hardy emptiness near West Farms. Barry was not a skillful hunter and I was little help, unable to chase or pounce or grab. My best contribution was to menace the cats with a stick, hoping they would run in his direction and he would do the rest. After a discouraging hour he lunged full length at a small gray-striped cat and, with her body pinned under his, slipped a noose around her neck, then pulled her, mewling and choking, to his darkened house. He unlocked the cellar door and dragged the cat down a long flight of wooden stairs that led to an old kitchen table, to jars and cans, scissors and knives and chemical stinks. Out of one of the cans he took a large wad of dirty absorbent cotton, gesturing to me to bring him another container. I didn't know which he meant; I probably didn't want to. He dropped the absorbent cotton, tied the cat with its lasso string to the table, then picked up the dirty wad of cotton and poured a sweet-smelling liquid out of a bottle he recapped quickly. He muttered 'Chloroform' as he approached the struggling, shrieking cat. As he held the cotton to her face, her legs churned, her body twisted and trembled under the tight cord. Her tail stretched, lashed, stretched, and dropped. She was quiet. 'Start cutting the string from her – there's the scissors, there, on the table.' 'How do you know she's dead?' 'Oh, I'm pretty sure she is, and when we start dissecting she'll die anyhow, won't she?' I had been willing down the vomit that kept rising to my throat. Now it was in my mouth. I ran up the stairs and vomited at the side of the cellar door. Heaving and in a gelid sweat, I rushed to the subway station, sure I would be apprehended for murder any second now, seeing accusation on each face in the street. Everyone in the subway car knew I was a murderess; at the next stop a policeman would take me off the train and drag me to prison. I made it home and to the bathroom, where I vomited again. I heard my father mutter that I was learning to drink, too, with my bum friends, drinking the homemade stuff that made people blind. When my mother asked me what was wrong, I said I must have eaten something rotten in the cafeteria near the laundry, a real greasy spoon.

The terror of being arrested diminished after a week or so, but Barry and I hardly spoke though we still shared the same frog. I never found out if he had actually dissected the cat, never asked, never wanted to know. It was enough to acknowledge that although I had not killed the cat, I had consented to its death. Was I a murderess? Was Barry a murderer? Did everyone conceal a killer? Could be. (The cat stayed with me for decades. During an experiment with hallucinogenic mushrooms in Mexico, many years later, the cat returned as myself, my brain scrambled as hers must have been under the chloroform: sounds became visual images and what I saw was tapped out in rhythmic sounds while I made mewling, strangled attempts to talk, to protest, to stay alive.)

The springtime of that year stayed clouded by the dead cat, and all of school, everything in it, even the English and music classes, became loathsome. Morning after morning, I would approach the red-brick school building with its dead doors and brutal hinges, turn back to the subway, which took me to Grand Central and the majestic lions and stairs of the 'big library' at Forty-second Street and Fifth Avenue. No one questioned students in those days and I had the royal privilege – a most adult privilege – of going through the immensity of card files, submitting slips for books, and when my number showed at the delivery desk, carrying my treasures to a dignified chair under a dignified lamp. Here I stayed throughout the day, reading Robinson Jeffers, Robert Frost, T. S. Eliot, and Ezra Pound, poets whom I didn't always understand but whose company flattered me, as did the company of my serious, elderly, learned neighbors, who permitted me to breathe of the cultivated atmosphere that was theirs.

This idyll of freedom and respect, of politeness and dedication to learning, lasted about two months, until I was called to the assistant principal's office and shown that I had cut school a shocking number of days, without a note from my mother or a doctor to justify the absences, and that I had attended only one gym class during the semester. That day my faithful double, the me who stood off observing while I acted, burst into laughter when I assumed the grotesque position – ass out, face pushed stupidly forward – for swinging a baseball bat. So I decided to skip the whole nonsense and started for the door, still laughing. The stout gym teacher, infuriated by my insouciance and laughter, called me back and began to push at my legs for their proper planting in the baseball stance and to pull my arm into the approved bend for wielding a bat. I wouldn't and couldn't obey and she began to shout at me. Suddenly I began to cry, loudly and heavily, and sank like a sack – the bat rolling away from me – to the floor, to sit there sobbing. I was playacting and yet not altogether: confusion about the cat and fear of the results of my present lawlessness, a mist of unhappiness that enclosed me when I was not in my library, were authentic ingredients of the theatrics.

I would flunk the gym course, the assistant principal said, and possibly others, and would be handled as a truant, constantly watched. Not quite ready to be expelled, I cut down my pure, serene days downtown but continued to avoid gym classes, Neanderthal pleasures.

In spite of the thickheaded school authorities, the melancholy fogs that touched me, life gradually became multistranded and rich. Having finished dripping rain, the trees began to shed blossoms; suddenly a yard yesterday fit only for a doghouse sprang yellow flames of forsythia; my laundry gave me a small raise, the library job for which the English Department recommended me stayed easy and pleasant. The apogee of that singing, dancing springtime was my acquisition of two suitors. they were in their late twenties, not boys, men, and close friends. Joe was a short, barrel-chested man with a droll, lopsided face. He had a mean job, dull bread-and-butter hours between happy lunch breaks which he spent searching out second-hand records on Sixth Avenue stalls: one movement of a Mahler symphony, Chaliapin singing 'The

Song of the Flea', Rosa Ponselle singing 'Pace, Pace' – a little scratched on one side but wasn't she gorgeous? Evenings he took high school classes to prepare for City College extension courses. His Sundays were fiestas of pleasures: the Lower East Side early in the morning to look for more cheap records, then tennis in some free park court or other, and in the evening, visiting friends, playing his balalaika to Russian songs – longing for birch trees and half-forgotten villages – robustly roaring the beauties of 'Kalinka'.

His host on many Sunday evenings was Mark, who looked like Marcel Proust, hooded dark eyes and sadness to the bone. Mark's family lived immediately below mine in the 'coops'. Since I spent little time there, I didn't encounter him for some time after we had moved in. Or possibly I paid him no attention, assuming he was one of the local young fathers. It was my mother who told me, when I stood still long enough to listen, that the woman downstairs, Mrs. Rosinsky, a talker with a bunched-up face, claimed to have been rich in Russia, before the Bolsheviks took her house and her husband's business. The jewels she had hidden in her skirt hem fed the family, two sons and herself (the husband seemed to have disappeared), as they made their long way to Shanghai, and slowly, after years, to America. Could I believe such a story, with lots of strange details she didn't remember? It didn't matter whether the story was true or not; people who could invent such a tale – if they did – were worth knowing, and then there were the alluring Russian songs that stretched themselves on long, sad chords of nostalgia from their window to ours. How I got to know stricken-faced Mark Rosinsky I don't remember, but I somehow managed it and soon was a frequent Sunday evening visitor, petted and spoiled by friend Joe. To celebrate a minor school achievement, Joe gave me a record of a Schubert piano sonata played by Alfred Cortot. He tried to teach me to play tennis, but anything I couldn't do well immediately I wouldn't do at all; too much exposure of gracelessness and ineptitude, a painful display of frailties that were to be kept hidden. The lessons trailed off. So he took me to the Lower East Side on record hunts and taught me a few Russian songs. It was Joe who managed to get to the Lewisohn Stadium early enough to buy (Mark always included) the twenty-five-cent concert seats, and it was Joe who knew friendly Carnegie Hall ushers who let us climb, for fifty cents, often for nothing, to seats in the top balconies. Being with funny-looking Joe was light and laughter, too often clouded by Mark's silent darkness. During my short tennis career, Mark had stood at the side and watched me scoop at the ball and miss it, fall over my own feet, serve in wild, unexpected directions, every awkward mishap made more hideous by his fixed, critical gaze.

He wasn't appraising me critically, it began to appear. He kept the door to his apartment open so he might rush to the door to greet me when he heard my footsteps. At unexpected times, I would find him standing at the subway station, ready to walk back to the 'coops' with me. At other unexpected times – when he should long have been at work – I would find him at the foot of our staircase asking politely if he couldn't escort me to the subway. I lied wildly in several directions simultaneously. No, thanks; I was going to walk to the library this morning. No, thanks; there were no classes and I was going to visit a sick friend. No, thanks; I had to do an errand for my mother. No, thanks. No, thanks. But he found me going up, going down, going out. The solemn face and voice became importunate, distorted in his urgency. Why couldn't we meet alone? He had important things to say to me that were not Joe's business. He would take me to a theater, or a concert, or a nice restaurant downtown It wasn't so much to ask, was it, to go out with him alone, to talk? He wouldn't touch me, he would do anything I wanted. He would try, if we got to be real friends, as I was with Joe, to get me a room of my own, which, he knew, I so much wanted. That would come in time, though. First, please, please, let's spend a few hours together and let me tell you how I feel about you.

One night when I found him at the bottom of the stairs of the subway station, I began to run and he to run after, pleading breathlessly. I felt choked, sick, tormented; I could neither understand nor meet this thing that tortured and drove him. It was not a crush as I knew them, goggle-eyed and mute. This was love, grown-up and terrible, and I had done it to him, as if I had actually crippled or blinded him. I was netted, trapped in this ring of fire I had set unwittingly for both of us. Feeling as much a victim as he – or was this torture pleasure for him? – I wanted him away, out of my sight, out of my life. The following Sunday, when I knew he would be at home, with many opportunities to wait and listen for me in his patient, suffering way, I hitchhiked to the place, an hour or so from the city, where I had a friend with whom I could shelter for the day. I found her reading and bored and we decided to walk to the village grocery, where we might find other friends.

As we approached the store, at the main crossroads of the village, the bus that connected with the train from the city stopped. Off stepped Mark. I ran, I don't remember where, or where I hid that day, or how and when I got back. Under the door at home I found his note: 'You don't have to run away from me anymore. I won't bother you again.'

My inability to cope with Mark, the sense of undefined and undeserved guilt I felt toward him, did not impair fun with Joe, but rather enhanced it. For one thing, Mark was afraid of Harlem, and now Joe and I were free to attend rehearsals of the Hall Johnson Choir, to which Joe had, as was his habit, gracefully wangled an invitation from someone he happened to meet and charm. We went to German and Russian restaurants – cheap, the cheapest and most generous those of the national homes, community centers that offered legal advice, ward heeling, sociability, lessons in English, dancing, and unfamiliar foods at minute prices to members and guests of various immigrant communities. Our favorites were the Polish National Home, near McSorley's on Seventh Street, whose bowls of food danced on the tables to polka rhythms one tin ceiling above; and the Bohemian National Home, uptown, which decorated itself with peasant motifs in unabashed colors and with blond, very white-skinned, Art Nouveau women, the women who still sing the heroines in *The Grand Duchess of Gérolstein* in Budapest, the type that later became known to us as the Gabors.

It was Joe who introduced me to Dr. Caligari's Cabinet, his cubist ashen makeup and his sinister gloves and broken hat. Joe told me Charlie Chaplin was a comic genius and I believed him but resisted Chaplin films because I had wept through all of *The Gold Rush* when I was a little girl and was wary of having little Charlie tear me to bits again. On overtime pay we went to a small Russian nightclub on Fourteenth Street near Second Avenue, where men in wide-skirted cossack coats glided swiftly on their toes like ballet dancers and threw knives around each other; exciting, foreign, *muy macho*. Across from the nightclub (was it called The Two Guitars? The Three Guitars? The Balalaika?) was a Jewish restaurant as sweetly solicitous and talkative as the national homes, and as cheap.

Chronology, an elusive, slippery thread of my memory, leaves me uncertain as to whether or not it was Joe who introduced me to early Russian movies; I think it was. At any rate, it was in his time that I saw the landmark *Potemkin*, whose rushing masses meant nothing to me because, although I had heard of Soviet Russia as the new Utopia, I knew nothing of its historical facts. One beautiful, sadly exotic film was *Gypsies*, so moving and impressive that I still remember, over the span of decades, the tune of one lovely melancholy song. Other Russian films seemed to be concerned with people in love with tractors, condensed for me as one large woman, significantly pregnant, standing in profile before a crude farmhouse at the edge of endless wheat fields full of tractors, and calling in a shattering voice to an unseen, faraway comrade, 'K-O-O-O-lya-a-a'.

At one rock-bottom financial stage Joe found us a ten-cent movie house, under the Third Avenue El, one of those dim, tattered houses that spread their aisles and toilets with perfume like melted lollipops to disguise the smell of past and present urine. Joe muttered apologies, but I didn't care; this dump was like the five-cent Lyric Theater on Third Avenue near 180th Street, where my brother and I sat entranced, oblivious of perfume and urine, watching Elmo Lincoln cut off the outlaws at the pass. Joe's dump was showing a version of *Camille* with Nazimova and Rudolph Valentino, in my recollection a vast bed of lacy pillows, nervously quivering nostrils, heaving chests, and a surrealist excess of long, narrow-eyed, staring passion.

It was Joe, with friends everywhere, who introduced me to the freezing tenement studios on the East River later torn down for the U.N. enclave, and to the big misshapen houses in Hoboken, reached by ferry from the end of Christopher Street, not yet the 'meat market' it would later famously become. Like Mr. Brandon at James Monroe, Joe was one of my Marco Polos, leading me into many realms and holding forth, as future forays into Cathay, night walks through the Fulton Fish Market and maybe boarding one of the Portuguese fishing boats swaying under the Brooklyn Bridge. He had a friend . . .

Although Mark kept his promise not to bother me, not to trap me on the stairs, not to trap me at the station, not to trap me at all, his mother remained a nuisance via my mother, who was amused while I was both annoyed and amused. The little woman came almost daily to tell my mother that Mark could not support a wife yet, not for a long time; his job paid too little. She had a lot of medical expenses and needed a whole set of new teeth, and although the younger brother had a part-time job, they had to help

support him through two more years at City College. And didn't
my mother think me much too young for marriage or even being
engaged? Though I was a big, well-developed girl who looked and
acted older than my age, I was, we all realized, only fifteen and we
weren't Old Country peasants who married their daughters off so
young, were we? My mother and father surely had higher ambitions
for me than her Mark, a poor workingman. I was so brilliant I could
marry a doctor or a professor. I was so beautiful I could marry a
millionaire. My chances were boundless, and why trample on them
now? My mother answered that neither she nor I was interested in
marrying me off; that I didn't want a husband, or any man, who
would get in my way of finishing high school and maybe – who
knows? – college.

Whether the situation I was in, courted by two *men*, not
impetuous, ignorant boys, put it in my mother's mind, or
my father's, a new suitor was brought in. A family that was
distantly related to my family, the Woolfs, who lived in a large
house on the edge of Morris Park and were obviously prosperous,
had several daughters and one son, Jerry. The son, when I thought
of him at all, became a vague romantic image; he was a sailor –
that impossibly extraordinary thing a Jewish sailor. Nevertheless
he had to be a tall, bronzed Viking with keen, far-seeing blue eyes,
wearing dashing tatters (there was a touch of the pirate in him, too).
It was somehow arranged, probably by my father, that on one of his
leave days he come to visit and take me out. I opened the door to
a slight man with a pleasant smile, wearing a conventional brown
suit, a brown tie, and well-polished brown shoes. After greeting
my parents pleasantly, modestly proffering thunderous words –
Hong Kong, Nagasaki, Bangkok – in response to their questions,
he turned to me and said he had theater tickets for us and maybe
we'd better hurry a little.

Conversation was easy. He said he read a lot between ports
and he understood that I read a good deal, too. We talked books, I
rather impatiently, eager to know about all the places he had been
and what they were like. He told me there were beautiful painted
caves in India and canals full of floating markets in Bangkok and
that the Chinese who hung around the ports were the cleverest
traders; you had to watch out for their quick tricks. From Union
Square we walked east to a Russian restaurant, where he ordered
for me delicious, expensive things, and to cap my delight hailed
a taxi – I had never been in one – to take us westward on

Fourteenth Street to the Civic Repertory Theater, whose cheap upper seats had taught me every line of Chekhov's *Three Sisters* and Ibsen's *Master Builder*. Now we were sitting in the orchestra, and on the stage was the great Nazimova playing Madame Ranevskaya in *The Cherry Orchard*. So moved was I by Nazimova – the real, actual Madame Ranevskaya, I felt – and by the old servant losing his life with the cherry trees, so moved by being treated like a grown, dignified woman on a grown, dignified date, that I had to sit straight and stiff in my seat, to contain everything that was going on in me. Now and then Jerry smiled at me, as if understanding and enjoying my heady pleasure. After the performance, the courtly acts went on in their classic design: he asked me if I'd like a soda. While I was sipping the unaccustomed nectar, he took a small box out of his pocket and saying, 'I brought this for you, I thought you might like it', lifted out of the box a string of light-brown, carved beads. I looked but didn't reach for them. No one ever had given me such a present; hand-me-downs, loans, discards, yes, but not a new special thing of my own. While I hesitated, smiling and dumb, he said, 'Smell them. They're carved of sandalwood'. I took the string from his hand, put it to my face, and pictures of antelopes and huge flowers in jungle groves and birds of a hundred colors swam through my head. My nice, polite brown Jerry really was, if not a Viking, a world wanderer, an intimate of places whose names I didn't even know, someone who might, were he older, have been a drinking companion of Gauguin in Tahiti.

I was not in love with him – that was our only encounter – but I cherished him and the gala evening. I wrote him sporadically for a number of years, until I overheard Mrs. Woolf's pained voice whispering to my mother that he was settling in Japan with a Japanese wife. The beads remained my most important possession and stayed with me until I began to live in places where things disappeared.

Mrs. Rosinsky took heart when she saw me walking down the stairs with Jerry, but when he didn't reappear she renewed displaying her wounds of concern and banners of praise to my mother, who reported it all to me. That is, when we weren't fighting about my smoking, my erratic eating habits, my crazy, schleppy coat, and – one monumental fight that lasted for hours – Isadora Duncan. I knew she was a great woman, an artist, a heroic world spirit. My mother said she was a bohemian bum who drank too much and had too many lovers, one of them a billionaire, one of them a Bolshevik. I marched out and went to sleep with my friend Minnie, complaining into the night about the vulgar conventionalism, the narrow-minded insensitivity, of my bourgeois mother.

17
The Children

The summer following my first year in high school, my mother had announced that she had saved enough money selling corsets – ready-made and those she devised – during our school hours to buy us all a vacation for three weeks. She disliked the clusters of *yachnes* who invaded the rooming houses of the Catskills and fought for space in communal kitchens. She had heard of a farmer not far from the city who had remodeled large chicken houses, put in beds and minute kitchens, and rented them out during the summer. We took off for the full, joyous three weeks of three kids in a bed, a spigot of cold water outside for washing dishes and faces, an outhouse with two holes and a chemical-plus-shit smell and clouds of buzzing large golden flies. And boundless grass to run on, trees to swing from, buttercups and daisies for chains and chaplets. There must have been rain and the discomfort of huddling in the narrow space, but I remember the time as a steady glow of golden sun. Dignity hit me every once in a while – I was still awed by my menstrual periods – and I left my running and leaping brother and sister to wander through the chicken house community and beyond, meeting girls my age who lived near a lake, where I was occasionally invited to swim.

Among our immediate neighbors there were two families I was smitten with. One consisted of a silent old man, as stiff as a sword under his discolored, swooping Panama hat, and his two silent daughters like swans, floating by us gracefully in splendid discolored linens and gauzes, their hair pulled taut to back knots, like ballerinas. The truth was difficult to find out surely, but these aristocrats, we were told, were a Prince and Princesses Dolgoruky – an ancient noble Russian name – who had escaped Russia during the revolution and were waiting to return to their blue-and-white palace in St. Petersburg when the crazy fury that had seized their country abated. This information came from another neighbor, a stout, heavy-browed Russian woman with a glorious accent, all rippling *r*'s and no 'a's or 'the's among her fast, tumbling sentences.She knew all the names and faces of the Russian aristocracy, and they should burn in hell; those who were still alive, like Dolgorukys, should slowly starve to death while the people's revolution went on to full triumph all over the world, as Trotsky said it had to and would.The lodestar of her life, several shades above Trotsky, was her son of three or four, a fat little brown berry who ran around naked, much to my five-year-old sister's amazement and amusement as his penis dangled and sung – like a pink bell, she said. The child had few companions but his mother; his English was precisely like hers in accent and syntax. He was an engaging, trusting innocent and we fed him Fig Newtons and Lorna Doones surreptitiously (his mother forbade all sweets) under the guise of teaching him to speak more correctly. We thought that learning songs in English would improve his pronunciation. The accent was, however, obdurate and all we got for our pains – no pain at all and for many years an entertaining memory – was a song called 'Cvementime', whose chorus, sung musically and with feeling, was 'Ooh mine dahving, oo mine dahving, oo mine dahving Cvementime'. We soon stopped trying to improve his accent; this performance, often repeated at our request, was a perfect thing, not to be marred by correction.

During a walk to the community near the lake a mile or two away I encountered a girl picking blackberries at the side of the road. As I helped her pick, she asked me if I would like to be a mother's helper the following summer; that is, would I like to live with a nice family named Bergson and take care of their children? The pay wouldn't be much above bed and board, but they were decent about time off and Mrs. Bergson was especially sweet and generous. She herself had to turn the job down because her family was moving out to Detroit, where, her uncle had written, her father might find an auto factory job. I said I was very much interested and, wiping the blackberry stains from my hands and mouth, followed her directions to the proper house. Stammering a little, I told the lady who opened the door that I would like the job, that having taken care of my brother and sister most of my years, I was well experienced in caring for children. She thought I would be satisfactory, the gentle-faced lady said, but in the meantime could

I baby-sit in their city apartment once or twice so we could get to know each other and to find out if I really wanted and was suited for the summer job? Of course, and I gave her my name and address and the phone number of a friend who took messages for me.

There was some baby-sitting that following winter, but I did not actually learn the Bergsons and their community until the following summer. The community was a stretch of flat undistinguished land about an hour and a half by train from New York. The original settlers were dissenters of several shades of left – anarchists, socialists, communists, whose assembled weapons were the words of their tutelary gods, Lenin, Trotsky, Emma Goldman, Rosa Luxemburg. On each acre or two of inexpensive land they put, at first, the simplest of bungalows, which, with the years, grew more livable but never wholly 'bourgeois'. Among the other dissenters there were the vegetarians, and the supervegetarians, who would touch nothing but roots, fruits, nuts, and berries. There were some of no clear political faith except that they despised all Republicans (except Abraham Lincoln) and all Democrats except Franklin Delano Roosevelt and Henry Wallace, who was saving a hungry world with his new strains of strong, fast-growing wheat. Although the majority were Jewish, they named themselves 'agnostic' or 'atheist', and thought that fasting on Yom Kippur was as barbaric as drinking the blood of Christ at Catholic services. The only passion that, in some, almost resembled religion was the passion for wholesome, whole-grain breads and biscuits, lumpish things weighed down with sincerity and no leavening of skill. One woman with an invisible husband and several zesty children produced an almost palatable loaf and gathered to herself a near-monopoly, bested only by the unbeatable monopoly of the local food shop which sold the great American goody, squeezable, rubbery white bread. Stuck between the impenetrable dark bread with its half-raw grains and the drooping, feeble white slabs, those of us with a taste for palatable bread occasionally hitchhiked into the city to drag back sacks of bagels, seeded ryes, and crusty Italian rolls to be dispensed to friends as payment for favors past and future.

Those who had rejected the artifices of the city completely, the people who endured the winter's cold in poorly heated houses, depending on fireplaces and heavy homemade sweaters for warmth, sent their children to a school the parents devised and established, a free-form school that prized artwork above reading (the playful, bright ten-year-old twins of a master carpenter didn't know how to read at all and their parents didn't seem to care), 'freedom of expression' above disciplined learning. It shocked my Bronx public school ear to hear teachers addressed by their first names and parents called 'May' and 'Harry' by their young, although I approved heartily of this advance in civilization.

As an adjunct to the schoolhouse there was a social hall, large enough to hold a stage and seats for about two hundred people. Although there were occasional appearances by visiting guests who sang or danced in Duncan peplums or recited poetry in English or Russian (Yiddish was rarely heard, a rather despised speech of the stupid Zionists who were dividing an already excessively divided world, which should be united as one universal humane government), young local talent was given its chance. After I had been with the Bergsons for some weeks and become acquainted with some members of the community, I was asked, along with several young musicians, to take part in a recital. I played my stellar achievement – the peak of my capacity in speed, in rubato, in sweet pathos – Chopin's 'Fantaisie Impromptu'. I had practiced it for many months before I quit practicing altogether, and still played it in friends' houses. It was well in my fingers and memory, and I thought it was going beautifully when I heard a giggle as I played. It may have been meant for me: in my pianism as in my general conduct there were often affectations that were designed to lend me greater probity as a bona fide artist, necessarily eccentric, and I might have displayed some peculiarity in my playing. Although I never tried to change or in any way modify Chopin – the awe was too great and he was, especially as a doomed tubercular like Keats, one of my most moving and enduring loves, a love who sang my nameless yearnings – I may have raised my hand too high in letting a lyric passage float away, as I had seen Ossip Gabrilowitsch do, or bend low to the keys seeming to snuffle among the keys like a hog, as old de Pachmann did. The giggle may not have been attached to my performance at all, but, the great artiste insulted, I rose from the piano halfway through the piece and stalked out, my eyes set on the door, not to look at any face. One girl of my acquaintance, who sat in the audience after performing a Polish folk dance, came after me. They were dopes and didn't know music, and she wasn't going to perform for them again she said as she looked at my stiff face, the shut dimmed window through which no one could see the burning in my veins and entrails. I couldn't cry; I hadn't since I was seven or eight, after I was accused of crying too easily; so I ran in several wild directions until I found myself on the road that led to the Bergsons' house. The children were asleep, the mother about ready for bed. There were no questions or comments after Laura Bergson looked at my deadened face. I couldn't sleep but seethed in anger against the giggler and, more, against myself. Why did I do such a dumb thing? I could play the 'Fantaisie Impromptu' without mannerisms and still seem to be an impressive young pianist. What did I think I was doing with the gestures borrowed from anybody who did something I thought looked artistic? Why did I have to try to impress everyone around me with the fact that I was unique? Did I really impress them as special, outside the common herd? Or as crazy?

The cocoon of self-contempt in which I was bound pricked and burned for several days, but I was since early childhood prepared to fulfill prescribed duties no matter how I felt, no matter that I wanted to roll up in a corner to die. Laura, who was genuinely sympathetic and becoming attuned to my moods, didn't ask why I was so quiet. She, too, was preoccupied, polite, silent, and dutiful, as she carried her own sack of pain. I knew that her husband Ivan was not coming up on the following weekend and I had gotten to know him well enough to understand that this was one of his frequent declarations of independence from marriage, a chance to unleash his irresistibility on wider spheres.

Our silences were broken into, gradually, by the needs of the children and by visiting neighbors, several of whom carried petitions to halt the execution of Sacco and Vanzetti, scheduled for late that August. I wasn't sure of just what they had done, but I had been told they were Italian radicals being victimized by the American capitalist establishment. They were undoubtedly innocent; many important people said so; and who didn't know that Boston was the seat of xenophobic, throttling conservatism? Knowing little of the details, I nevertheless aligned myself body and soul with the immigrants and against the natives, a throwback to the Them and We schism innate to the immigrant neighborhood of my childhood. Sacco and Vanzetti were, as well, Italian workers like those I had known intimately; in a sense, close relatives. There was nothing I could do about their situation but go to rallies in the community and, on a day off, give out leaflets in the city. I tried to imagine, for the first time in my life, how it might feel to await certain death, how it actually felt – the buzzing, the piercing, the burning in the body – to be electrocuted in a big, hideous, wired throne, like the murderess Ruth Snyder in the picture in the *Daily News*.

Sacco and Vanzetti's deaths interfered minimally, however, with the last community dance, a farewell among mothers' helpers, young masons, and some of the chosen whose families had the money to send them to the University of Wisconsin, an Olympus ruled by a liberal genius-educator named Kirkpatrick, who was freeing his university of the barnacles that hung on most colleges. I was invited to the dance by one of the summer delivery boys, accepted happily, and then regretted having accepted. I was a mediocre dancer and had nothing festive to wear; a small sun blister on my lip looked like a chancre; my hair was wild, sun-bleached and uncontrollable and except for a polite dance or two with my date, who else would guide me to the floor? When I told Laura I wasn't going, she took from her closet a dress of dark rose linen which I had admired and coveted; the wide skirt danced of itself and the deep-cut bodice dangled small silk flowers. 'Wear this dress; it will fit you. Tie a ribbon around your hair, put some powder on your blister, and go.' I went and felt airy and like poetry in Laura's dress and because I was asked to dance by several boys. I was only lightly bothered by my friend Anne, who stood off to the side, straight and tight-mouthed, rejecting possible invitations to dance by her 'Don't you dare. I'll turn you down, you simp' manner. She might be critical of me in the beautiful low-cut dress, wearing a hair ribbon, dancing ineptly and heartily. What the hell. I didn't, for once, care what anyone might say, and grinned as I bounced past her.

When I stepped into the Bergsons' house the summer I was fourteen and a half, I had no sense of the fascinating, often puzzling world I was entering, a new world full of corners to peer into, to observe and to learn. The job had presented itself as rather ordinary: responsibility for the children when their mother went shopping or visiting, taking care of them when both parents went off on their own. The children were three-year-old Eric and six-year-old Nancy. Laura, the mother, looked like a sorrowing cherub, her smile infrequent and small (maybe she didn't want to show the gap between her front teeth, I thought). She wore no makeup except pale powder and her hair was coiled in rolls rather like those of nineteenth-century English ladies I had seen in pictures. The style suited her, it suited the old-fashioned, many-buttoned dresses on her small, round body, suited her subdued voice and old-fashioned manners, her sobriety and lack of humor; suited because I liked her and chose to hold her unusual, distinctive. It was from her that I learned a sort of child-rearing I had not known before: to persuade with respect in a calm, reasonable voice, to be truly, gently patient. Her concentration on the children's physical welfare and their behavior was so serious and constant that there was little tendency or even time for play. I supplied the games, the nursery rhymes, the stories, and the nonsense songs like 'Old MacDonald Had a Farm', which I enjoyed along with them. They had books but few toys and were expected to entertain themselves with a pot, a few clothespins, bits of cloth, empty cereal boxes, to invent games with whatever was around. Getting into the spirit of things, I devised an outdoor game we called 'music stones', exploring the myriad sounds that were to be found in clacking different types and sizes of backyard stones together. Laura approved of the musical game and applauded my imagination.

Intelligently malleable, in the main, with each new situation presented by a child, the mother was utterly rigid in a few respects: like it or not, the children had to drink almost a pint of hot water heavily laced with lemon juice and brown sugar (never, never white) each morning. This was meant to help them move their bowels, and well-trained from infancy they did, shortly after finishing the morning elixir. When cause and expected effect did not properly meet, there was considerable consternation, especially on my part when I was alone with the children, as disturbed by the anomalous event as if the whole world had become unhinged. Not entirely a health nut, not entirely not, Laura fed her children the locally baked wholegrain bread, and honey, a 'natural product' – the key words – rather than jam. Instead of the classic bologna sandwich for lunch, theirs were filled with avocado mashed with lemon juice. (Lemon, much used, appeared to have a mystic power; yellow like the sun, it might share the sun's life-giving force.) They yearned but never asked for the slice of salami or hot dog they saw in other children's hands. I was tempted to buy some for them when their parents were away, but I was afraid, too burdened by their mother's principles and sure that one bite of the forbidden food would poison their cosseted baby-pink intestines. However, the same envy with which they watched a boy chomping on a limp gray slice of liverwurst marked the faces of the children who watched Nancy and Eric sitting on their back porch tearing at lamb chops. These were the children of the nuts-roots-fruits-and-berries, who were allowed nothing but those basics and were, some of them, desperate little outlaws, ripping a bit of cheese or a lollipop from another child's hand; a sudden wail as often as not signaled the rape of coveted food. The desperadoes, after reports to their parents, were reproved and punished both for theft and for breaking the health rules. But the determined (and very hungry) ones became cannier and bolder, capable of snatching packets of candy and sliced ham and boxes of cookies from grocery shelves and fleetly disappearing into tall meadow grasses or up trees, chattering like thieving monkeys.

Laura's rigidities about her children's food and drink were stern but rational, as was her conduct generally – except when ominous clouds streaked the sky and winds roared and tore through the trees, promising the thunder and lightning which terrified her. She called the children indoors, tamping down all fear and urgency in her voice. Having settled them with books on the floor in the middle of the room, she quickly took the many hairpins out of her rolls of hair and put them on an outer windowsill of the toilet. It was fascinating to watch the ritual – a particularly primitive ritual it seemed after she told me, out of earshot of the children, that she would surely be killed by lightning if she did not rid herself of the metal hairpins. The children liked to stroke her loosened long hair and never questioned its appearance during storms, and as far as I know, because of the iron discipline that covered her terror with false calm, they were never disturbed by the sights and sounds of weather.

Her husband, Dr. Ivan Bergson, was a dermatologist – the specialty he chose to free himself of house calls and shrieks for help at inconvenient times – and one of the most puzzling people I had yet met; trying to make the pieces fall into an understandable portrait was one difficult course in that summer's dense curriculum. I advanced, in time, to the point where I realized that there were people made of diverse pieces that shouldn't hang together but did; that a lover of the arts was not necessarily a lover of the truth; that elegance abutted on brutality; that my foursquare judgments and evaluations of people had to be loosened, a major push toward maturity. Ivan was slight and exquisite, his enameled smoothness enhanced by shining baldness and shining swells of forehead, like an Oriental ivory figurine. He had a delicate, perfectly bowed mouth that echoed the slight bow-curve of his thin, high-arched nose. Always distinctively dressed, he it was who gave me the golden Borsalino hat and the still dashing old dark-gray raincoat which became the basic components of a costume that, for a couple of years, made the distinctive, unique 'I'. He had, or had invented, an aristocratic European background, replete with 'von' relatives, a faint 'Continental' accent that slipped when he was angry, forgetting that he was connected to a 'Statspalais' (as he called it) in Vienna; like all young aristocratic bloods, he had seduced bevies of chambermaids before he was twelve. He was the first anti-Semitic Jew I had yet encountered, denying anything but a distant, dim stain in the blood and speaking of some of his neighbors as kikes.

The superior baronial manner and looks were, in my eye and mind, fortified by a large library of books in several languages (something I had never seen in a house before) and a collection of contemporary paintings, much of it gathered in lieu of payments from artist patients. He was baronial as a father and husband as well. A harsh voice emerged from the sleek head to thunder at his timid little daughter – long afraid of him, to judge from her cowering stance when he was around. 'If you spill a drop of milk out of that bottle' – a full, heavy glass quart bottle – 'I'll kill you'. Pale, trembling, her thin little arms taut and twisted, she almost always spilled some milk, once smashing the whole bottle as it slipped from her nervous fingers. She hid from him in the toilet for hours. I wondered why Laura rarely sprang to her rescue. I once ran to help the child, furious with this shade of my own merciless father, and was thrown back with 'Mind your own goddamned business'.

By the end of the summer I understood why Laura did not rescue her child from Ivan's cruelty. She was, as thoroughly as none of the tough immigrant women I knew had been, his creature. It was for him that she devised the exceptional coiffure and it was to his design that she had her evening dresses made – Renaissance confections of satins and velvets, one Elizabethan gown of panels of pale-blue velvet over white satin, bordered with gold paillettes. (We were of about the same size, and when she let me try on one or two of the dresses and I became rare and beautiful, I could understand her Patient Griselda attachment to a man who could be so brutish with his child and also devise such loveliness.) She had puce silks that looked like great dark rosebuds, and hand-embroidered lawns and linens for winging through lyrical summer nights. To adorn the gowns he bought her delicate, ornate ornaments from a dealer in Chinatown. An exquisite storybook couple, they went to recitals by a young dancer called Martha Graham and to openings at the gallery of Alfred Stieglitz, and were the dinner guests of artists who were filling state capitals and county courthouses with murals. They entertained friends who brought messages from Raymond Duncan in Paris, from Mary Wigman in Berlin. Eating with the children in the kitchen of their long, old-fashioned Village apartment I heard from the adjoining dining room names like O'Keeffe, Varese, Picabia, Bodenheim, James Joyce. (They had, of course, a pirated copy of *Ulysses*, which I lifted off their shelves and still own.) This was the style of life designed for me, I was sure. I would wear dresses like Laura's and dash around in the stupendous Peruvian llama poncho owned by the wife of one of the painters; I would talk art and books, dance and music, and serve exquisite dishes. Meanwhile I eavesdropped keenly from the kitchen to hear gossip from Rome, Paris, London, laced with exalted names I carefully memorized to make part of my discourses. (Of my several sets of parents, real, fancied, adopted, the Bergsons had, I think, the most telling effect.)

For the glamour, the clothing, and the jewelry, Laura paid in heavy coin. It was understood that she try to disregard – certainly not complain about – Ivan's extracurricular flings, which he, in turn, preferred not to keep too secret; there was no joy in being a closet Don Juan. A piece of jewelry he purportedly took back to his dealer for repairs smiled brightly from the neck of a friend's wife at a Christmas party both Bergsons attended. And there were several such etceteras of which she told me when we had known each other for some years and I had become a member of the household, old enough to understand the patterns of their lives and keep my silence.

One set of demands he made on her came to me slowly. He would give her long looks after the children went to bed and waft winsome looks and smiles at her – a vicious little boy – with hints of 'If you'll do it, I promise you something nice'. Sometimes she giggled and nodded a little, sometimes she looked irritated, frowning as she whispered 'No'. I began to know that she had consented, after repeated importunities, to some sort of sexual variant when he presented her ceremoniously, the Earl of Essex addressing Queen Elizabeth, with a jeweled mask, small and exquisite ('Maybe a Cellini, who knows?' he said) or a seed-pearl collar hung with Indian enamels. Or he would announce that next weekend she was to come to town and they would go to the theater, eat in her favorite restaurant, and shop for furs for a new coat.

It was during these absences of both Bergsons, sometimes longer than a weekend, that I felt aged, bent with burdens. First there was the momentous matter of bowel movements. Nancy, in all matters an obedient child, gave me no trouble. Eric sat readily, smilingly, on his pot and for fifteen minutes, a half hour, an hour, refused to perform. He was not angry with me for keeping him on the pot; he beamed and sang a long recital of tuneless songs. I, certain that all the hot lemon drink he had swallowed would explode his intestines if he didn't rid himself of it, was in twisting anguish. I couldn't let him sit, his behind growing redder and redder as it pressed the pot rim, indefinitely, though he didn't complain. I took him off after a long while and continued to watch him closely, waiting for catastrophe. And so it went one time from day to day, for four days, he singing on the pot for an hour and more each day, I shriveling in terror; if anything happened to either of these children I would have to kill myself. After the interminable time, the Bergsons returned, Eric ran to his mother, embraced her, then rushed to his potty and quickly relieved himself of four days' meals and quarts of hot lemonade, the present for his mother which he would not give me. As he emerged from the bathroom he gave me a sweet, villainous smile and asked me to button his pants, which he usually managed without help. The need to strangle him was tempered by admiration of his control, his poise, and the three-year-old wisdom that devised such clever weapons. He became increasingly interesting, this potbellied miniature Machiavelli who knew how to manipulate almost any situation, a knowledge that kept him confident and charming, ready for anything. When he was a bit older, no more than five, I overheard him teaching his sister how to handle Daddy, who terrified her but never him: 'Don't let him see you're afraid; try to make believe you're not afraid and he won't bother you. He likes to see you cry, don't let him' – infant wisdom to which I bowed in respect. He was a lot better armored at five than I at fifteen or, I later thought, at twenty-five. Having had a brother who lived in the sun while I lived in the shade, he always young, fleet, and shining, I dun and slow, I could feel with

Nancy and tried to show her favor. Helping her with her reading, inventing number games to make her quicker at adding, teaching her to play one-finger tunes on a neighbor's piano, did to a degree diminish the polite, silent distance from me and, slowly, painfully, from the world around her.

Eric and his father had their worlds by a string their women never found. Nancy stayed nervous, retiring, and although she could be lovely and appealing, often covered her heart-shaped face with a hangdog, defeated look. Forced by her father and the irritating ease of her brother, she would sometimes become spiky and brash, frightening herself as a screaming baby is often frightened by its own noise. She then quickly retreated to her usual scared shyness and mute passivity. Her mother, unlike the child, had certain unassailable strengths – the sexual adroitness her husband apparently prized, for one, and her extraordinary skill as a cook. It was one of Ivan's pleasures to search for ancient recipe books (he was a lightweight classicist and medievalist, from whom I picked up greedily names like Phidias and Herodotus, Thomas Aquinas and Grosseteste). From his old books he would pick out a recipe or two and demand that Laura present him with the accomplished dish. I watched her one day with pleased awe as she prepared the feast served a fourteenth-century Archbishop of York on his visit to Durham Cathedral. For one course she stuffed a deboned half-roasted duck with nuts, raisins, currants, ginger, and other spices and herbs, doused with Madeira wine. She then stuffed this duck into another, slightly larger, also painstakingly deboned, then duck within duck was put in the oven, watched carefully, and later served as slices of mixed nectars. The performance and the taste (a slice was put aside for me in the kitchen) were intoxicating to a girl brought up on barley soup, *klops*, and chicken boiled down to shreds, as they were to the *feinschmecker* friends – all male – for whom Laura prepared the high ecclesiasts' spread of which the ducks were the centerpiece. Like Mrs. Roth, like Mrs. Roberti, Mrs. Rosenstein, Fannie Herman, and all the other immigrant women I knew as a child, Laura did not sit at the table but picked bits off the almost-empty platters in the kitchen. (It was always shocking to see this 'advanced' woman in the antique role of slave servitor.)

One of the men never invited to the connoisseur dinners – men who wore gray vests and Vandyke beards, showy watch chains attached to heirloom watches, one sporting a monocle which he never seemed to use – was a favorite cousin who was a caricature of Ivan, the elegant face and tight lean body reduced to a yellow-pink melt. They were occasional partners – as I learned as I lay in bed next to the kitchen, where they talked late into the night – in womanizing, comparing notes on women they both had known and conjecturing about a few they hoped to know better. One dawn I was awakened by their voices close over my head. It was the cousins peering down on my breast – my loose nightgown had slipped – admiring, in their words, the pretty pink skin in its light shine of sweat, the youthful freshness of the nipple, which the cousin was about to touch when I sat up and stared at them. I wasn't afraid of the cousin, whom my mother would have called a *graubyon* or a *ballegullah*, both expressions for coarse, foul-tongued, and dirty-minded men. I could have dismissed him with 'What the hell do you think you're doing? Get away from me, you fool.' Ivan was another matter. Why, with his fine tastes and affairs with worldly women, salivate over an adolescent breast? (I was still naively trying to put disparate pieces together.) I was also afraid that any protest from me would produce an angry shout, as he shouted at Nancy, and I would be paralyzed, as she was, as I was when my father had shouted at me, as I was – and still am – whenever I heard a loud male voice spraying anger. If Ivan was sufficiently annoyed with me he could, over Laura's ineffectual murmured protests, fire me and I would have to go home, to stay there as little as possible, to wander for hours if I couldn't find a friend at home or sit in a library growing hungrier and hungrier because I would have no money and was stubbornly reluctant to take food from my father's kitchen. So I said nothing, Ivan said nothing, and pulling the sheet well over me, I turned toward the wall. The cousin smirked at me through breakfast, but no one said anything and I soon discarded the incident, no new experience in a progression of encounters that are now headlined as child molestation and are as old as the earth.

I enjoyed the job when I was in town, enjoyed the children and even the effort to infuse life and ease into Nancy, but found it more difficult when I was left all alone in the country with a three-year-old and a six-year-old. Intensely a city child, I was afraid of the country dark and its inexplicable sights and sounds: the scratching of a field mouse, the swoop of a bat outside the window, the scramble of a raccoon on the roof. Like most of the local houses, the Bergsons' was a plain, loosely built bungalow of wood, a house vulnerable to rain and winds, and I often considered Laura's pale, mute hairpin rituals justified when lightning cut the sky and thunder shook the small house. As in most of the bungalows, the kitchen was centered around a kerosene stove, ours distinguished by erratic habits. One night, when the children were in bed and I was frying a couple of eggs for my supper, the flames from the burner suddenly shot up, attached themselves to the butter in the pan, and, strengthened by the extra fuel, soared. I couldn't reach the screw to turn the fire off; it, too, was lapped by the wild blue flags of flame. As I watched the flames shoot up to lick and tease the wood of the ceiling (there was no canopy over the stove), I became knots of nausea and pain. 'Don't panic, don't panic, don't panic', I repeated, because I knew no prayers. when the flames actually began to eat the wood I would waken the children and get them out of the house. There was no phone, no fire department to alert, no one within earshot to yell to for help. I could save the kids, but before I walked them to the nearest neighbor, the house might burn down. I would be responsible for the immense loss and how would I pay for it? I would have to commit suicide, the solution for any huge guilty burden. 'That's for later. For now stay calm, don't panic, watch the flames.' (The control I soon managed must have stemmed from early admonitions to take care of my crippled little brother, to watch and comfort him at times and in places in which I felt as lost and frightened as he but was already trained at five not to betray anything but calm capability. He was not to cry; see, I wasn't crying; I would take care of him.) And suddenly, as the flames danced before me, I was sitting on the street tending my baby sister in her carriage, cut by a whiplash of shock and horror in finding that the carriage was overturned because I had been reading and let it tip over. She was not hurt or even surprised, but I never recovered. Here, again, I had not taken care of them, an accusing voice shouted at me. It never occurred to me to blame the Bergsons for keeping such a faulty, dangerous stove, for putting *me* in immediate danger. The fault was mine because I was there, because I must have done something wrong. My fault. My fault. Always my fault, as cripples were my fault and beggars and cross-eyed people.

The flames did not chew up the roof boards, but slowly ebbed and died. I did not have to awaken the children, but I kept staring at the kerosene burners after I had turned them off, suspecting anthropomorphic malevolence – the sneaky

nastiness of inanimate objects. Contenting myself with cheese and
bread for supper, I dumped the kerosene-soaked eggs down the
toilet and leaped back immediately into mea culpa – maybe the
fatty mess would clog the toilet. My God, more trouble. I had heard
of girls leaving houses and children who were too troublesome, but
I could not resign, not only because it meant a return to the Bronx,
to be delayed at all costs, but because I had learned that there
was no backing away from difficulties and had become almost
arrogantly proud of my endurance, and control.

From month to month, my life became almost inextricably
bound up with that of the family, in the country and the city,
relied on to take care of the children at any time, under any
circumstances. In spite of Eric's attempts to poison my life
with his empty potty, I found him enchanting (as my little
brother had been at three), shrewd and ready to give advice
– anything from how to feed a cat to making a folded paper
hat, an unctuous Uriah Heep smile, as he spoke, on his rococo putto
face – yet baby enough to sit stark naked on the street before the
city apartment, waiting for Birthday, a benevolent friend who was
to arrive imminently, carrying a sack of toys. I learned him better
when we were quarantined, he with measles, while his mother took
care of Nancy, who had scarlet fever. We were in widely separated
sections of the many-roomed apartment and in contact with each
other only as voices through doors and the swift handing in and
out of food trays. Laura would not go near Eric and kept her
distance from me when we accidentally met in the hallway. When
Eric turned restlessly I was afraid, and afraid of his hot, blotched
face. I had no knowledge of fever except as a dreamy long time in
bed when I was a child. But I learned to put cold compresses on
his hot forehead – his mother did not believe in medication for
children (or possibly reliable remedies did not yet exist). Carefully
following her instructions from the notes she slipped under our
door, I became as involved in his symptoms and as anxious as
a young mother, coaxing him to eat, loving him greatly when his
fever ebbed and he became coherent again. Troubled by the fear
that he might retain scars if he scratched his measles, probably
confusing it with smallpox, I devised finger games, taught him
to play 'Church and Steeple' and to walk his fingers on me as the
'Teeny, Weeny Spider'. I sang endless songs, to which he beat time
on the bedrail – spirituals, Irving Berlin songs, Russian folk
songs with impromptu mock-Russian lyrics, and songs from the

endless store given me by P.S. 58 – 'Funiculi, Funicula', 'The Minstrel Boy', 'Jingle Bells', 'Drink to Me Only with Thine Eyes', 'Believe Me, if All Those Endearing Young Charms'. When he had learned most of these, I resorted to the blues and what were then called 'race' songs, as sung by Ethel Waters, which I just about understood and he not at all, though he was mesmerized by the slow, sinuous rhythms and the rough, salacious voice with which I sang them. (It might have amused him in later life to know that his musical life began with 'Get off, get off your knees, Papa. Turn in, turn in all your keys, Papa. You can't get me back that way', and with the 'Handy man who churns my butter and strokes my fiddle', songs I learned from records owned by the 'fast set' in the summer community.) Eric and I also pushed the long days away by drawing pictures and tracing letters, which he had begun to learn by himself, sounding out 'Cold' and 'Hot' on the bathtub spigots and transferring those sounds to other words. We traced his hands and mine and pasted paper stars and suns and animal shapes on the wall, on his headboard, wherever his short arm could reach.

Through the passing days I became more sure of his needs and responses, of his affection for and dependence on me and my affection for and dependence on him. It was living with Eric alone and constantly that created another dream image of a future me. I saw myself vividly, and felt comfortable, as a mother of twelve children, a large, benign, patient earth mother who looked like Aline MacMahon; a mother who never flashed her hand at a kid, who never said 'Scratch your ass on a broken bottle', never said 'Bang your head against the wall' to a bored child; my children would never be bored. This dream of myself in yet another ideal role shaded but did not erase the me that would be Joan of Arc, Shaw's Candida, Portia, ugly, courageous George Eliot. (They were full-costume portraits, with more to come of personae to try on to keep testing for their attractiveness and suitability, all but the perfect *one* to be discarded at some wonderful, revealing time. I did not know then the adult character in a Sartre play who says that 'every morning I put on the me that matches my coat' – suggesting that the adolescent collection is never entirely closed but keeps seeping thoughts, gestures, words.)

A different sort of mothering, not as satisfying as being Eric's mother-vassal, came to me when the Bergsons went abroad for a month after the children were well, and the employment office in school called me to fill a temporary job that required an experienced baby-sitter – really a teachers' helper, they assured me – in a boarding school that was part of a castle in Washington Heights once owned by the sculptor George Grey Barnard. It was a very long trolley ride from James Monroe High School in the East Bronx to the rustications and crenellations that housed the school which viewed the Hudson. I enjoyed the ride, learning new neighborhoods, new streetcars, new houses, new kinds of dress and faces. Sometimes I walked the distance, as I frequently did from school to home, taking pleasure in my swinging legs and arms and the fine machinery of my lungs and heart.

The school, whose name I cannot remember, was owned and conducted on the principles of leaving the children almost entirely unbridled, an educational tenet popular among advanced groups like those of my summer community. I had often wondered about the 'freedom' of the Bergson children. Certainly Laura allowed her children greater freedom than the shouters and smackers and 'Where were you?' mothers of my childhood street. But her children were bound in other ways: they had no street life to bang and roar through, no stickball and fights over who held the ropes in Double Dutch, no cabals of plotting, no breathtaking, bizarre sexual revelations, no alignments in fealty or enmity, no politics; in other words, no society of their own, without adult interference.

The castle children had their group societies but were, in addition, permitted to shriek 'No' to food, to baths, to going to bed, to lending or returning a toy. 'No' was the battle cry of the castle, and it was my role to relieve the regular teachers of the most exhausting nursery group, abundant babblers and wetters, to ease them into quiet for supper and sleep, actually the toughest job of the day. I was ready for them thanks to Laura and a few instincts I had grown on her soil: how to hold a child who was by his own shrieks and sobs being tossed into a wild jungle of hysterics from which he didn't know how to emerge; how to divert a 'No' by a smile, a joke, a pat; how to speak in a whisper so that a curious child, interested in the words and manner of the new teacher, would stop his yammering. After working in the castle of the tall, dim rooms most afternoons and evenings for several weeks, I was asked to stay on – not as a substitute, but a regular assistant teacher. My prior loyalties were, however, to the Bergsons, already returned to New York, from whom I could continue to learn of the ways and riches of the world, about what Stein and Honegger were writing and Soutine painting, about Eugene O'Neill and Susan Glaspell and the Provincetown Players, about the experimental Habima Theater; to hear haunting, incomprehensible poetry, to conquer bits of their world, which would become my landscape, my native climate. In any case, I had missed their children.

Slowly and sporadically I had begun to sense other people's feelings, growing up to sympathy, and some of the castle school's children had an extraordinary effect on me, a girl who had felt until recently only her own discomforts and pains. One wide-eyed hyperactive eight-year-old boy, still a bed wetter, a ceaseless masturbator, a stammerer, and omnivorously eager to be patted, embraced, or merely touched by anyone, was the son of a showy free-love couple. The parents had been legitimately married for a few months but now loved freely wherever they lit. The mother was made up and dressed to resemble the legendary vamp Theda Bara, wearing massive rings and heavy ropes of multicolored beads, the effect reduced by bony wrists and ankles and a flat chest. An actress of now and then small parts and a maker of lame little poems, she comported herself with the petulant allure of a star. Papa was a writer, rather popular in a limited and pallidly radical way. He was disheveled, dirty, and given to long lectures – into the air, to a captive audience of children who stood politely still and bewildered for a few minutes, then slid stealthily away – on the subject of poetry, on the joys of drink and revolution, on the ecstasies of sex, a wonderful astonishment to me, who had never met a writer or a parent who wandered so loudly in such forbidden forests. Nor had I ever met a parent who was drunk, as he seemed frequently to be, though I knew little of the comportment of drunks other than the wobble and drag of Mary Sugar Bum, who used to warble and beg on Lafontaine Avenue. Both parents came on most visiting Sundays, she with her coterie, he with his, taking care to meet now and then for the exchange of a couple of cliché insults that slammed at her sluttishness, his drunken filthiness.

She greeted her boy, when he ran wildly at her, with a light kiss and a pat on the shoulder, asked him if he'd been a good boy, and left him, to stroll the grounds like an artiste at a society rotogravure lawn party. The father tried harder, too hard. He insisted on joining baseball games with the other fathers but was so unsteady on his feet and so dangerously inept that another man had to take the bat from him. Little Sitwell, named for a literary crush of the father, began to howl, outraged. Because his father was not allowed to play? Because he was so shamefully drunk? We tried to explain to the child that the sun in his daddy's eyes made him dizzy and he couldn't see the ball to hit it; lots of people had trouble with batting when the sun was in their eyes. The child's mother made no attempt to comfort him and we didn't urge it, keeping him away from her anticipated mutterings of 'That stupid, shitten drunk.' My childhood had been replete with domestic quarrels, in my house, in houses that blasted their furies through courtyard windows, but I had never heard a parent shamed in this way before his children; our parents' fights were mano a mano, shouting mouth to roaring mouth, no snide mutterings.

Broken little Sitwell hurt me and I was hurt by six-year-old Franny, who played peaceably near the other little girls – washing toy cups, dressing and undressing dolls, smearing the paper on her easel with water paints – all done quietly, slowly, while she wept. She never made a sound, no sob, no pull of breath, simply a ceaseless well of tears out of an unnamed sorrow. The most moving adult was one of the 'old' teachers. 'Old' to an adolescent might be forty, and that was probably the age of the very plain woman with coarse hair and potato features, an intelligent, dignified woman who had – the gossip went – approached a man of her acquaintance and asked him to impregnate her; she desperately wanted a child. Whether she didn't know the hazards of a late first pregnancy or would not succumb to the information, she carried the pregnancy to term and produced a boy with marked symptoms of Down's syndrome, a sweet, docile child, open-mouthed and oblique-eyed, who could learn almost nothing. His mother spent interminable hours with him on her lap, after her classes were over, trying to help him count on his fingers, to say his name clearly, to say hers, with little success. Watching her and living intimately with Sitwell and the tiny blond Niobe became insupportable. I was pleased to leave the school and its pain, although life there with its vamps, drunken poets, and curious variety of other aberrant parents was, in its troubling way, a revealing journey into the widening world for which I was insatiably greedy.

I returned to my role as assistant mother at the Bergsons', where the climate was less charged but as highly colored: the new book, the new picture, the swooping capes, the flaming hennaed hair, the bushy beards, the paint-stained overalls, the African jewelry, a vat of bathtub gin in the kitchen, women stomping in batwing fancies, shrieking like banshees, and no next-door neighbors to complain because they were also stomping and shrieking.

During my second summer with the Bergsons, when I was fifteen, I had met Martha, probably at one of the entertainments so frequently and ardently staged by the community. I became enmeshed in her. She was Diana, the lithe Diana of the hunt, her movements like the graceful sway of tall reeds; her fingers were long and she joined them in circles and arcs as she spoke, the compelling punctuation of an East Indian dancer. We were the perfect pair, I thought, she dark and vertical, I fair, short, horizontal. She must have been aware of the striking contrast we made, because she wasn't averse – I yearned for it – to walking very close to me, her arm around my shoulder, my arm around her waist. We caught a good number of glances, a few amused, a few censorious because we were being showy in this place that pretended to have no pretenses, because maybe we were attempting to appear to be lesbians, a fashionable stance among those teen-age girls who were avid to read Radclyffe Hall's *Well of Loneliness* (difficult to obtain), of which we heard and spoke a good deal. And there were the titillating shadows on Virginia Woolf and Vita Sackville-West, etched a little too subtly in *Orlando*. And what about Willa Cather and what about the poet H.D.? It was a distinguished company, and a number of intellectually ambitious girls, not prepared to join it, liked to feel linked to its members by dress and gesture, no more.

Martha and I didn't see each other as often as I liked and I never surely knew how important it was for her to see me. We hid potentially emotional words in smart, light commentaries on the stupid world and its stupid people. It was easier to be with and worship her when the summer was over and I could cut classes to meet her downtown at her school and ride the subway with her to her house. I eagerly performed errands for her: a music book in one of the secondhand music stores then on West Fifty-seventh Street or downtown on Fourth Avenue, where I might also pick up a copy of the *Oresteia*, for a classics project in which she was to read Electra. I was willing to do anything for her; the long subway rides to search out music and books were holy ventures, as a devout young soldier might march in the Crusades, as the palace slave Charmion might serve Cleopatra.

Although she invited me to her house, I rarely went, preferring to meet her away from the angry glare in her mother's onyx eyes. As she slowly took in my long, worn mouse-gray coat, my black stocking and black sneakers, the golden man's hat, she stripped me of all charm, character, intelligence, of my very being. Behind the tight lips, behind the thick eyebrows and the hair harshly pulled back as if she were trying to tear it off her skull, I could guess the thought that moved through the minds of several mothers I knew: 'Dresses like a crazy, not like a girl, not even like a boy; practically homeless, no ties to anyone, obedient to no one. So she works, she says, in a laundry and library and takes care of a doctor's children. I wouldn't let her touch my children. And she's spoiling my Martha, interfering with her practicing, teaching her to answer me back.' I never heard her rebuke but knew this sort of rapaciously possessive parent of a talented child who would carry the family into riches and glory – shades of my father. To fulfill her mother's fantasy Martha must succumb to the unceasing vigilance of the harsh eyes under the aggressive eyebrows and to orders from the sharply defined, almost metallically edged lips. Priding myself on being a rebel, my raison d'être of the time, and working the role for all it was worth, I had expected attention, possibly admiration, or at least acceptance, from a family of avowed Marxists, who should approve of the freedom I had wrested from capitalist convention. Faulty logic or great innocence. Mrs. Alpert's politics had nothing to do with the fact that Martha belonged, all of her, every breath, every cell, every thought and word, to her mother and to her ambitions for her daughter's success in the capitalist world. Her attitude toward her husband was even more chilling than her disdainful manner toward me. I could escape but not the brown man who looked like a pumpernickel loaf and was as simple. He adored his daughter and liked to make little jokes with her, into which Mrs. A. cut with a phrase of contempt: 'Stop already with your idiot jokes.' Or worse still, called Martha away from her father into the kitchen on one pretext or another, leaving him foolishly suspended in midsentence. I liked him and was sorry for him; I had never seen such a steady attempt to annihilate a person totally. When my mother and father fought they gave each other full size and sound, equal, well-matched adversaries.

The only other member of the household was a young cousin who was registered at City College from the Alpert address although his parents lived in New Jersey. He seemed to come and go at will, without comment from his aunt; she had no ambitions for him. His attitude toward me, the few times we met, was familiar: an awkward nod and a dash for the door after we were introduced, a few muttered words on the second meeting, a third meeting during which the fear of appearing friendly bred nastiness. He told me that I looked like a horse when I made my nostrils flare. He had me; it was one of a number of affectations I tried on during those years – the flaring nostrils meant sensitivity. I dropped the flaring nostrils, which must truly have looked grotesque, flapping and waving like fish gills, and took on other mannerisms that attracted me and were, in turn, discarded when they became a source of embarrassment. I pitched my voice very low and kept forcing it lower, for dramatic effect, until I was addressed on the telephone as 'Mister'. Simultaneously with the dramatic contralto voice, I devised a manner of walking in a slow, stately stride (as stately as five feet two inches would allow), with my eyes fixed poetically on a far horizon. The seer's stride and vision once knocked me hard against an unyielding subway turnstile, and the blow to my stomach pushed a loud, pained grunt out of my spiritual, otherworld face. I was wrapped in hot shame, as if a large, critical crowd saw the blow and heard the brutish grunt, although the station was actually almost empty. It is difficult to know when the putting on and taking off of affectations altogether stopped, certainly not until later and not until I became easy and trustful with one or two people whom I loved and who seemed to love me.

The censor of my nostrils left for another college. Life and love with Martha dwindled to a halt through a progression of causes. Her mother had learned that we had slept together in their country house while she was in the city. Although we lay stiffly holding hands and carefully not touching each other's bodies, Mrs. A. forbade Martha to have anything to do with me. Martha wasn't completely obedient, but she had been invited to work with an amateur chamber group who were more experienced and older than she, and felt the need for more practice; her mother's admonitions not to spend time with an undisciplined sloven folded smoothly into Martha's ambition. I continued, however, to meet her at her school and ride the subway with her. There seemed to be less and less to talk about; she was becoming increasingly laconic and I too discouraged to continue babbling on my own, sensing the futility of being constantly bright and arresting.

When I went early the following summer to live with the

Bergsons, I found that Martha had acquired an attractive new friend. She was very blond, delicate, curly, and, compared to my dun shabbiness, dazzlingly chic. She had a cute, feminine name – Bettina, or something like that – and apparently had a clothing allowance that permitted her to wear several striking costumes: from flirtatious headband and hair bow down to her shoes, she was all in one color – a yellow set, a green set, a lavender set, with bag and handkerchief to match. She talked quickly and smiled a good deal and flirted with man, woman, child, dog, cat, and, of course, herself. I was envious and jealous, furious with Martha for taking this froth of bubbles as a serious friend, of paying so much attention to her breezy burbling and, worse, admiring her meticulously matched wardrobe. Bettina refused to notice my presence and never spoke to me, closing a ring around Martha and herself, locking me out. That Martha consented to my being excluded was a terrible blow, not, though, as deadly as I had thought it would be were we ever to be separated. Shocked, bitterly displeased, and yet a little amused, I watched Martha and pert Bettina walk as Martha and I had, an arm embracing a shoulder, an arm embracing a waist, and decided that the effect was posed and fakey, Bettina, so blond and curly, hanging on the straight, flat length of Martha like a parasite vine.

I tried to make Martha's indifference, her heartless perfidy, a dagger to my heart and venom in my veins. Her cruelty was the black swift path to a noose or a leap off a high roof, to the suicide I had promised myself if she ever left me. She *was* leaving me, and I found (though acknowledged reluctantly since it contradicted the view of myself as boundlessly faithful, in spite of love's wounds, to the death) the fact acceptable. What sustenance would Martha get from Bettina? She didn't know Dostoevski from Elsie Dinsmore, nor César Franck from Irving Berlin, but was endlessly informative about where to have yellow shoes dyed pink. And what about Mama, who would certainly not permit the child of her plain-thinking, low-living house to listen long to such decadent frivolity and its little threats; maybe soon even boyfriends. I was – it took some time to admit – growing tired of them, the pumpernickel father who smiled as no one smiled back, the forbidding mother, whom I later recognized as the twin sister of the famous Grant Wood woman, and Martha herself, turning to me, when we met by chance, her mother's disapproving face. There was no farewell speech, no dramatic act of parting, as

I had envisioned it, my eloquent, accusing monologue battering at Martha's shamefaced silence. We faded from each other like objects in a fog. I heard considerably later that Cutie had taken her rainbow wardrobe to a boarding school and that Mrs. Alpert and Martha had moved to Philadelphia, possibly to be close to the Curtis Institute, and probably leaving behind – almost absentmindedly – the unimportant father.

The Bergson children inevitably grew more self-sufficient. Since I was no longer needed as mother's summer help, the children now capable of bicycling and running around on their own, I looked for other summer jobs, the most memorable one in a loft on the Lower East side, where fifteen or twenty girls of my midteen age pasted 'diamonds' into junk jewelry. It was easy and monotonous and earned five dollars a week. We were probably illegal child labor, without protections, with little air and no fans in the hot loft, but we were pleased to be working and earning. At first I was captivated by the shape of the stones, whose unpolished tails were cut as shallow cones. A small cupped stick dipped in glue picked the gem up by its face and the tail was embedded into the cone-shaped hollow in the metal. We had to be careful that the jewels were well planted, using a pushing twist, that there was enough glue, but not too much, on the stick. When I learned there was a bonus of a few cents on ornaments filled beyond the daily quota, I stopped being entertained by the cones, the holes, and the sticks and worked fast, trying to earn money that would buy me total freedom – an importunate need for some years – from my father's house and earnings. (I seem early to have realized how vengeful independence – from some fathers, some lovers, some husbands – could be.)

The job had other satisfactions. It was near Joe's place of work, and it was a glorious thing to show off a cavalier, not good-looking and with a slight accent, and yet a man friend who waited night after night for me. Once in a rare while Mark came along, sad enough to excite the other girls with his air of intense, doomed love, like Ramon Novarro. From the loft we wandered through the East Side streets and into a line of shops that made long-tubed Russian cigarettes, which I smoked as I had seen it done in a movie, held between the tips of thumb and third finger, the hand cupped under the cigarette. Practicing the exotic gesture on the streets – streets of *sheitels*, of young girls in long black stockings and long-sleeved dresses, streets of the Orthodox, of yarmulkes and prayer shawls – I was halted by the broad body and blazing eyes of a bearded, black-hatted man, as wide and firm as a wall. He called me a *kurveh* (whore) and cursed me in Yiddish with black years and cholera. Then he spat on the ground before me, wetting my shoes. He frightened me, not as my father had, with punishments here and now, but as a supernatural force who would hate and doom me forever. He was the messenger of a Jewish God who would drown the world, the messenger of a furious Jewish prophet who, I once read, howled imprecations at the 'Daughters of Zion with their stretched-forth necks and eager eyes'. Bold and immodest, I took it to mean, and un-Jewish, as I was being. There had been times when I squirmed away from my parents' accents as they revealed them to strangers on the El or in Crotona Park, and times when I was pleased with my mother's pert 'Polish' nose and the fact that I had *goy* coloring, blue eyes and blond hair, and the small nose as well. In spite of these passing breezes of anti-Semitism and having been raised in a nonreligious house, neither Yiddishist or Zionist (my father was more fervid about the union movement than about the striving of Jews to return to some distant Arab desert hole), I could not think of myself as anything but Jewish, if it meant only loving Jewish songs, very funny, very sad. The spitting old Jeremiah threatened a firmness, a spine, a strong support that I didn't want shaken; I might briefly, tacitly, deny Jewishness, but it mustn't deny me. (Encounters with groups of black-clad, bearded men striding purposefully through the Orthodox streets of Jerusalem are still a threat, still capable of spitting, cursing and denying me for my unsheiteled, unshawled head, my lipstick, my cigarette, abominations all.)

Occasionally I would visit with Laura Bergson as with a friend, sitting in the kitchen with her, talking about school and jobs while I watched her prepare an interpretation of a menu once ordered by Tiberius, or maybe Napoleon, and to be served to Ivan and several special guests, a writer on food and wines among them. Why had I not learned to cook from Laura, nor even remembered clearly any of her dishes other than the duck-stuffed duck? My mother's contempt for all matters domestic except child care had seeped into me and left a stubborn stain. Her worse than mediocre cooking, I sometimes suggested to her, was a form of revenge on my father. No, she said, laughing, it was a nice idea, but it didn't work; he was accustomed from childhood and the years he was a boarder in America to just the kind of food she made. And we certainly had become big and fat on the repetitions of stuff she cooked. And what about the potato latkes and blintzes, a lot of trouble, of which we couldn't get enough, and the fried matzo we consumed in great mounds during Passover? 'In your own house you'll cook more fancy, more Yankee.' As for cleaning, polishing, neatening, straightening, and all the other domestic busynesses which, I once complained, she didn't teach me as other mothers did their daughters (obviously a plea for intimate mothering that I unexpectedly wanted), her answer was dismissively curt: 'Any girl who isn't an idiot can learn everything there is to keeping a house clean and neat in a half hour. All it requires is that you must want to do it. If you want to show off to your neighbors and relatives what a *baleboosteh* you are, you do it a lot. I'd rather go to school or work. So it isn't so shining neat here. For who? Your father, who doesn't notice anything except where is his paper? For you? You and your brother make the disorder and I'm not going to run after you both all the time, straightening, cleaning up. If you want your books and pencils neatly kept, keep them that way. It's your business, not mine.' She was right; when the time came I found the skills of housekeeping quite simple, arranging the time and will to do it much more difficult. I learned to cook fairly well eventually, never in Laura's class but, like Laura's, acts of slavish devotion. When devotion seeped away, with it seeped the willing passion for ornate, painstaking cuisine. A trustworthy, objective barometer of my love life was the plunge from Grand Marnier soufflés under the most effulgent of suns to burned hamburgers for the storms and shipwrecks.

When the Bergson children went off to college and their parents moved to the country, I saw them rarely, and they gradually left my life except as vibrant memories and gratitude for all, in myriad ways, that I had learned from them. It might have happened in any case, without them, but I prize them as the first spurs and witnesses of my growing up. They trusted me with their children, their houses and the money and jewelry they contained, their paintings, their records, and their books, of which I stole, as mentioned, only one. They were not critical of me or my appearance, rather abetted its singularity with their esoteric Villagey hand-me-downs; they accepted me as the adolescent I was, with a mature sense of responsibility but otherwise a bright kid shouting into all the corners of the earth for answers to her own ill-shaped, garbled questions, searching for an 'I' into whose shape she could nestle comfortably, a form that didn't pinch or prick. Laura, especially, understood the rattling handful of mosaic bits called Kate and was certain, as I was not, that they would sometime join each other smoothly. Noblest of all Bergson virtues was that they never said or even suggested that I was a *meshugge*, a word thrown frequently at me at home.

18
Harlem, etc

A new friend, May, was my number two Carola Polanski (the daughter of our janitors on Lafontaine Avenue and the first and only professional prostitute I've known). May was not as good-looking but a lot smarter, fixing a schedule with a couple of traveling salesmen rather than playing the broader, more hazardous field. Her school attendance was about like mine, full of holes, though she didn't spend her truant time in the library; she curled her hair and polished her nails and slept and shopped. Nor did she shop in Klein's on Union Square as we did, and that rarely. Her clothing looked like the ads of the big stores in the Sunday papers and she had reached the supreme acme of her own place, a one-room kitchenette apartment in Manhattan. Other than a double bed, a small table, and a couple of chairs, it had little furniture and the icebox was almost empty, but this was *living* and I felt honored each time I visited. One Friday evening she asked me if I'd like to go to Harlem; she had a date with some friends there and we'd have a good time. As usual inwardly leaping forward with eager curiosity and at the same time cowering back in fear, I said coolly, 'Sure.' She, dressed in her low-necked purple satin, squeezed me into a black silk dress with long tight sleeves. 'Black makes you look skinnier and older'. After a long subway ride from her place on West Sixteenth Street, we reached Lenox Avenue and made our way among clusters of houses and people I had never known before. They were, for one, several shades of brown, talking, laughing, and dragging at bottles on the stoops of their houses. Their clothing was frilly and brilliant and their children slender sprites who nudged and teased and ran restlessly among them. At one corner, we stopped at a stall lit with kerosene lamps and the shine of fatty meats with a rich hot smell. We had pork sandwiches – particularly delicious because so defiantly nonkosher – and some conversation at the stall and walked on the short distance to the dance hall where May was to meet her friends.

It was a large, low-ceilinged room, dimly lit except where the band sat at one side, under bright lights that glistened on the saxophones and the oiled hair of the drummers. On the opposite side, a series of small lights over the faint gleam of glasses on a bar. (Prohibition concealed the bottles.) On the dimmed dance floor shadowy figures twirled, dipped, kicked, turned, made grotesque shapes as in a dark etching of a witches' sabbath I had seen in an old book. May and I were greeted by a couple of Negro girls. Her chumminess with them, a foreign breed to me, was awesome, as if she had easily floated across a great abyss; my friend May was a citizen of several worlds and I was very proud of her, flattered to be in her company. The girls pointed across the floor and we snaked among the dancing couples until we came to a tall, middle-aged light Negro man walking toward us and, immediately behind him, a younger, darker man. Introductions were made. May began to dance with the younger man and I was taken onto the floor by the older one, a sturdy man with a round, pleasing face. I knew how to dance, somewhat, but usually refused to because I thought I was too fat and felt ugly and was always aware of my feet as Chaplinesque – my father's description. Almost, I could lindy hop, but I had seen it described as 'riotous' and as 'a flying dance done by couples in which girls are thrown away'. I couldn't stand the idea of being thrown, flung like a large, heavy sack, so much manipulated; I resisted, square and stolid. (I often think that fifteen overweight pounds changed the course of my life. For one thing, the sheltering in intellectual pursuits might have come later and less avidly if I could have lindy hopped really sensationally, and I might have known less serious and more playful boys, with whom I might have spent more playful, foolish hours.)

I told the man I didn't know how to dance. With, 'I'll teach you, honey', the man put his arm tightly around my waist and I was skimming the floor, turning, bending, swinging, acquiescent to the skillful suggestions of his arm and fingers. He seemed pleased with himself and me and kept me on the floor for another dance and yet another. During the third dance his guiding arm grew tighter, his other arm joined it at my waist, and he began to grind his belly against mine. As I tried to pull away, the arms held tighter. He smiled down at me. 'You're a nice piece. A friend of May's? How come I haven't seen you here before?' Still trying to pull away, as politely as I could, I said that I had never been there before. 'Well, I'm glad you finally came. How old are you, honey?' I gave him my stock answer, usually acceptable. 'Seventeen.' He laughed. 'The time of the sweetest, juiciest peaches.' Still holding me tight against him, he began to lead me to the edge of the floor, toward a dim area near the bar. He then backed me up against the darkest wall. His hand with the big onyx ring began to rub my breasts while the other arm held me tight to him, his erect penis pounding at my belly. I couldn't run, scream, or try to hit him. Nor did I want to. I had gotten myself into this, maybe actually wanted to, and should have known what to expect. I struggled timidly, but couldn't act offended or angry; it was all my fault. Still clasping, rubbing, pounding, he said huskily, 'Let's get out of here. I've got a nice place down the next block and we can come back to dance later.' 'No, I'm sorry, I have to get home, my father'll kill me if I don't get back soon.' 'Aw, come on. It's too late to worry about your father.' He looked at me, studying my face for a moment or two. 'You're scared, aren't you? I'll bet you're a virgin. We'll fix that; no use carrying around a thing you don't need. That cherry's going to be busted one of these days by somebody, why not me?' I didn't know what to say or do, I didn't know how to escape, and if I did were the subway trains running? Where was the station? I was bound in panic, doomed forever, lost to whoredom and disease, as my father had promised. The man, feeling my terror, released me and led me to the bar, where he bought me a bottle of soda which I tried to drink. My strangled throat couldn't swallow it. He stared at me for a long while. 'You're no May. You're no seventeen. White girls who come to Harlem come for one thing, black prick – supposed to be bigger than the white thing – to buy or to sell to, and everybody knows it. You're not ready and I hope you'll never be. Come on, let's get your coat now and I'll walk you to the station.' As we left the dance hall, he grasped my arm firmly, angrily. 'If I ever see you in Harlem again I'll whip the shit out of you, much worse than your father would. I mean it. You know I mean it.'

At the station he paid my fare, told me where to change and to stand in the middle of the platform, where I could yell for help to the man in the change booth if anyone bothered me. There was no one else on the platform and no one came except a rat, out of one hole, a nervous shrewed look around, and into another hole. The subways were not then dangerous places, but I was afraid, afraid of the rat, of the station, of the black tunnels on either side of it, of the silence, afraid of my lack of courage, afraid of May's contempt if she would ever bother to see me again. After an endless time, the welcome rumble and the roaring light and I leaped into the nearest door, to sit near a sleeping black woman in a ragged coat held together by safety pins, a shapeless knit hat slipping to her eyes. She roused herself at 149th Street and stumbled out with me, to slant to a bench, asleep as she fell to it. I left her there, bereft of the comfort of her sloping presence, and waited for the East Side train whose slow progress would take me through familiar stations – Freeman Street, Simpson Street, Intervale Avenue – stations that were the addresses of my schoolmates, friendly stations that allayed fear; home, if I would admit it. When I got off at Allerton Avenue, the clock on the candy store window near the station accused me with two-thirty; the street lamp glared balefully. It was an innocent, peaceable neighborhood and there was little reason for fear, but I had acted like a bum, a whore, and I must be assaulted and raped, fulfilling my father's prophecy. As I ran, my own footsteps were those of a pursuer, someone who would tear me apart.

Relieved by the sound – as soft as I could make it – of the key in our apartment lock and the door shutting behind me, I stood trying to calm my breath in the dark entrance hallway; ebbing panic gave way to resentment over our peculiar sleeping arrangements. The bedroom that might have been mine and my sister's had been given over to my cousin Bessie, for the duration of one of her long separations from her husband; my father's niece of the weak bladder was especially appreciative of the room's proximity to the bathroom. This left a convertible couch in the living room for my younger sister to use, and either my brother or myself with her, depending on who arrived earlier. (Its eccentric machinery suffered when my brother, now a large, well-fleshed adolescent, disturbed its balance as he got in. The couch began to fold slowly of itself, rolling both occupants toward the center and threatening to crush them like insects in a Venus's-flytrap. My resigned sister would wearily call 'Sandwich!' and both would pull themselves out to push the sides down again.) The person to arrive home last had to take a cot out of the hall coat closet, extending its folds, dropping its feet quietly to the floor, and reaching high on the closet shelf for blankets and pillows, careful not to pull down a shower of clattering hangers and their coats. I could have pushed my way into my cousin's bed. Unthinkable. With the determination to keep late hours which my brother, a lover of sleep, hadn't yet achieved, I had learned to set up the cot smoothly, without much noise.

It was doubtful that I had awakened them; they must have been awake for some time, to judge from the intensity of the whispering that came from my parents' bedroom, off the hallway. As I lay on the cot, fully dressed, I could hear his voice: 'Where does she go? With whom does she run around so late at night? You don't know? Why don't you know? Are you her mother or not? Who but an idiot, a criminal, lets a girl so young run around in the black hours? You're making a prostitute of your own daughter.'

'No, I'm not. Maybe you like the idea, you talk about it so much, you've been talking about it since she was ten, even younger. Another father would worry about an accident, maybe, but you always find your way to the same idea – street girl, whore. I know she isn't and won't be and she's a lot older than fifteen. Do you know any other girl who since thirteen has earned her own lunches and carfares and even clothing, a girl who stays on through high school in spite of a father always putting rocks in her way? How long is it that she's taken money from you or me? She's even stopped eating here because you keep talking about how much butter costs and chopped meat, while you feed the fat, ignorant sisters you brought to America. And maybe soon another niece, and who needs her and the expense she'll be. And why is Bessie in the bed that should be your daughters'? She's fighting you and has the right to. She has a right to a father who encourages her, who helps her. Why do strangers, teachers in school, praise her, push her on, while you try to break her legs? She won't let you, she's becoming a *mensch* in spite of you. Leave her alone!'

'Leave her alone? Leave her alone wherever she likes, with whoever she likes? No-goods, street people, dirty people, diseased people, drinkers, maybe gangsters even?'

She broke in on his customary litany of horrors. 'Stop it, already. She's foolish, all kids are, but she isn't a fool. Shut up and go to sleep.' But he was wound up, driven, and couldn't stop, repeating and repeating, his voice growing louder, his words stronger, more urgent. I could easily picture his distorted face and flailing arms and suddenly imagined that he was about to hit my mother. I jumped off the cot and yelled, 'Shut up, you in there. If anybody was going to make me a bum, it would have been your shitty nephew Yankel. Ask him what he tried to do to me. Ask your pal Mr. Silverberg, who took me to the movies to feel me up.' I was about to mention Bessie, who had had her kind of fun with me when I was younger, but she was standing at her bedroom door, staring. (And anyhow, my bed experiences with her had been more curious than menacing.) I shouted, 'Ask your friend the one-hand-under-the-sheet barber, Tony, who gave us all such cheap haircuts. And it could be that you knew about them all.' As I felt again the anguished turns under Tony's pinstriped barber sheet, the twisting under Yankel's thrusting body and onion breath, the imprisonment by Bessie's grabbing thighs, the crawling of Mr. Silverberg's fat spider hands, my fear and shame in Harlem that night, I burst into an explosion of weeping. Sobbing, bellowing, 'I always thought you knew it all, and didn't stop them, didn't try to protect me.' I pulled my coat on, kicked the cot over, and started out the door. My mother, tight-faced and pale now standing in the hallway, asked where I was going. I didn't know, but I was never coming back. I would let her know when I had a place. She said nothing, she didn't ask me to stay, she didn't cry. When we were out of the apartment, near the stairway, she thrust five dollars into my hand, saying, 'Take care of yourself.' No embrace, no kiss. We didn't do such things, and in any case I needed to stay untouched, firm, gathered on myself. As I walked down the stairs, Mark opened his door, dressed in his bathrobe. He had of course heard my shouting and weeping, and repeated his offer to find me a room and pay for it; he could be dressed in a moment and we could find a room together. I hated him, too, and his wounded dark-eyed Russian love, another burden to cope with. I told him it was too early in the morning to look, for the time being I would stay with a friend, and dashed down the stairs.

There was no friend. After I had so profoundly disgraced her in Harlem, I couldn't go to May, who was probably not at home yet and wouldn't be for a while. Minnie's mother, who said I was a bad influence on her daughter – I lived like an unbridled *shikse* – certainly wouldn't let me in at four in the morning and I really didn't want to see or talk to anyone. I walked and walked swiftly in the damp morning, winds swirling leaves off the trees as I wanted dank, ugly things to swirl off me. I strode through the gray dawn and rainy morning, clutching my five dollars in my hand, my coat open to the healing cool dampness, from the upper Bronx to the big library at Forty-second Street, my safest haven. The library was not yet open when I got there. I sat on the stairs watching thousands of people rushing to work, some of them quite young. Almost as young as I? Could I learn what they did, filing and stenography and good typing? Could I lie about my age and sell things in a store? Maybe I could get a full-time job at the laundry near school for a while? That is, until I got a job as a chambermaid on a ship to Europe and then hitchhiked slowly through France and Italy and Spain. Or until I went to a far-off college and worked my way through as part-time librarian among thousands of books in ivy-covered buildings on wide, long greens. Lulled by these dreams, I went into the library as soon as the doors opened, to wrap myself in noble words, to weave a soft cocoon of words around my life and being, to make smooth the lumpy, irritated, confused thing I was.

Reluctant to break the five-dollar bill tucked deep in my coat pocket, I had no lunch but did feed well that night for fifty cents at Childs near Grand Central. White-tiled and unadorned, like a public rest room, the restaurant suggested the women's waiting room in the station as a place to sleep. I had seen, in the several times I passed through, many sleeping women looking forever glued to the benches. After strolling along Madison Avenue and Lexington and glancing into the local hotels (a quick look; I didn't dare go in), I entered Grand Central Station and, hesitating, made slowly for the women's rest section. There they were, the women I would rather die than ever be: the cracked shoes, the swollen, splotched naked legs, the frayed, stained sweaters, the matted hair held by one comb or a twisted rag. I thought I could sit with them, at least through the night (or until the police threw us out) but it was the open eyes that weren't seeing, the ears that didn't seem to hear, the haggard faces without expressions, that soon drove me out of the station and to circling the emptying nearby streets.

Where to get some sleep on four dollars and change? I knew nothing about the Y's and their accommodations. The only possibility that presented itself was to tempt Minnie's mother with my four dollars. She was no poorer than the rest of us but had a passion for hats, and I might tempt her with the price of a new hat for two nights of sharing Minnie's bed. She and Minnie were about ready for bed when I rang the bell of their apartment on Fox Street. Mama opened the door with 'What are you doing here this late? My husband's in bed already and we're going to sleep in a few minutes.' She didn't shut the door on me, though. Very quickly, bold with fear of defeat, I said, 'I had a fight with my father and I'm afraid to go home. Would you let me sleep here for two nights? You don't have to feed me and I'll pay you two dollars a night.' I took the four dollar bills out of my pocket and offered them to her. She muttered some sort of assent and took the money. Minnie gave me her towel so that I could wash up. Face and hands clean, my underwear dingy with a couple of days' wear and wanderings, I slipped into Minnie's bed, hugging the outer edge. I had no right to crowd her, particularly since I was going to lie to her, make up a story of a beating by my father because I came home late from a party. Since I had to lie to her, she was not that night an intimate friend, and I kept my careful distance as I told my quite ordinary story.

Without books or notebooks, I went off to school with Minnie, who had put an extra slice of buttered bread into her brown paper lunch bag for me. School registered only dimly. What did it matter that I hadn't read the chapter on the Civil War for my history class? I couldn't describe the fission of amoebae in the biology class and I wasn't embarrassed. It was all far away and unimportant. There were two dimes and two nickels in my pocket. There was no choice of action but to go home at three o'clock, long before my father would be there, to see my mother, to whom I could admit defeat, with difficulty. She greeted me with a surprised smile. She didn't ask me where I'd been, what I had done, where I had slept. She suggested I could use a bath and a change of clothing and, if I was hungry, there were some fresh rolls in a bag on the kitchen table and farmer cheese in the icebox. After I had bathed, dressed, and eaten, we sat down together, looking at each other. After a long while, I said, 'I don't want to live here anymore, but I don't know where to go.' 'I know,' she answered, and added, 'I have an idea you might like. What about the Goldens? They're nice people, and with all those relatives coming and going, they must have lots of room and beds. Maybe you could teach little Clara the piano – and sit with her. If that won't cover your rent, I'll give them a few extra dollars a month; they won't ask much.'

Mrs. Golden and Clara were at home and both enthusiastic. Clara wanted a big sister to share her room, Mrs. Golden liked any new, interesting situation, any change, and she sparkled at both of us out of her Tartar-slanted ice-blue eyes. Mr. Golden, she said, would have no objection; we knew how good-natured he was and how much he thought of me. As for the money, don't worry about it. We're doing all right, thank God. That evening I moved my books and clothing into Clara's big closet and was launched, on Mr. Golden's courtly welcome, into the merry, talkative family, of which I soon fancied myself a member. Memory exaggerates, but I hear constant laughter as I think of them, laughter when they were arguing politics, laughter when they ridiculed distant relatives (of which there seemed to be thousands), laughter when the overcooked spaghetti became a wad of paste. It seemed as if laughter lived of itself as a member of the household, and ruled it during the almost incessant playing and partying. There was a gaggle of young people – whose nephews, cousins, and nieces they were I never found out – who traveled almost constantly. With each arrival and departure, bottles of homemade wine, steaming heaps of stew and noodles, bowls of fruit compote, cakes stuffed with raisins and nuts, dishes of chocolate kisses and nonpareils. Relatives came from Brooklyn and from New Jersey and even from other sections of the 'coops'. I was always invited and maintained a balance of 'Of course, thank you' and 'No, thank you, I have a date,' careful not to overuse their kindness. The happiest part of the parties was the dancing that followed the feasting. It was unstylish, laced with a touch of horas and Russian kazatskes and polka hops, everyone dancing, even grandma. The couple I found most engaging – and educational – were a slender cousin and his fat young wife, a pretty tub of happy pink cheeks, ripe moist lips, and a full, broad, round bottom. They had their own immutable style: she clasped her arms around his neck while he kept his hands outspread, covering as much of the juicy flesh as he could, on her bottom. It was fun to watch as a frank, mutual expression of sexuality which I had never seen before – and would not again until I began to frequent French movies.

All good things must end, and too soon, I had learned. The summer was coming on and the Goldens were going to spend the vacation months with their ebullient tribe in a big communal farmhouse. Everything in me – my blood, my breath, my uncertainties and hungers – urged, begged, 'Take me with you, please. Don't leave me.' But of course one never said such things, never betrayed such weakness. We all embraced, promised to see each other soon, and that was that, except for 'Where am I to live?'

19
The Women

It may have been talk among my teachers in the music and English departments, it may have been my artistic 'Lower Depths' costume, it may have been an expression of her own needs, but an English teacher, Marian Wood, with whom I had no classes, engaged me in conversation in the lunchroom one day. She continued to seek me out in the lunchroom and in the halls, to arrange that I walk to the subway station with her after school or, if I wasn't working, to have a cup of hot chocolate with her in a local coffee shop. It grew and grew, the relationship she fostered so vigorously and which I didn't understand. She had learned that I was running the risk of being expelled from school, that I was exploring perilous courses like Harlem dance halls (I couldn't resist broadcasting my adventure, with some fancy edging to embroider it); she could assume that I was poised for all sorts of flights into enlightenments and trouble. (She was one of a numerous breed of teachers in her time whose efforts went beyond teaching: efforts of involvement, of persuasion, and, if need be, rescue, generously and often astutely achieved and I may have appeared, in the beginning, simply a subject for such help.)

One Friday afternoon she asked if I'd like to go to a matinee on Saturday, if I was not working. I dashed to my laundry and begged to be allowed to work two extra evenings the next week instead of Saturday afternoon. The boss was good-natured about my hours, possibly because I was such a dumb bargain as a worker, and I met Marian at the theater she had mentioned. This was the opening of a remarkable series of events which I don't think I ever completely understood. I was a bright girl, a raw girl, a well-read girl, a self-destructive girl, who it was hard to imagine merited all the attention, time and money she lavished on me. We went to frequent Saturday matinees or to afternoon concerts (to Marian I owe, among many other debts, Lotte Lehmann and the German lied) and then on to a dinner at a large, amiable Italian restaurant favored, she told me, by liberals and intellectuals. After dinner, another theater performance. I never paid for anything but my subway fare. It was a glittering world and I danced through it with joy, with delight at being chosen as a companion to an educated adult, a teacher at that, still a word as exalted in my lexicon (though I would never admit it) as it was in my mother's. No one ever had valued me with such steady enthusiasm. And always, in the pleasure, the nagging little 'why?' Why me with the Luna Park mouth and the 'blond-nigger' hair, according to my father's description? 'Why' slowly faded when I began to visit her house on Sundays, with increasing frequency. Although she did most of the talking, she was careful to ask me my opinion of the play we had seen the night before and of the chicken cooked Tuscan style we had eaten. In the main, she taught in her own lively, nonstop fashion. She told me about places in Paris where she had lived for a while, she told me about Socialist friends in Berlin and the bitter, political drawings, banned in the United States, of George Grosz, about *New Masses* magazine and its cartoons by Art Young, about anarchist friends in London, and in each city she sketched the shade of a lover. Women with lovers were supposed to look like Camille or Nefertiti, while Marian was slight, with the full, round face and the bright, alert eyes of a squirrel. Yet I never doubted a word she said or listened for false tones under the words, as I did with other adults.

A new note soon crept into Sunday conversations, these mainly with her crony Helen, who seemed always to be there. Marian would point to me as if I were inanimate, a statue, a puppet, and say to Helen, 'Look at that gesture! And that long neck and the subtle smile! She will be a fine lover someday.' I had no notion of what she was talking about – a lover for whom? And with my fat thighs and ugly big mouth? Whatever she meant, it came peculiarly from a small squirrel lady, a schoolteacher who wore navy skirts and oxfords. Was she being sexy – and to what purpose – as well as maternal, as well as my best teacher? But I refused to worry long about the odd words and observations, preferring to remain the choice protégée of a royal household which had so much to give me. I actually saw the forbidden George Grosz drawings, in a folder she had smuggled from Germany. She showed me

European artbooks I had never seen, by artists I had never heard
of: Bonnard, who painted with brushfuls of sun; Braque, thoughtful
and honest; the sinuous, delicate menace of Japanese courtesans;
the Coney Island blare and the despairing streets of artists she
called the Ashcan School. Art was not enough; there were music
and books in her rather frantic rush of force-feeding culture. From
her large record collection she picked out *Fidelio*, too much for me,
too heavy, too hortatory. I wasn't ready for Beethoven's opera and
she cleverly went back to Chopin mazurkas, her recordings carrying
little gems only vaguely related to the battered shreds of sound
I had heard from too many tenement windows. Marian gave me
books to read: Maupassant stories, the poetry of Heinrich Heine in
a German-English edition, a bilingual copy of Baudelaire's *Flowers
of Evil*. Though deeply impressed with the hot, tangled phrases, the
perfumed odor of decadence, the '*luxe, calme et volupté*', I could no
more cope with these *Flowers* than with *Fidelio*. Eager to appear
capable of understanding anything that was written, since Marian
seemed to expect it of me, I went to the library for a book about
French poetry and quoted, as my own, in my own vocabulary, the
judgments of Baudelaire I had picked up. Marian was impressed
with my critical acumen, turning to Helen with 'Just listen to that,
will you?' I didn't like lying to her, but lying to adults was still not
too difficult. I absolved myself by buying a recording of Debussy's
'*Après-midi d'un faune*' for her. The gift moved her, as an offering
out of my meager earnings and as a reflection of the advanced
musical taste toward which she was speeding me. (I see myself,
over much time and distance, as a project, a piece of work toward
a degree of prime importance which had to be achieved rapidly.
Or was she, like my father, wrapping a fantasy about me, a dream
daughter who would make *her* life glow, enacting a most subtle
form of child abuse?)

When summer arrived and with it the departure of the merry
Goldens, Marian put several English Department heads together
and a summer camp job emerged, as assistant to the dramatics
counselor and supervisor of a group of fifteen- and sixteen-year-old
girls, one or two of them older than I, who had as usual represented
myself as older, eighteen. It was a difficult summer, much tougher
than my summers with the Bergsons, a time of trying to cope
with campers' adolescent cruelties and furies, of desperate
improvisations on the design and execution of costumes, about
which I knew nothing but had to seem knowing. I didn't think

much of the broad green horizontals and dense green verticals of what might have been a pleasant landscape; the landscapes that spoke to me were city streets. Never having been to a summer camp, never having known anyone who had, I found it essential to learn quickly the vocabulary and to use it in recounting fraudulent former camp experiences to my bunkees. There wasn't much else to learn from them, actually, besides the routines of games, crafts hours, and meals, and to appear authoritative, even commanding, to girls older, richer, and – I had to think in self-protection – dopier than I. The sour grapes that made acid scorn of their white shorts bought at Best's, the skirts from Lord & Taylor's, the fluffy angora sweaters and exquisitely boxed cookies from B. Altman's, were one weapon of self-protection, another my superior vocabulary and overprecise, careful speech.

None of it has stayed with me, not one girl, not one counselor, not the name of the camp; nothing, no one except my boss, the drama counselor. She had informed me as we sat together on the train going to the camp that I was to be responsible for the costumes for two big parents' day productions, *Alice in Wonderland* and *Peter Pan*, and they had to be showy, impressive proofs of the camp's creativity, among its other excellences. Unless I wanted her advice or criticism, the designs for all the costumes were to be my creations, and for putting them together there was somewhere in the camp a sewing machine, and a lot of varied materials in the storehouse. I had doodled costumes in my history notebook and had watched my mother use a sewing machine but had never tried it, encouraged by my mother to avoid the skills that, she felt, had imprisoned her. The only sewing I had ever done was the fine hand stitching that went into the awkward, slightly musty graduation dresses we made in the last grade of elementary school. Insisting, after several troubled days, that I couldn't find the sewing machine, that it must have been discarded, I began to sew all the costumes by hand, working through the nights on the challenges I had set for myself. The *pièce* of *Alice in Wonderland* was a close-fitting coattailed suit made entirely of black patent leather for the Mad Hatter. The costume for the dog in *Peter Pan* was made of pieces of rough rope, unraveled into hairy matting, then painstakingly pasted and sewn to a pair of pajamas. The costumes elicited fervid admiration from parents and my bunk charges, who showed surprising pride in their counselor's achievements. I was called out of the props tent to take a bow after the creditable performance.

After she had taken her second bow, the drama counselor joined me in the props tent, spoke her gratitude and admiration, and unexpectedly enfolded me, murmuring endearments and kissing my eyes and hands. I was too tired, too relieved that it was all over, to be much impressed; maybe she was acting out of relief and exhaustion too.

Amy was a tall, slender woman with close-cropped shining brown hair, who wore boys' shirts open at the throat and trousers – not then common among women. She was both graceful and awkward, as a young boy often is, sometimes mute with shyness, at times lyrically voluble. After the costumes and props were put away and the parents left, dropping souvenirs of money and candy as they departed, we both had more time, time for me to walk with her on a tree-lined path outside the camp and to row with her on a nearby lake. She liked to point out slivers of moon and the stars nesting in their curve, she asked me to admire the changing silhouettes of the trees as we glided by and the diamond sparkle of drops as they fell from her raised oars. She spoke of her friends, poets and actresses and painters. It was a delicate courtship, no more kissing, no more words of endearment, simply lyricism as it glowed and sparkled around us and unrevealing bits of biography, tentatively offered.

After a few weeks of walks and rides, when we seemed to have grown comfortable with each other – a little formal, but easy – I found her in the washhouse, scrubbing my laundry, left earlier. For a moment I hated her. How dared she? What colossal nerve, to invade my privacy, to be intimate with my socks, with my shirts, with my bras, my panties! She was trying to close in on me, as Mark had, burdening me with a weight of devotion I couldn't and didn't want to understand, affection that must demand more in return than my limited gratitude, all I could and would give. And maybe now not even gratitude. I hadn't asked, never would, for this bit of slavery, this ugly symbol of devotion, of a grotesque dream marriage. I had heard the girls in my bunk giggling about her and other counselors. They said the women were lesbians, girls' camps were full of them, and they teased me for being the pet of the most conspicuous of the local lot. They were an uneducated but shrewd bunch, frequently justified in their rude judgments, but I was not going to be instructed or intimidated by them. And then there was my insatiable curiosity to be fed. So in spite of the invasion of my laundry and the threat of cloying devotion, I continued on the walks and lake rides, sometimes winsomely, flirtatiously trailing my hand in the water like the lissome girls in English films who spent their blond youth punting on the Cam. The hand stopped trailing the waters prettily, the curiosity waned, the discomfort swelled, when Amy began to recite love poetry and described in greater detail, with more glowing praise, the friends she would like me to meet and whom she was sure I would love. She was slipping more and more of Mark's ropes around me, trying to pull me closer and closer. I knew I would be forced to free myself, forced by a too exigent gesture she must soon make.

The night it happened was a soft night with a pale moon, the stars misty. As we walked, Amy put her arm around my shoulder, turned her face toward mine, and kissed me, long and deeply. I pulled away from her as gently as I could. Here again, as in Harlem, I had gone to the edge of a cliff and couldn't blame the cliff. This was my fault; I should have stopped it days and weeks before and chose not to, flattered and curious, wrapped in a light delirium of power. As I tried to find words to discourage but not hurt her, she grabbed my hand and in an urgent voice begged me to come to live with her. We would go anywhere I liked – France, Spain, Italy, Greece, where she would dedicate her life to me, to keeping me happy forever, and I would never have to worry about money or jobs again. Drowning in this flood, I turned quickly in the direction of the camp, walking rapidly as she walked behind me, calling, 'Think about it, please think about it seriously. I mean every word I say to you.' Had I known then that many sexual approaches carry the words 'forever' and 'I want to make you happy,' evanescent clichés, I would have been less impressed but with little experience, I took the phrases in their full, solemn, literal weight, made heavier with the guilt of having evoked them.

To avoid Amy in later days I told the girls to say I was out when she approached the door to our cabin, or hid in another bunk when I thought she might be looking for me. She soon stopped asking for me, but I could see her sitting on the stairs of her cabin looking across to ours, and soon that, too, stopped. In a cruel mess of contempt, guilt, and mockery, I joined the other girls in a teasing game of nude night swimming, posturing, leaping, revealing as much of ourselves as we could, watching to see if Amy was watching us from her cabin near the pool. We all insisted gleefully that we could see her – there, behind the trees, in a corner of the porch, behind a window. We probably never saw her after a first glimpse and her swift recognition of the hurt we were trying to inflict on her; she was a sensitive, dignified woman, who wore away the remaining camp days in as much seclusion as her job would allow.

When I jumped off the train in Grand Central, my summer job over, it was into the great vault of a Byzantine church, the information desk its exquisite chapel. The surrounding skyscrapers were clustered like majestic, gleaming waterfalls, the slender city sky was alive with forms, with gorges and hills in red brick and shining white stone. The women in their city dresses moved like dancers, the men were as slick and taut as toreros. Over them all – sky, buildings, men, and women – a heat haze, a tremulous, delicate mist that tasted to my skin like honey. This was my habitat and I floated through it in a state of grace. Woolworth's and its enchanting city gimcrackery was my first place of welcome. Having feasted, I took the subway to Marian's apartment and spilled a witty stream of complaint: all the greenery I could accept was about the size of a city block, more was too much; the girls in my bunk were crass and ignorant, when they weren't outright stupid. (Not then, or in letters before, did I mention Amy, except flatly as the dramatics counselor for whom I worked. For reasons that weren't clear, I had a feeling that more talk about Amy would open a Pandora's box and I wouldn't know how to handle its evils.) Marian told me about her summer, in a distant corner of Connecticut, and the interesting friends she had made, people I would meet when we went there for a weekend, soon. Would I like a sandwich before I went home? No, thanks, and I wasn't going home. For the time being I would probably stay with Rosie, whose mother was a grumbler, but a quick forgetter of grievances, and between her job, no husband to look after – the legend was that he had run off with a greenhorn boarder some years back – and her Workmen's Circle meetings, not much at home anyhow. In the meantime, I would look for a full-time job and transfer to an evening high school. Marian looked dismayed; so much of her effort and expectancies to be washed away in drabness, in ordinariness. 'But you seem to forget,' she said, 'about the college scholarship my friend is trying to arrange for you. I haven't talked much about it, but now it looks almost sure. They don't require math, and your English record, and the very good chance that you'll get the English medal when you graduate, should get you a creative writing scholarship, maybe as soon as next year.' As I leaped at her with eagerness for more details and assurance, she said, 'Before we discuss anything else, go to see your mother, who's been worried about you and it would be cruel to keep worrying her.' (Something I rarely thought of and will feel dreadful about into my grave.)

The visit home was stiff. My mother didn't ask me why I hadn't written her all summer, why she had to find out if I was all right by calling Marian every Saturday morning from the corner drugstore. When I told her, as I had before, as flatly as I could, that I was not coming back to live with the family or with the Goldens, that I was going to work and attend evening school and find myself a room somewhere, she said she couldn't blame me for leaving. Only keep in touch and if I needed a few dollars to let her know; she would send it with my brother if I didn't want to come to the house. Her pretty mouth was tight in her white face, her fingers tightly clasped in her lap. I put the things I had left in a big paper bag, said good-bye, and went to the door. I would have liked to speak the sudden wild sadness I felt and, as sudden and profound, the sympathy I felt for her. But I didn't know how. Hesitating at the door, I said good-bye again. She didn't move. I walked out, closing the door gently behind me; no abrupt final noise.

Rosie's mother was not especially pleased when I appeared, but she was busy preparing to visit friends and hadn't much time to object. More important, Rosie was the sun in her life and she didn't want to displease her, possibly lose her as my mother was losing me. Instructing us not to burn the chicken when we reheated it, not to leave her our dirty supper dishes, not to track up the kitchen floor; I was to wash my hair, it looked messy, and wash the sink afterward; there was a blanket folded into the cot in the corner of Rosie's room (no sheets, but I was accustomed to that), and Rosie wasn't to forget her Jewish homework for her Shalom Aleichem school, and we weren't to talk all night, she threw a fringed Russian shawl over her skirt and blouse and dashed out. School was not yet in session and Rosie and I spent delicious days visiting with friends. I told highly colored stories of my life in camp (no mention of Amy) and they talked about new boyfriends they had met as mother's helpers in the country, their stories as richly embellished, I suspected, as mine. On the money I had earned during the summer – mainly tips from parents – I treated Rosie to the movies and big ice-cream cones, and to win her mother's favor, supplied the breakfast bagels and farmer cheese. She was impressed; such an adult, nice gesture, maybe I was outgrowing my irresponsible *bummerkeh* stage.

The days with Rosie and her mother exhausted my money. Reluctantly, I decided to visit my laundry to ask for a full-time job; it would be infinitely easier to talk to Vito, the Italian boss who liked to pinch my cheeks and my behind, than to search want ads and stammer my way through interrogations about my age and experience to an inimical business face that I always imagined as lean, hard-jawed, gimlet-eyed, as immobile and unresponsive as a mannequin in a store window. I was also worried about job applications that would ask my religion; 'Jewish' might damn me and I refused to lie, bound not at all by religion but by a firm tribal loyalty. The day before I was to see Vito, however, a letter arrived from Marian's place in the country, addressed care of Rosie. She had a job for me that offered room and board, it wouldn't interfere with my part-time jobs nor with continuing at James Monroe High School. One of Marian's friends needed a mother-sitter, someone to stay several afternoons and evenings with her elderly, widowed mother, someone to run errands and keep the old woman company when the daughter went out.

I knew the forbidding, sharp-voiced Miss Sonntag slightly, and had a premonition that I wouldn't please her. She was quite amiable, or at least very polite, as she explained my job and asked if I could start – bring my things – a few days later. There was no bedroom for me, but a convertible couch in the living room, which contained, as well, bookshelves, pictures, and a baby grand piano. The coat closet in the hallway had enough room for my clothing, and a cabinet next to the closet would serve for the rest of my wardrobe and my schoolbooks. A Negro lady came to do general cleaning and the laundry – not mine – once a week. I was to see that the bathroom and kitchen were clean and to do some light dusting between the cleaning woman's visits, said Miss Sonntag. As she spoke, I wanted to like her. I couldn't; her voice was too commanding, she was too large, blocking out all the space and air around her, and her square head reminded me of the people of my unfavorite painter, Léger; her big jaw was like part of a machine. I can't think that she liked me either, but she needed me and it was her social duty, Marian undoubtedly told her, to help a gifted girl who was drawn to the brink of trouble.

It was a proper, respectable, uncomfortable place, everything placed squarely and neatly, the furniture always highly polished, the window shades always at the same level, the white-enameled garbage pail always gleaming in its immutable niche.

The shining white garbage pail, infinitely more refined than the tin bucket kicked around in my mother's kitchen, seemed too fine a container for used sanitary napkins – I had long graduated from strips of old sheets – so I stashed them for a couple of days shortly after my arrival in a paper bag in my cabinet, intending to dump them in a street basket. But I never seemed to find the opportunity to take them out of the hallway quickly and inconspicuously. I hoped the Sonntags wouldn't notice the hideous stench that was growing out of the cabinet and filling the hallway. Reproval came dryly, tersely, from Miss Sonntag: That terrible odor, it was rotting sanitary pads, wasn't it? I was to wrap the soiled pads in the old newspapers under the kitchen sink and put them in the garbage pail, which was placed outside the door for the super to collect every night. Intensely miserable, feeling loathsome and filthy, I wrapped the bag in huge wads of newspaper under her unmoving eyes and jammed it into the pristine pail. The shame hung on my chest like a big rock. I took everything out of the cabinet and scrubbed it. I bathed carefully every night – not my Lafontaine or camp habit – and still the stink was on me for many days.

Miss Sonntag remained correct, stiffly kind, and even persuaded me to play piano duets with her. I was out of practice and resistant, nor was she very skillful, so the results were halts and starts and abused passages, but when we were able to do a page or two properly together it was so satisfying, so happy an experience, that I liked her in spite of her Léger face and voice. Those times I called her Sara, as she had several times asked me to, though I usually had difficulty forcing such intimacy from my mouth.

The mother was small and round, with little features, like my mother, and, like my mother, eager for merriment. She walked with difficulty – I never knew why – and few neighbors visited her; Sara discouraged what she called 'tenement sociability'. There were no grandchildren for impromptu, after-school visits; her other children and their spouses visited only on week-ends, though they spoke with her frequently on the telephone. She read a good deal, she talked long with the once-a-week cleaning woman, learning much about her dour days,but it was still a lonely life and a limited one for such an animated, intelligent old woman. It was at least partially because she was lonely that she greeted me so effusively when I got back from school, and quickly told me what the cleaning lady had recounted that day, the funny joke her youngest son had told her on the phone, and that the super's wife was pregnant again. Then we made a grocery shopping list, the last item always, 'Buy yourself some cookies or chocolate or whatever you like.' The evenings that Sara was out, Mrs. Sonntag told entertaining stories about her youth and early schooling on the Lower East Side, and remembering, she laughed as my mother laughed, with a flood of tears rushing down her cheeks. Convinced that I was not lovable, was a self-centered slob, I had to admit that she probably loved me, or something close. Although I was confused by the many uses of the word 'love' and wasn't at all sure of how it should feel, I almost certainly loved her, the grandmother I never knew, and like the baby brother I once took care of (now embedded in a sturdy pubescent boy), weak in the legs and dependent on me. To keep her entertained during our evening hours together at the kitchen table, I would note and record everything I saw and heard around me: the two bedbugs that crawled out of the library book of a girl who had been boasting to a friend that her mother was an ardent cleaner; the old woman who approached me at a bus stop on a cold night to say, in Yiddish, 'Don't be such an *elegantke*, wrap your shawl around your head.' (How did the woman know I was being Eleonora Duse, the romantic shawl lifting and dropping picturesquely on my shoulders as I heroically braved the wind?)

I told Mrs. Sonntag about Mr. Goldberg, in whose English class we had spent one whole semester listening to him read *Green Mansions*. He looked, I told her, like a counterman in a delicatessen, round and moist, and he had the expected concomitant Yiddish intonation. That was an exaggeration, but he did have a cantorial lilt, usually controlled, except when he was carried away. And Rima, the heroine, carried him away; he was in love with her as if she were real and his own true palpable love. I liked to imagine fat-nosed Mr. Goldberg imagining himself a slim, blond lover in a loincloth, a poetic Tarzan, caressing the long, shining hair of his beloved. Mr. Goldberg was abetted by a unique accompaniment, almost a musical obbligato, to his reading. One of the girls in the class had riches of red-brown hair, her star attraction, and she pinned it around her head in a variety of inventive styles that required a battery of pins. As Mr. Goldberg's Chassidic cadences trembled in adoration of Rima, the girl slowly removed the hairpins, one by careful one, releasing

one long red-brown loop and then another, placing the hairpins in
her lap carefully so that not the faintest tinkle might sound. She
ran her fingers through the garlands and swags of hair until it was
all down, shook her head a little, and then sat enraptured, elbows
on the desk, fingers intertwined beneath her chin, half-hidden and
mysterious in her silken tent. We all waited for the moment in the
reading that would inspire her act; inevitably it came; inevitably we
called her CooCoo the Bird Girl, a then-famous freak attraction in
Coney Island. Mrs. Sonntag was enamored of Mr. Goldberg, Rima,
and CooCoo the Bird Girl, and I reported the events of each class,
introducing as many entertaining details as I could invent. I also
told my responsive old lady about Mr. Cantaro of the History
Department, a short man who looked a bit like Adolphe Menjou and
was a passionate admirer of Napoleon, stressing his hero's amours
as he looked out the window at the schoolyard, searching for the
lost, heroic world that was rightly his and, we generally agreed,
to show off his supercilious profile. She also learned from me all
of Dr. Huebner's primitive, effective teaching jokes. Her favorite
was the story of a soprano soloist singing with an orchestra led by
a very animated conductor. Boy in a distant seat: 'Why is the man
with the stick beating the lady?' 'He's not beating her, he's leading
the music.' 'Then why is she screaming so?'

Eavesdropping in the grocery store, on the bus, in the school
lunchroom, everywhere, I brought to my old lady vignettes,
witticisms, stupidities, weather reports, news of dry stringy
bushes losing their last leaves. I complained to her about a movie
hero singer who looked and sounded like an empty can, probably
affected by my mother's earlier judgment of him as 'a blond shitter'
(much more contemptible in Yiddish). I remembered for her and
described the shapes and corsets and bras I had seen in the crowded
communal dressing room of Klein's and the eager-eyed girls who
sat on ladders to watch for the thieves who put on one new dress
over another and their own old dress over the new obscured
acquisitions, then waddled out carrying nothing, paying nothing
if they weren't caught. Bringing to my old lady these gifts to color
her narrow life was my first experience of prolonged, voluntary
solicitude, and a pleasing one. It also made me look at my mother
in a new light and imagine her growing old and lonely. I began to
visit her more and more frequently when my father was at work,
and after slow, formal beginnings – 'How are you?' 'All right,
how are you?' – I began to tell her the stories I told my old lady.

I lost my plump Russian-doll grandmother and my two surrogate mothers, the hot and the cold, within a year. The first move was Sara Sonntag's. Sara liked to keep up with youngsters she had met and encouraged in her years of settlement work, her favorites in my time a group of boys, some in jobs, a couple in college. A few of them were invited on frequent weekend evenings to eat rich cakes and drink big glasses of cream soda and to sing to Sara's accompaniment selections from Franz Lehár and Victor Herbert operettas. Being myself in a pure Bach period, particularly the unaccompanied violin music, which I found dry and undigestible, therefore the acme of great music, I scorned their silly stuff, but as a member of the household – and Sara considered this type of socializing part of my education, too – I was asked to join in and reluctantly did. Between wondering what she saw in them, what they saw in her, didn't they have anything better to do on weekend evenings, and why was Sara's color so high and her speech so excited, I carefully, critically examined them. Tom – a suspect name for a Jewish boy – was tall, with strong features; he sang loudly, talked a lot, moved quickly and flashily, and was very arch with Sara, already the actor he was determined to be. Davy was slight, quick, and funny. I would have liked him more if he weren't obviously enjoying the dopey stuff and if Sara weren't so hectically bright and grotesquely flirtatious when she spoke to him. Danny was quietly polite and clearly there because his friends had dragged him along and he had nothing else to do those evenings. Conversation over the slabs of cake were nostalgic bits that referred back to experiments in amateur theatricals and the fun they all had together. 'Remember when Ralph kept tripping on his sword in *The Gondoliers?*' 'Remember when Millie forgot the words of "The Moon and I" and we had to shout them to her from backstage?' I sat and smiled with their laughter, taking time out for several visits with my more entertaining old friend, reading in the bedroom.

The boys' attitude toward me was minimally polite, and vice versa, until Davy began to talk to me, to ask me questions, to say my blue dress looked nice on me. As I stood in the kitchen one evening, filling glasses of soda, he came in with a loud, 'Let me help you,' and in helping, whispered, 'Let's meet next Sunday and maybe take a walk, you and I.' He was clearly Sara's property and I suggested, also whispering, that she might be mad. 'Let her be,' he said, and rattling the full tray of glasses, said, 'Three o'clock at the elephant house, Bronx Zoo.' Sara was home that day, writing

reports, and I was free to meet him. We fell together as if we had
been waiting for this for a long time. Since it was late fall and there
were few people to see us, we huddled together like the animals
and kissed and kissed. In front of the indifferent snakes, before
the censorious eyes of the eagles, and the curiosity of the deer
and pacing tigers, we kissed and hugged. On later excursions,
because public kissing was rare, we staged farewells at subway
stations, at smelly El stations, at bus stops, and expanded our
field to Penn Station and Grand Central, where many tracks
offered many places for fake leavetakings of high emotion. The
very best place was the top of a Fifth Avenue bus, designed for an
infinity of kissing and necking on its long route from Washington
Square up into Washington Heights. We were soon spending all
our spare time together, if only for an hour. The happy, excited
dashing and Davy's phone calls should have explained themselves
and I decided that lying, a first impulse, would be too complicated
and too demeaning. When I announced that I was leaving to meet
Davy and would be back at seven o'clock so Sara could get to her
concert, the old lady said, 'That's nice. Give him my regards.' Sara
said nothing.

The half-expected complaints began to roll out. Sara had offered
me shelter, she said, because she wanted me to be in a steady
environment that would make me a good student and possible
college material. It appeared to be a wasted effort since I wasn't
studying or doing much homework. And I was jeopardizing Davy's
record as well; City College made high demands on its students and
dropped by the score those who didn't meet its standards. I might
consider him and his career, too. How come the top of the piano
was so dusty? I had left grease spots on last night's dishes, washed
too fast and carelessly, always ready to run. The washcloths in
the bathroom were for the face, not scrubbing the basin. She
did not, could not, complain about my concern for her mother.
Davy and Grandma liked each other, too, and we often spent
evenings together, a contented threesome, cracking nuts, peeling
tangerines, laughing, when Sara was out. I sent Davy home early
those evenings, not so much afraid of Sara's jealousy, but sorry
– I was becoming almost human in the refulgent climate of
love with Davy, with my old lady, love with myself – for a
plain middle-aged woman too much moved by an eighteen-year-old
boy, the chosen boy, who preferred a rough-edged, uncouth girl.
The smart old mother must have been aware of the unrequited

attachment. She was probably sorry for her daughter and impatient of such foolishness, but said nothing about her and rejoiced in us beamishly.

Sara announced one evening that she was bringing in a practical nurse to care for her mother, a woman who would sleep on the convertible couch and would be in attendance all day. There was no obvious deterioration in the mother's condition, but something like this had to happen, this maneuver for getting rid of me. As usual and because I was too happy with Davy to worry, I had no alternate plan. He helped me pack and waited for me outside the house while I said good-bye, now with sadness and open affection, to my old lady, promising to phone her frequently; she was too wise and honest to ask me to visit. Davy took me to his parents' house, a poorer and smaller apartment than our tenement flat on Lafontaine Avenue, crammed with cots for relatives from Williamsburg who carried their own hard-boiled eggs and *challa* because Davy's mother was forgetfully semikosher. And she, direct and fatalistic, said, 'What the hell, one more,' as she shoved her young daughter to the side of a single bed to make room for me. 'You, Davy, sleep where you always sleep, in the bedroom with the other boys, and stay there. No gidgee in this house.'

20

'Birds Do It...'

School continued and the part-time jobs, including Vito's pinches, and I continued to see Marian on the weekends – theater, concerts, education, restaurants, and all – when Davy had to work or study. Among the techniques of Cubism, the symbolism of Kandinsky, and the novelty of Schönberg's scale were interposed expressions of boredom with my virginity. Again a return to the wonderful lover my neck and shoulders and big mouth promised (flattered always and occasionally appalled as I saw myself as some sort of roast of mouth, neck, and shoulders, followed by rich undefined desserts). Marian knew just the man to lead me into elegant sex after a poetic deflowering.

One spring weekend I met the man, whose first name I never knew; we'll call him Jones. After a mottled career of wandering and working at several trades, he had found himself the leader of a leftist group – several kinds of left, from pity socialism to bombing for anarchy – which settled in a far reach of Connecticut. Largely self-taught, he was remarkably well-read and well-informed, especially in American history, whose most attractive personage was, to him, Brigham Young. On a reduced scale he duplicated Young's life quite successfully. He, too, was chieftain of a small, polygamous tribe, though, as a devotee of free love, he did not take his women in marriage. He had in his wanderings found a Mexican tribe whose design for living he also admired and tried to adapt for himself. The Indians kept one woman, he recounted, for household chores and carrying water from a distant well; another took care of the children, everyone's; one woman was the prime producer of babies; the youngest and prettiest was for love alone. Though it was difficult to find the proper number of women of the proper dispositions for so exquisitely efficient a scheme, he managed well in his narrower pattern. Three of his women were in their forties, career spinsters with enough money to keep a man, at least partially, in exchange for his favors and as pioneers in this unique manifestation of equal rights. One woman paid the rent for his well-equipped, warm cabin. Another kept him in utilities, woodsman's boots, and virile woodsman's shirts. Marian was the best cook, so she provided his lunches and dinners. Preparing breakfast was the ceremony performed by the woman who had 'been pleasured', as he put it, the night before. A continuous surprise to me was the fact that the women were polite, even hospitable and kindly, with one another. There was a number four, but she was not of the circle. She was younger, in her early twenties, singularly pretty, it was said, and her cabin a distance outside the settlement. Thus she was rarely seen, but strongly felt, especially since Jones stayed with her for two or three days at a time. It was an impossibly long walk to her house he explained, there was no bus, he had no car or bike, so he had to stay a couple of days. (Clearly, this was the youngster to be used for pleasure in beauty and sex in the Mexican style, I thought, and the others probably thought, though she was rarely mentioned.) Marian explained the various details of their design for living rather proudly, as if it were a privilege to be a member of so singularly advanced a society, a bold step in man's evolution. Wasn't she ever jealous? I asked. Of course not. Jealousy was a primitive thing, an atavism of an urge to possess that was a root of capitalism. How could free, intelligent men and women justify owning each other? I didn't ask again, lost in admiration of these heroic women who could do what I certainly couldn't. I seethed and my stomach churned when a girl tried to link arms with Davy or even touched his shoulder.

A later weekend in Connecticut, a picture-postcard weekend of blossoming trees and blossoms in the grass, Marian invited several local friends, including Jones, for an evening of large, good eating, followed by singing. We sang spirituals and Russian folk songs (the combination a telling symbol of left leanings) to a guitar and a mandolin. Between songs, the mandolin player, a skinny man with a Russian accent and doleful eyes, stroked my arm, brushed pink by the sun, crooning, 'Byoochiful, such byoochiful,' and asked me to walk with him in the woods the next day, Sunday, to look at 'byoochiful tris end flowvis.' Marian quickly took me aside to say that Jones expected to take me to the woods tomorrow for

my deflowering ('really *flowering*,' she said) ritual. I thanked the
Russian, promised him another time, and turned to look longer
and harder at Jones. He was good-looking in a history-book-picture
way, clear and American, like Thomas Jefferson. He looked almost
as old as Jefferson, I thought, certainly much older than my father.
But Marian was a conoisseur of lovers, and anyone who pleased as
many women as Jones did must be remarkably skillful. I tried to
comfort myself with that thought while I worried, still, about the
pain my friends told me to expect, a fact that Marian pooh-poohed;
a little twinge, a moment's discomfort, a drop of blood, maybe,
nothing to it – and cured by passion. This technical matter
had, of course, nothing to do with Davy though it might provide
instruction for both of us.

Sunday was warm and fragrant, and we were given a light
lunch by Marian, who thought it would be best for what was
to follow. (Her planning offended me, so lacking in poetry, but
maybe that was the way of sophisticated, incomprehensible worlds.
And then again, almost every situation and person I encountered
seemed strange to some degree or other. I had long accepted life as
meshugge, to use the favorite parental word.) As Jones and I left the
house shortly after lunch, I half expected Aunt Pandarus to shout
erotic blessings on us, but she just continued to smile from the
doorway as we headed across the fields toward a deep stand of
birches and flowering shrubs. As we walked, Jones talked of the
beauty and fecundity of nature; the millions of blossoms waiting to
give way to fruit, their seeds to become more blossoms, more fruit,
more seeds. Had I noticed the stuff that looked like spit when we
crossed the brook? That was the beginning of frogs, thousands of
them. Those nests in the trees before us held new eggs, the birds
soon ready to break the shells, then learn to fly and mate, to make
more eggs. All these profligate, beautiful cycles were the music with
which the male element awakened nature's spirit in the female. In a
less exalted mode, I had heard all this in biology class, in another
mode in poetry, in yet another in the movies and novels, and in
yet another in dirty jokes. He wasn't telling me anything new but
was telling it in a rich, measured voice and a cadenced vocabulary
– like a ballet to baroque music. At one particularly welcoming
and sheltering clump of trees he sat down and gestured for me to sit
with him. He continued to speak of the overwhelmingly generous
fruitfulness of nature flowing from the mysteries of sexuality, the
divine power of sex. A city girl assaulted by the warmth of sun,

the odor of leaves and grasses, and breezes of delicate air, I grew sleepy. I tried to keep my eyes wide open, rubbed them awake but couldn't resist leaning against a tree trunk, and fell fast asleep.

An easy explanation, among a couple of others, might be that falling asleep was an act of avoidance. Losing one's virginity was not like having a tooth pulled, as I had tried to tell myself; it was being a citizen of a new country, a new person forced in among the motley others I was: scholar, aesthete, writer, the woman in a coarse country cloak who devoted her virgin talents to a greater one, like Dorothy Wordsworth to brother William, like Mary Lamb, when she wasn't mad, to brother Charles. What would happen to my life with Davy when I became an experienced nonvirgin? In spite of my failed, clumsy foray into Harlem, I didn't want to be a 'lay', a thing I might become, a thing of submissiveness and victimization, of being flattened and mounted, maybe spreading for someone I hardly knew. I was troubled, too, about the potential looks of Jones's elderly penis. I had never actually seen one close up (subway flashers were too fast) except on statues in the Metropolitan Museum, and in spite of the sleek white perfection of the classic bodies, or because of it, the genitals looked like pasted-on afterthoughts, brutish clusters inappropriate to the androgynous grace of these demi-gods. If that's what they looked like on Apollo, imagine the kind of grotesquerie an old man dangled from the bottom of his belly.

And Jones had let me fall asleep; his dozens of allusions and illustrations, his spate of poetic clichés, might have been *his* avoidance. As soon as I opened my eyes after a gentle nudge from him, he began to say he had chosen not to disturb me because I looked so much like a sleeping wood sprite, a dryad of ancient myths. Under my fake smile of flattered pleasure, there was a silent grumbling: 'Shut up, please, shut up.' Yet I kept nodding and smiling as we started back, trying to look responsive and intelligent while he went on, this time roaming in Greek mythology, singing the glorious life of Zeus, who could become a swan, a bull, anyone, anything, and cause any nymph to become enamored of him and eager for mating. By the time he reached the cruel, destructive jealousy of wife Juno, we had arrived at Marian's house. We both put on sly, contented smiles as we opened the door. Marian was alone, sitting on the edge of her couch, holding a book. To her questioning smile I answered nothing, torn between a light regret at having disappointed her and the pleasure of having foiled her.

Jones said I had fallen asleep with too much breeze and sun and looked so enchanting among the trees that he didn't want to wake me. Another time; there was no rush and shouldn't be about these matters, should there?

A later weekend we were taken on a long drive by the Russian in his rattling, last-breath car, Marian, Jones, and I, to a beach where the tide was very low and the water shallow for a long distance into the sea. As I walked into the water, Jones came to me, put his arm around my waist, said something about Ibsen's Lady from the Sea, and paced our steps to a slow, ritualistic walk, suggesting that we might keep going forever until the sea covered us. A sucker for any poetic idea, any extreme gesture, I was almost ready to try. Having grown familiar with his hyperbole, however, I knew at the same time that he was no more interested in drowning, however poetically, than I. The long solemn progress, as to a temple, stopped when we were out of sight of our friends on the beach and still only waist deep in the water. He turned toward me and kissed me fully and breathlessly long. Still holding me, he pulled his head back to look searchingly into my eyes. The act had to be played out, so I kept my eyes centered on his, hoping they suggested something profound and moving. I couldn't keep it up as long as he did; that other self, my doppelgänger (a word I had borrowed from Schubert), was standing a few feet away, saying I looked like a dolt and why the lying gestures? I wasn't lying, I answered. This was an attractive game I might never play again. Where would I find another Jones? And anyhow, now was not the time to hurt the old man's feelings, fake as they might possibly be, as fake as mine. As my eyes dropped, they stopped at his wrinkled neck, slid down to the sag of breast, down to the belly pouch slanting sadly like a half-filled sack, down to the back of his hand, which carried a purple tree of thickened veins. And he talked too, too damned much. In spite of Marian's injunctions and recommendations and the important fact that Jones might be the instrument of a college scholarship, as Marian had half promised, it was not this one who would lead me to Orphic joys. Davy would do me for the time being; to hell with the technicalities. They would come, I was sure, sometime.

In spite of his frustrating experience with me, Jones didn't altogether lose interest in my butterfly-blue veins under my peach-down skin, in his phrase. He dashed at me unexpectedly, some months after the walk into the sea, in the lobby of Carnegie

Hall, where we were separately attending a performance of Bach's B Minor Mass. Behind him stood the woman who paid for his rent and, apparently, for his concert tickets, looking around, carefully not observing us as he fervidly kissed my hands and face. A few days later I received a letter from him, an elaborate tapestry of words about the Lady from the Sea, about striding into the belly of the Amniotic Mother Sea together, about a long kiss that was a mystic seal, about the exultant celebration of Nature and man in Bach's music. The mingling of Ibsen, Bach, the sea, the long kiss, the birthing fluid – the extravaganza of phrases – was beyond my patience, old-fashioned and ludicrous to the aficionado of stark Hemingway prose and sharply etched Frost poetry I then was. Enclosed with the letter were two tickets at five dollars each for a weekend festival and dance in his Connecticut community. An attached note explained that the tickets were a gift, one for a boy I might want to bring along, and not to worry about accommodations; he had made all arrangements.

Youth trampling middle age, shrieking in triumph, it may unconsciously have been, but it seemed natural – I didn't question or hesitate for a moment – to show the letter to Marian. She was my closest friend, my teacher in all things important, the begetter of my friendship with Jones, and should be interested in the letter and the tickets. I dashed to her lunchroom table, waving the letter, on the very day I received it. The letter didn't seem to impress her. She skimmed it quickly, muttering, 'The usual seduction junk', but the tickets flung her into an astonishing fury, a storm I would never have suspected in my ideal of the cultivated, worldly woman, the revered mentor. Like a coarse market woman, like the immigrant peasants of my childhood when they threatened their kids, Marian's face became distorted and poured out sour words in a harsh shrillness. 'He sent you two tickets, two, for free? He never spent a cent on me or Lydia or Maggie! And now for a snot of sixteen he uses the money we give him, hard-earned money! And don't think he'll find a bed for the boy you're supposed to invite; he'll put you in his own bed and let the boy sleep in a cold cellar! Ten dollars! Ten dollars! I just bought him an imported shirt for ten dollars and was going to buy him an English raincoat for his birthday.' She spat out at me, 'You buy him the goddamned raincoat! Take my place, see if you can support him and his lordly tastes on your part-time pennies.' I protested that I didn't want the tickets, I had no one to go with, I didn't want to go, I didn't even have the bus fare. She didn't listen but kept spitting venom on him and me.

The next morning, when we met in the hall, she wouldn't speak to me. She turned away from me in the lunchroom and rushed by when I waited for her after school. She never spoke to me again. Distraught and bewildered, the earth dissolving under my feet, the college scholarship she and Jones were to arrange fading from sight, I wrote her explaining that I had not seen or been in touch with Jones except for that chance encounter in Carnegie Hall. She knew everything that had gone on between us and nothing but words really had, I had no wish to become one of his harem, I didn't want to sleep with him, ever, I was not going to the festival – had returned the tickets, in fact – and I couldn't understand why she was so angry with me for an act of Jones's. I had not meant to hurt her and was deeply sorry if I had. I would be grateful if she explained to me just what it was I had done to make her hate me so. She didn't answer the letter and I cut school several times during the next two weeks, mainly not to meet her and see her turn her head away. Afraid of the hazards of cutting, however, I returned to school, avoiding the lunchroom, the sections of hall and stairways near her classroom. I went to school early and left late to avoid meeting her in the street.

She had in several ways given me a Promised Land and had taken it away, leaving me abandoned, foreign to myself and my surroundings. No more theater and Italian mussels, no more artbooks and operatic records, no more verbal cadenzas about sex, no more the feeling of being a cherished child at the same time that I was a grown-up among grown-ups. Who would care what I thought of the design of an Art Nouveau chair, if I read Montaigne, if I knew what Heywood Broun had said that morning, whether I had money for a pack of cigarettes? I became again the raw armature of the piece of sculpture she seemed for a while to have been so vigorously shaping. Who would be the next armature? What would happen to her life with Jones? Would she leave him because of me? What happened to the woman who scorned jealousy?

Eve expelled from Paradise, with Davy-Adam at my side when he wasn't working, I began to explore the city: streets of the Lower East Side Joe had not taught me, the Greek flower market in the West Twenties, and to the east, restaurants Moroccan, Lebanese, Armenian, wafting spicy odors. We learned the Czechoslovakian, the Hungarian, the German craftshops of fine cabinetmaking and violin repair in the East Seventies and Eighties, and the red-checkered tablecloths in their kitchenlike restaurants. We found the Ukrainians with their blouses and painted eggs and honey on Seventh Street. We walked across the Brooklyn Bridge toward stately unused warehouses and, above, old houses and their magnificent views of Manhattan. And back and forth, back and forth, on the Staten Island ferry and the Fifth Avenue bus. Once cloistered in the ghettos of home and school, we were becoming tireless, impassioned New Yorkers. The incomprehensible world of Marian faded slowly, gradually; pictures I saw were often those she had taught me, music I heard was hers, books I read had her stamp on their pages, and from place to place in my restless youth I carried a small bilingual leather-bound volume of the poems of Heinrich Heine that she had given me. I still have it.

21

Hunter College

Through an agent I despised, viperous Ruthie, I was pushed along my peripatetic journey from bed to bed, room to room, to a small room on Commerce Street in the Village. I was quite contented with its modest virtues – hooks for my undemanding wardrobe, the two shelves that held my underclothing and books – and particularly pleased with the small, arrogant mouse who would stare at me from the curtain rod as I stared at him; banging, shoe-throwing had little effect: he left only when he had enough of me. My landlady, Mrs. Essen, was the handsome, graceful mother of vicious, ugly Ruthie, the source of the most poisonous gossip in James Monroe, designed to knife friendships she envied. The girl lived with her father, hating her mother and her stepfather ('She isn't really married to that shit, she's his mistress and the kid is illegitimate' – Ruthie speaking) and especially her radiant bright-haired younger half-sister. What might have been Ruthie's room became mine, for a small fee and the obligation to sit with the little girl when the couple went to the Yiddish theaters on Second Avenue and later sat with their actor friends in the Café Royale, across the street from the most influential theater. We all got along very well, I often treated as a guest, invited to listen to the poetry readings of Mr. Essen, a director, and a failed poet. The Yiddish of his verse was simple enough to understand. What was difficult were his narrow fields of simile: children, women's eyes, small flowers, were all *ziggalach*, young goats – a disconcerting dullness as I made unfair comparisons with the great Romantic poets.

On New Year's Eve Mrs. Essen asked if Davy and I would like to accompany her to the Café Royale, where we would celebrate with her husband and their friends of the theater. We eagerly would and did. The deep, wide room was dazzlingly

lit, as noisy as a market and as brilliantly, gaudily colored as a
Gypsy camp. We recognized a few of the actors as Essen guests
and as Second Avenue billboard posters, all of them in full stage
makeup, cheeks hectic, eyes blazing. Several of the women wore
large embroidered Spanish shawls with deep tassels that they
tossed, stroked, and wound around their crimson-nailed fingers.
One famous tragedienne wore a tall, blaring-red turban; another,
with heavily kohl-circled eyes, sported a yellowed ermine capelet,
her hands buried in its matching Anna Karenina muff. They called
and waved and hugged each other and ran from table to table
to exchange laughter and fervent affection. Davy and I were
introduced to a few people, who kissed us roundly, admired
our youth and beauty, then turned back to praise magnificent
performances, superb costumes, imaginative direction, admiring
each other extravagantly. Left on our own after the initial
welcomes, Davy and I made our way through the darting bodies,
the tassels, the furs, the dashing hats and billowing neckerchiefs,
to the crowded table of a quiet, smiling group listening to one
droll-faced man. He was the famous journalist of whom we had
heard, who could maintain a conversation or a long monologue
on almost any subject in rhymed couplets in Yiddish, quite a feat.
He was adroit, funny, and gracious enough to invent a lilting set of
couplets for us 'rosy baby lovers'.

It was a happy time. The mouse stayed faithful, Davy was always
welcome, I had my very own keys. Except for sitting with the little
golden girl once in a while, I was free, after school and work hours,
to be an envied denizen of the Village, to buy a couple of cookies
at Sutter's on Bleecker Street late at night as they came out of the
redolent ovens. I could stare in at parties through the long windows
of Horatio Street, imagine myself behind the flowers and the New
Orleans ironwork on Eleventh Street near fifth, drop in to talk with
the Sicilian shoemaker on Carmine Street who baked orange rind
on the top of a small stove to rid the narrow shop of the smells
of glue and polish. I could buy apples at Balducci's broad fruit
stall at the corner of Greenwich and Sixth and stand across from
the women's prison on Tenth Street hoping to catch a significant
criminal happening or at least a roundup of prostitutes. I could
walk in Washington Square Park on a Sunday morning to watch
the children on the swings and slides or sit down with a book
near a young man rocking a baby carriage, estimating how long it
would take him to ask what I was reading and pull a conversation

out of that. Several times conversation with men no longer very young – late thirties or forty – turned to nostalgic, dreamy narratives of how they played in their childhood parks, in their streets, and what movie stars they worshiped, accounts that were both wistful views of a lost world and a gift, a gift of a kind of lovemaking, subtle but unmistakable.

For another sort of small lovemaking I could go to the cafeteria on Sheridan Square to find a saturnine young composer I had once grappled with at a party. He always sat at a window seat, covering lined music paper with rapid notes and quick strokes of bars, waving the paper about from time to time to help the notes dry and, my bitchiness told me, to gather as much attention to himself and his art as was possible from a cafeteria seat. Since our grappling evening, he knew that the attack direct wouldn't work with me. A newer tack was meant to work on my sensibilities, my sympathy. He told me in one manuscript-waving cafeteria conversation that his hearing was growing dull, dim, not as sharp as a musician's should be. I knew, of course, that Beethoven was deaf and couldn't hear his last great works at all, didn't I? And the same was happening to him, he was afraid. But if Beethoven could live and work in deafness, so could he. The lips quivered a bit, the eyelids drooped, as if to hold back tears. I would have been deeply moved had I not witnessed this act once or twice before, and seen him respond to seductive pianissimo voices when he chose to.

I had the small conquests, a vivacious neighborhood, a room of my own, money, meager but my own, a boyfriend of my own, a life of my own, responsible only to those for whom I felt responsible, and they were few. I would always be unassailable, unconquerable. I would never die.

Life's rains washed out my lovely parade. Ruthie the viper had to leave her father's house; his new wife wouldn't have her another day, the lying little bitch. Her mother dreaded having her but had no choice. In genuine sorrow compounded with many fears, my landlady with the vulnerable face explained that I had to go. Expulsion from Paradise I could brook but not expulsion from my vivid and, at that time, only a shade self-conscious Village. An ad in the local paper – *The Villager*, I think – led me to 'a loft on historic Bank Street' (historic because the banks of the eighteenth century were moved up here for the summer months when yellow fever attacked the crowded city to the south). The loft was a papery attic, cut into three or four segments. My room, at three dollars a week, was wedged into the slant of a steep roof gable, offering low snug shelter for the shaky cot and a few feet of space to sit and stand in normally. My neighbor, a taciturn woman who appeared to keep the nine-to-five hours of a job, seemed to live in the same arrangement at the opposite slope of the gable. We were the elite of the attic. On either side of our closed rooms there were open areas like large playpens, furnished with pads on the floor and surrounded by slats that marked territorial borders. It was one of my firm principles not to complain, to be an endurer like my mother, and it suited me to tell my friends amusing stories about life in the cold attic, like that of the artists in *La Bohème*. I tried valiantly to be charmed, and when I couldn't manage that, tried to warm myself in my cloak of independence. Independence turned another face, fearsome unsafety, when I was molested by my crib neighbors. One was a woman who seemed never to dress, although there was some clothing hanging on her territorial slats, but stayed wrapped in a tattered comforter. She must have been half mad with loneliness, with no space to move in, and chose me as confidante and playmate. She stood at the head of the tall stairs when she heard my step or outside the communal toilet when she thought I was in it, to grab me for stories of past riches and glamorous travels – the commonest collection of fantasies. I would listen for a while, then, on the excuse of having to leave soon for a job, would pull her insistent hand from my arm. The encounters were only mildly disconcerting until she began to suggest, with lumpish, embarrassing coyness, that I spend the wet November nights with her, cuddle under the blankets together and keep cozy and warm.

She could accept no, however, unlike the large drunken man in the other crib, who would bang on my door, turn and turn the doorknob at all hours of the night, calling, 'Let me in, pretty baby, I just wanna give you a drink and a kiss.' Between wary avoidance of the woman, the sleepless noisy nights, and fear that the drunk might be able to force my door open, I felt myself sinking and sinking, and finally sank into a racking cough and a high fever. It had never occurred to me that I could be ill and might need help, need someone to buy food and medicines for me – to take care of me. If I could leave my bed to telephone – if the landlord would let me use the hall phone near his kitchen – whom would I call? Not Davy, who was in school, or at work in a place whose number I didn't know; nor friends, who had no telephones. Certainly not my mother; it would be another confession of frailty and I had to be indomitable. The drunk kept banging on the door, the blanket-woman kept following me to the toilet; it was the taciturn working woman who brought me cans of soup, already heated, several times. The amorphous days crept by, punctuated by the night noise and the toilet encounters, until, early one morning of no classes, Davy came. After a distressed look at my disheveled hair, my damp pasty face, he burst into tears. As if his tears were a flood that washed away my fortitude, I began to cry, too, as I had not cried since I was a very young child. He said he would quit school and find a full-time job to keep us. I sobbed no, and where would he find a job with so many experienced people out of work? Anyhow, one incident of the flu or pneumonia or whatever it was I had shouldn't change the course of his plans. Whatever we decided, I couldn't stay in that cold attic,with those crazies, he said. Still crying, he packed my books and clothing in the old suitcase Marian had once given me; still crying, I washed and dressed and pulled a comb through my matted hair. We knew nothing of emergency services in hospitals. With St. Vincent's Hospital nearby and Bellevue not too far away, we walked, wobbling, to the subway and after a number of exhausting stairways and changing platforms, arrived at his mother's house. Davy, usually tactful and engaging in his approach to everyone, said curtly as his mother stared at me, 'She's staying here until she's better. She can use the living room couch. You won't have to do anything. I'll take care of her and I'll pay you next week's wages for her food.'

Davy didn't have to take care of me; his father did when Davy was in school or working. Being long unemployed, as I had noticed among the fathers of several friends, seemed to silence and emasculate them and they became quiet, slow-moving old women. Davy's father seemed to like serving me, urging me to eat. I ate as little as a convalescing young appetite could manage of the two- or three-day-old bread that was bought cheaply at a local bakery and the improvisations on bones, stock of wilted soup greens, beans, and homemade noodles – types of minestrone, the classic poverty dish – that Davy's mother cooked up in large kettles. She saved a little each time to use as the base for the next invention, which might be a stew of carrots, onions, and potatoes, strengthened by another bone or two wheedled from the local butcher. I knew that Depression was the country we lived in, but my father was never out of a job; we had fresh rolls and generous helpings of meat and chicken, and my mother bought her soup greens fresh and perky.

Under Davy's father's care and the comfort of hearing ordinary human voices around me – children fighting in the tenement hallway, the dumbwaiter rattling its call for garbage in the kitchen, the slap of playing cards on the dining table – and the resilience of seventeen, I turned my attention to the matter of conquering the squat Victorian Gothic world of Hunter College.

Besides the illness and unhappiness of Bank Street, it was a trying time. Davy carried too heavy a load of courses and jobs and I had drawn tight the struggle to graduate from high school with my English medal, in spite of my truant's record and the anger of the physical training department en masse, which considered me the most recalcitrant, unathletic student they had ever encountered, probably a young Bolshie, certainly one of those know-it-all Yid kids. They were all, in my prejudiced view of them, humorless, foursquare, anti-thinking, what now might be called 'jocks', with thin *goy* hair and thick chins. As soon as I learned the word 'fascist' I was delighted to cover them with it. Since Marian and Jones, the androgynous Pygmalion to my cloddish Galatea, were no longer in my life and there was no scholarship on the horizon, I had to do my college education on my own.

I had to, to please my mother, to apologize to her for having been so many times so merciless, including the most recent act, refusing to attend my graduation exercises, denying my mother the pleasure of seeing her firstborn celebrated in the ranks of the well-educated. I had to, to show my father that in spite of him, I could make it. I had to show Marian I could, without her help; to thank Mr. Brandon and the English and music departments,who had been so steadily encouraging. I had to because of the light mutual crush between me and a history teacher who looked like one of the young officers in *The Three Sisters*, he insistent that I had to go on to college. I had to because, having dragged my independent and erratic way through high school, I deserved it, confident that I could drag my independent and erratic way through college.

The only college I could afford was Hunter, of the City College system, then virtually free. The only possible way I could be admitted, however, was to satisfy its requirement of five semesters of high-school mathematics, none of which I had had in James Monroe, all of which had to be conquered successfully in one semester. With the understanding permission of the authorities of Washington Irving High School, I registered for the five courses. For someone whose mind shattered at the sight of numbers and the sound of the word 'math', it was an order to climb Mount Everest. Sines and cosines, theorems, numbers into letters and vice versa, were a return to the incomprehensible kabalistic exercises I tried to learn, with no success at all, from derby-hatted, fine-fingered Mr. Roth of my Bronx childhood. For a while, the mingling of algebra, geometry, and intermediate geometry, swirling like Poe's malestrom in my mind, forced thoughts of giving up, of running away and maybe – doing what? But with Davy's help and an unexpected sudden view of algebra as rather simple puzzles, and geometry as strict abstract pictures, it all fell into place. The finest irony of that time was that my high math grades, plus my English medal made me acceptable to competitive Hunter.

According to the WPA *New York City Guide*, one of the finest works of the Depression, Hunter was originally the Normal College of the City of New York, established in 1870, its name changed, when its scope broadened in 1914, to honor the founder, Thomas Hunter.This indelibly remarkable school-menagerie gave me and my friends – or tried earnestly to – what might be called a quality education, requiring a great deal more of its students than is asked there now and in many other colleges. Several faculties required of their seniors studies that are today considered graduate courses, and everyone had to spend some time in all the major fields of learning, from the classics to integral calculus. The tacit ideal was to make cultivated women of us, and to a good degree the Hunter of my years succeeded, giving us solid expertise in one field, useful or at least entertaining knowledges in several others, and, best of all, numerous frames of reference which left us with lively curiosity and many threads to follow as and if we chose to.

In its change from teacher-training school to liberal arts college, Hunter still retained a faint tinge of semicloistered female academy (or was it nuns' school?), strongest when it floated out of the offices of several controlling officials with searching mother superior manners, who were looking into the moral *faiblesse* of that girl or the other rumored to be leading an 'irregular' life. Another lingering vestige was the paucity of male professors. Of the few men teachers, I remember fairly well two, both young and each in his way quite attractive, particularly to the many vulnerable, love-starved girls who had few or no dates and hadn't the luck to be bound, like myself, at least for the time being, in a solid partnership with a boy. One man was pale and enameled, with a high, Romantic poet's brow and the strayed lock favored by nineteenth-century engravers. Titillating whispers, freighted with words like 'affair' and 'divorce', normally the property of movie magazines, greatly enhanced his allure. I never had a class with him, never saw him as seductive, and furthermore was protected by my more advanced age (a year or two older than my classmates, thanks to the semester of math classes and six months as interoffice messenger with B. Altman and Company before I came to Hunter, and the precocity of some of the Quiz Kids who entered before they were sixteen) and my attachment to Davy. I no longer had any use for crushes and consequently found the other young professor, in the German Department, with whom I did have classes, interesting but not especially lovable. Nor did I want to run off with him to the Black Forest, of which he spoke with such *Heimweh*, nor did I dream, as some classmates did, that he would leave his robust German wife and blond children for me and that we would elope to Italy – maybe Bologna, maybe Padua – where he would teach German literature and I English literature and we would become the twin stars of an intellectual community that walked hand in hand with Browning and Goethe.

He was thin, angular, and moved jerkily, like a stick doll. His hair was spiky and willful, winging in all directions from his skull, a proper frame for the spiky mind and the witty, angular face with high cheekbones that pushed at slanted green eyes; a snaggletooth glimmered from his wide-lipped, mobile mouth. He was innovative and quirky in his methods and his opinions, which took on excitement as he dashed restlessly from one corner of the room to another, ridiculing the views of George Bernard Shaw and extolling the misanthropy of Strindberg in the European drama course I had with him. For improving the quality of the German in his language classes, he invented rhymes, riddles, and crossword puzzles, rather like the painless learning devices of Dr. Huebner in high school.

Some years later he left Hunter. He had, I was told, gone back to Germany to help in Hitler's Conquest of the World. This was difficult to absorb for a while, since he had appeared liberal, and was never known to have made any sort of anti-Semitic remark, though the opportunities were many in a school whose population included a large number of Jewish girls. But whether we believed it or not, the Professor O.K. whose voice we recognized on the radio spewing anti-American, anti-British, and particularly anti-Semitic propaganda was our erstwhile bright, swift, querulous man of culture, our stellar example of the cultivated European.

It was difficult to explain to Davy and other non-Hunter friends why I was registered in several German courses – a German major to a biology minor, in spite of my English medal – rather than concentrating on English classes. The simple fact of the matter was that examinations for English teachers had been suspended for an indefinite time – there were too many applicants – and in Hunter, at least, the English major, the base for teaching English, had become a difficult goal to achieve and maintain. It was a complicated process, too dull to explore in detail, that had some resemblance to climbing peaks which grew higher and higher until the atmosphere one breathed was quite rarefied. Or one could compare the achievement to beholding the Holy Grail after a long, wearying quest. We few knights who had made the full journey were rewarded with a juicy variety of arcane courses, a fine field for snobbishness: who else but we few could speak Chaucerian Middle English, quote long passages of Anglo-Saxon poetry, speak knowingly of Diarmuid and Gráinne, early Irish lovers in the Tristan and Isolde line, could write essays on King David as a mixed-up modern neurotic?

Who had the background for such dreams as mine? One night I was a noble lady of medieval times named Marguerite, the white daisy that was purity, the flower of the Virgin Mary. I wore a gold brocade dress, broad at the waist to accommodate the Second Coming; my feet were enfolded in soft leather, like gloves, on my head a tapering wimple from which floated a long silken veil. Accompanied by ladies-in-waiting wearing flower chaplets, I seated myself on a thronelike chair placed for me in the company of other nobles, at the side of the field of jousting that fronted my castle. Several knights tilted, thrusted, unhorsed each other. Then my lover and his adversary came to the field. He was not altogether my lover, but my lover in the manner of courtly love – the man who wrote me love songs, who vowed eternal fealty and protection, who made me deep obeisances and looked long at me from sea-blue Saxon eyes. As he rode toward the center of the field, I detached the white silken veil from my wimple and handed it to a handmaiden to give to him. My knight attached it to his sleeve, publicly acknowledging our profound union. While he turned and loosed and held his steed in a masterly display of horsemanship, while he urged his shining lance swiftly and skillfully at his adversary's cuirass and helmet, my veil – my spirit of love – swirled and darted and rode high above him in victory.

A second dream was less simple, less direct. I was a young monk, riding a swift horse past churches, past palaces, past vineyards, to bring an important message from the court of the Visconti of Milan to the Scaligeri of Verona. The message was actually an object, a small revolver recently invented by a Frenchman, an invaluable weapon and ornament for any gentleman, lighter than a sword and more deadly, and possibly useful in warfare. The Visconti thought they could buy the Frenchman, then kill him and keep all his little weapons for themselves, wielding a great advantage over their friends and neighbors. The dream then swam into details of tapestries and paintings, the Venetian velvets and fine lace on the court ladies, and the tight doublets and hose of court pages. (The analytic suggestions here are not too arcane, and anyone is welcome to them.)

The same rich brew may have existed in other departments – I'm inclined to think not, if only from the width and depth of the field and the variety of minds it attracted – but our particular cluster of female English professors of several ages, several styles of manners and mannerisms, degrees of chic and raggedness, the earthbound and those who flew with the high, wild geese, made a fascinating scholastic display. One smart, guarded young woman who had come from a school with an awesome name left Hunter after two or three years; we decided that an orderly Harvard professor had carried her off to an ivy-covered New England retreat, where, instead of sexing, they would read Milton to each other. She was a cold and discontented young woman – as one began to know her – who had no impressive enlightenments and yet was ambitious, it seemed, to become a memorable, legendary professor, like George Lyman Kittredge of Harvard, for instance. Impelled to guide us into adornments of English literature, she asked whether some of us might like to sing Elizabethan madrigals and write masques in the style of Ben Jonson, outside of class time. I was the only student to arrive at the appointed time and place for discussion of these projects. As we waited fruitlessly for others to arrive, she uttered a few sharp words, pointing out that we were called, and properly, 'Hunter girls', while Radcliffe taught 'women', as did Barnard and Bryn Mawr. After that insulting afternoon,

I only mildly insulted, she humiliated, I became her favorite, but soon fell among the contemptible 'girls' when she caught my sneaky, critical look as she read 'mastiff witch' for 'mastiff bitch' in a Coleridge poem. She knew I knew she was bowdlerizing, a cowardly act, a desecration of Coleridge and poetry, according to my unforgiving priggishness and wise-guy shots at teachers. She gave me an A nevertheless and I pushed on to the next perilous journey of the English-major quest.

It is impossible to describe the specific subject – purportedly a branch of English literature – of another instructor, who lived in an empyrean blue that scorned definitions and limits. She was small and elderly, with thin white hair and eyes that looked like pale grapes in sour cream; her vague, fluty voice matched her milky eyes and hair. She consorted with ghosts and spirits in a nebulous world through which she wanted us to wing with her. I was perfectly willing to adventure with this sweet mother of the Mad Hatter, but my pragmatic smart friends insisted on concrete proofs of the phenomena that were her familiars. After being pushed and buffeted, she stiffened her eighty-five pounds and proudly challenged them with 'Prove me the airplane!' leaving her adversaries wide-eyed and mute. No one answered, but I was, and still am, delighted with her. Another professor, visiting from Ireland for one year, held classes in her literature from the legends of Cuchulain to the plays of Shaw. (We managed to erase troublesome Oscar Wilde entirely.) The tall, gaunt woman with dark hair and ravaged face looked to my romantic eye like pictures I had seen of Yeats's rebel love, Maud Gonne. To our meager knowledge of Irish history and early literature, knowing Ireland mainly through its treacly songs, she added the revelation that these songs were 'fustian' masks. 'I'll Take You Home Again, Kathleen' or vows to mavourneen or Macushla, seemingly love songs, were actually promises of rebellion against the English, promises that Ireland would be free. Repeating the words of the songs, she grew increasingly proud and defiant. Reviling the greedy, ruthless English and recounting the rape of magnificent Irish forests decreed by Elizabeth I, she would burst into tears and weep as if she were a present witness and victim. I later heard the same present pain in the trembling voices of American Indians and refugee Jews.

There were also a few pragmatic professors who didn't scorn to pick up a stimulating idea from a student's paper to be used as her own contribution to a learned journal. What student ever saw the professional quarterlies? And if by some outrageous chance she did and found her teacher's article, who would believe an accusation of plagiarism directed by a snotty kid against a respected scholar? Then there were the foreign exchange instructors, poised pieces of exotica slumming among us. The German Department had imported a pleasant young woman who looked somewhat like Greta Garbo; she imitated the hairdos, the makeup and clothing, but did not know how to garner the magic. My course with her in Schiller and Goethe was a series of papers invariably marked 'Ideas outstanding, grammar repellent'. In spite of my contemptible grammar, we became quite friendly, she soon eager to have me meet the young millionaires who were her friends. They really were millionaires, or close enough, as I learned from having dinner with her and a smitten young man who languished in love like a heroine in a Victorian novel. After dinner in a restaurant famous for its Pimms' Cup (whose nectars I didn't appreciate), where I gorged on duck with fruit sauce for the first time in my life, we stopped at his house to leave a message for the caretaker. It was neither a house nor a mansion but some unreal literary thing in a foreign language, a *schloss*, a *château*, a *palazzo*, a castle out of chivalric stories. It was an endlessness of dark rubbed woods, of marble floors and ruby brocades surrounded by formal gardens and a park where white classical statues postured in the pale moonlight. Lisl asked me as we walked in the garden whether I thought she should marry this young man; could she live, did I think, in such a big, rich place with so many servants? Would his parents accept her, a foreigner and, although of an old line whose blood ran in the veins of a medieval emperor, not very rich? With the arrogance of inexperience I advised her freely, in which direction I cannot remember.

Whether she married this one or not, she thought I, too, should snag a young millionaire. Not all of them were afraid, as their fathers were, of Roosevelt and his liberal cohorts. Some of them were eager to join the shaping century of the 'common man.' Someone like myself, a girl of the people, a brave, independent spirit, Jewish, poor, and 'interesting', might attract a few of the boys who were bent on developing broad, tolerant, contemporary minds. A few days after the visit to the house of the patinas and brocades (with a stop in an implausible cut-velvet toilet) and the stroll through the cold, naked marbles, Lisl's friend invited me and a few cavaliers to a yachting party. As usual, my impulse was to run fast in the other direction. This was too foreign an experience, too demanding. What would I talk about? What did I know about polo ponies, about low, whippy roadsters and yachts, except from the pictures I saw in the society section of the newspapers? What lies would I have to invent to placate Davy? What would I wear? I had one cotton dress and one bathing suit, both shabby. Or was I supposed to appear shabbily working-class, and talk about Mike Gold and Floyd Dell, and tell the pretty young men about 'radical' movements about which I had strong feelings and feeble information? The impulse to accept was equally strong, as usual, and I accepted, borrowing ten dollars from a friend to buy a classy dress in Klein's and borrowing a bathing suit, quite new and slinky, from my classmate Dinah, like me generously padded. As I pulled on the bathing suit in one of the Hunter bathrooms to make sure it fit, I saw myself stretched like a houri on embroidered silken cushions, shadowed from the refulgent sun by a canopy of peacock feathers. Gathered around me were adoring young men in bright-buttoned blazers and visored yachting caps. They all had straight small noses and clean, straight, white teeth.

In the miscellany that is my biography, there frequently appears a caricature of bags of gold and jewels running away from me fast, like Virtue fleeing the Foul Fiend in old prints. If money courts me (a friend whispers that this smitten gentleman is Mr. OPEC), a bit uncertain of foot and tongue as we all are at a party or opening, if it charms, beckons, invites, glistens, pulls me into an alcove to make firm arrangements for getting together alone – the first seductive, treacherous phrase in the vocabulary of love and lamentation – it is sure, before telephone numbers can be exchanged, to trip on a large ashtray and so surprise its balance and alcoholic content that it passes out, never to be heard from again. My first such experience of swift abandonment by golden bejeweled butterflies was propelled by Lisl, unwillingly, I prefer to think. For days before the outing, I had been gliding into the world of privilege, preparing to abandon Klein's for Bergdorf's, to buy a bathing suit when I had a whim for one, or seven or eight. Exquisitely dressed, adorned with discreet baubles of emeralds and pearls devised centuries ago by Italian goldsmiths, I would drop soft clatters of chips on the gaming tables of Monte Carlo and Deauville. I would return to Park Avenue on the *France*, entertaining distinguished

statesmen in my suite, ordering champagne and caviar in perfect
French.

This moving-picture version of the high life was blanked two
days before the outing by a phone call from Lisl. She had had
too much sun the past weekend and was now in the hospital being
treated for burns; with much regret she had backed out, for both of
us, from the yachting party. Before I could find out which hospital
or whether I could do anything for her, she hung up. I didn't hear
from her until two months later. A note from Germany informed
me that family matters had demanded her immediate presence
after she left the hospital. She was returning to America in the
fall and would be in touch with me. I saw her only once again,
and then in a society page, as the splendidly dressed wife of the
importunate suitor I had met. Nowhere for me to go but back off
the movie screen and into the favorite fantasies – in spite of
Davy, who, I somehow knew, would not remain my *life* – of
cold, gallant pennilessness in a garret as the helpmeet of a great
artist or writer, maybe ultimately to do something famous of my
own, like Mary Shelley. I gave up the Mainbocher silks for a long
gown hand-embroidered in designs from the *Book of Kells*, maybe
like that of the wife of noble William Morris and the inamorata of
his friend Dante Gabriel Rossetti. All she and I had in common was
a wild thatch of hair, hers black and passionate, mine the color of
straw and hay, the unfortunate colors of bucolic innocence, but I
wanted her place. Not with Rossetti, though I envied the sonnets
he wrote her, but with her suffering giant husband, who would
forget Jane's cruelty in the nest I would build around him and
the beautiful houses which I would help him design when I wasn't
editing sheets for our Kelmscott Press. Or, quite possibly, I would,
like several intrepid British ladies, wander in the Judean wilderness
with a tribe of Bedouins. Or I would live in a black felt tent with a
group of Kurds and eat yak flesh with them, dressed in bright bands
of yak wool, with big dangles of glittering stones around my neck.

While I was rising and falling with Lisl there wasn't much
time or care for my Hunter companions. Now I was thrust back
among them and listening to much talk about a new crush that
had smitten a number of them. She was a teacher of zoology, an
energetic, dark young woman with a sturdy walk and an unabashed,
immoderate voice. I didn't like her earthbound looks or her brisk,
efficient manner as she marched through the halls. I had no classes
with her and my information was secondhand, often delivered in

exaltations, young saints adoring the Virgin. 'She understands so much, she's so friendly and informal. You can tell her anything, everything.' 'I've been invited to her house again, next week. The last time I went with Mary and she gave us coffee and cake and she showed us the artbooks she brought back from Europe.' (Shades of perfidious Marian, of my high school days.) 'She thinks friends, girl friends, often experience emotional pulls toward each other that they don't understand, are afraid of, and resist though close friendships with girls are more satisfying than with boys – they understand each other better – and less hazardous, like pregnancy for instance.' 'She says men are immature, unstable, and insensitive.' Developments waxed into further developments. She gave her chosen girls little gifts and little suppers, sent them on personal errands which they treated as royal honors, awed them with her wide-ranging conversation and unconventional attitudes, favored them with strokes on the cheek, on the shoulder, told them what alluring eyes and delicate hands they had.

The clay feet showed ultimately and uglily. She invited one of her adoring friends to supper, alone, to mark a special occasion, the first anniversary of their meeting. As naive Ida told it, they had bootleg wine, two or three glasses with dinner, a glass or two afterward. While they sat and talked on the couch, Miss Hennessey opened the buttons of Ida's blouse and began to stroke her shoulder and breast and pull her close. Ida tried to move away. It was a bizarre contest, as Ida described it, the sturdy woman pulling the girl toward her to be stroked and kissed; startled, embarrassed Ida squirming away and still trying to be polite with the goddess. Herself embarrassed and angry, the goddess rose, and looking down at her acolyte of the disordered blouse and frightened eyes, hissed at her, 'You stupid, stupid little kike.' The cult collapsed in my immediate circle, maintained only by a few strangers in short pasted-down haircuts.

22
Hunter Girls

The old Hunter building at Sixty-eighth Street and Lexington Avenue had only one shelter for girls who smoked, our most forceful symbol, other than pregnancy, of freedom from parental prohibitions. This unremittingly ugly cellar, furnished with chairs and tables that had the dull utilitarian stamp of Salvation Army furniture, was rarely used by the girls who had steady habits and controlled routines. These nonsmokers, our Conservative Party, invaded the cellar – dignified by the name 'Exchange' – only when they desperately needed someone's notes. Our incommodious salon was the hangout mainly of the slightly disheveled, the class-cutters; it was for gossiping, for borrowing money, and for borrowing clothing for the not too frequent date. My usual offering was a handsome old leather pocketbook given me by Laura Bergson; Stella offered her one good blouse and Liz her rabbit jacket. On Friday afternoons, we had loud calls from Anna, of the mischievous face: 'Who wants my pessary? I haven't got a date this weekend,' running around from table to table offering her supreme and rare gift. Since most of us were too inexperienced to wonder about fit and general usability, she frequently found takers, handing over the small, flat box with a large, benevolent gesture. One wit or another called her our 'infertility goddess'.

It was in the Exchange that we ate the sandwiches our mothers had forced on us in the morning or bought from a slatternly stand a five-cent bar of chocolate that would do for lunch. It was in this cellar that some of us plotted to join the City College boys who were preparing demonstrations to oust their president. Whether he merited removal, whether students could force it, we didn't know or care; it was protest, and we, particularly those firebrands who belonged to the Young Communist League or the Young People's

Socialist Party, were always ready for confrontation and battle, at least verbally. The cellar was also the place for gathering a group determined to cut afternoon classes to spend several luscious hours on sparse lunch money with long-legged, soft-lipped, delectable Gary Cooper in the nice, warm, dusty, dark movie house at Sixty-eighth Street at Third Avenue. The cellar was the place where two or three of the eldest of us met to go for a couple of after-school hours to the Aquarium, a speakeasy nearby. Its name derived from the large tanks full of varicolored fish which provided the only illumination for the dim, secretive room. One of us had been taken there by an uncle, and we used his name in our version of 'Joe sent us' to get in. There were few customers at three or four in the afternoon and it amused the proprietor to serve a group of schoolgirls, laden with books, the one drink over which they would sit, puffed with sophistication, until the five o'clock masculine trade began to pour in.

The money for this ultimate worldly gesture meant the sacrifice of several movie sessions, or overtime work. It wasn't come by easily, though well worth it. To earn little, to do with little, to give up one pleasure for another, was the atmosphere we breathed, our natural climate. Many of our houses held as prisoners abashed, unemployed fathers. A number of girls, though fairly well dressed – the *bella figura* syndrome – lived in apartments almost empty of furniture, the few sticks frequently moved from apartment to apartment to avoid paying rent or being shoved out on the street. Some of the fathers went to distant boroughs, where they were not known, to sell apples; some continued sitting with vacant eyes. Rarely cold or hungry, except when I chose to test myself, to see how much cold and hunger I could withstand (as I had practiced being lame and blind in my childhood, to see how it might feel), I was aware of the meager lives of friends, who, however, didn't feel singularly deprived, too young and gallant to complain, too familiar with the parallel lives that shaped their norm. The one experience of profoundest poverty that infuriated me, made me painfully sorrowful and ashamed that I could not alter anything, nor scream and yell and protest effectively, was the slave markets that were held in front of Woolworth stores in several neighborhoods, black women facing white women who wanted a few hours of household help at the lowest possible cost. It was dreadful to watch black women outbid each other downward for the jobs: 'I'll take twenty-five cents an hour.' 'Hey, missus, I'll

work for twenty cents.' Another offered herself for eighteen cents.
I don't know if the bidding ever went lower; after a few moments I
would run from the shameful scenes.

The group that preempted the Exchange table at which I usually
sat – preempted early and held stubbornly, as others held their
territories – was a kaleidoscopic mixture composed of a core
of intimate friends and visitors who admired our freeform ways
and nasty tongues. One girl who sat with us once in a while was
the princess of a long line – on both parental sides – of
dynasties of Chassidic rabbis, the Chosen of the Chosen. Malka
was afraid of the marriage, with the learned scion of another
dynasty of rabbis, already in negotiation. She had met him once
and found him pimply and little, his black frock coat hanging
limply from narrow shoulders, his earlocks thin and wispy. She
sat with us, we thought, to gather as if by osmosis the strength
to protest against the marriage. But she had exhausted the limits
of liberty allowed her by attending Hunter College rather than a
religious school. Enough. She married the little pimply Chassidic
scholar, who prayed and studied at the expense of her parents –
considered an honor to the family – while she shaved her auburn
hair, put on an iron-ridged wig, and grew belly after belly.
  Her opposite number in our gallery was a hummingbird who had
been brought up in the West Indies, or possibly Cuba. Sometimes
she alit wearing a tall bright turban, carrying a magic candle for an
obeah ceremony she was to attend later; sometimes she sat dully,
disappointed in 'all that primitive crap', sans turban, sans magic
candle and powders. It was a struggle, clearly, one we could neither
understand nor sympathize with; crazy mixed-up kid, a curio. Then
there was our fashion plate, Miriam, who lived in a large apartment
full of light. Her father had a well-paying, steady job and her
mother was a skilled dressmaker. The rest of us knew little about
fashion and were scornful of the superficiality in the little we saw,
but we could not deny style, and Miriam's clothing had style, copied
by her mother from glossy magazines like *Vogue* and *Vanity Fair*,
which we knew only from their covers on newsstands. There was
subtle insult in the difference between our coarse skirts and cheap
blouses and the soft swirl and gentle cling of her skirts, and the
blouses of sculptured silk shaped like morning glories, to frame
her limpid pale-brown eyes and her skin, the texture and color
of antique clay, which I admired in its contrast to my ordinary

white and pink. Her nails were almond-shaped, manicured by her
mother, her hair a smooth cap, shaped by her mother. She was her
mother's doll, as none of the rest of us had been since we were
three or four, some of us never. We envied, admired, and disliked
Miriam.

Esther was a studious, generous girl who had little to say but
liked to listen to our babble. Suddenly she stopped coming to our
table and no one saw her, in our out of classes, or at the subway
station. After several weeks, Stella went to visit her and returned
with a chilling story. She found Esther at home, pale, thin, and
terrified at the suggestion that they go out for a walk. No, no, she
couldn't go, she couldn't leave the house. Why not? Was she sick?
What kind of sickness did she have? The father shouted at her to go
walking, to get out of the house, her mother began to cry, Please,
please, go out with your friend. Esther ran into the bathroom and
locked herself in and stayed while her father banged at the door,
alternately begging her to come out and threatening her with the
fire department, the police department, who would get her out and
maybe send her to Bellevue, the current euphemism for an insane
asylum. The weeping mother told Stella that one morning Esther
decided not to go to school. No one thought anything of it, a heavy
menstrual period, probably. The same evening she canceled a date
to go to the library with a neighborhood friend. The next day, no
school, no going out anywhere, not even on an errand around the
corner. She hid in a closet, in the bathroom, when it was suggested
she leave the house. It was weeks now and they didn't know what to
do. The only agency they knew was the Board of Health, a foreign,
suspect power that might put Esther in a crazy cell and keep her
there forever. Event crowding on event, we forgot about her after
a while, but for weeks before thought about the gap between
universal, common craziness – the *meshugge* with which we
Jewish girls were often stamped and dismissed – and her black
pit of a world, like scenes of hell, called insanity.

It was the wet, gloomy days, when the Exchange smelled
of rubber overshoes and damp coats, that wafted the densest
mists and miasmas on which to float intimate self-images at each
other. The display was often led off by a fantasy phrase spoken in
a dreamy voice by someone on the fringe of our circle, impressing
her way toward the center. One such contender for our attention
was a large girl, all dark gold – hair, skin, and eyes – like
girls I later saw in Greece and northern Italy. Elena's perfection was

preserved by the immobility of her Minerva face. She rarely smiled because her teeth were short and her gums long, and the excessive display of wet, pink flesh, marring her Greek goddess look, tortured her. To match her immobile face she walked with slow, measured steps toward a distant vision, a seeress, a sibyl, a Cassandra. The majestic stride and the dignified face were dictated, she explained one gray afternoon, by the fact that she was the vessel of a special destiny; there was a pulsating, constant bubbling in her throat, a reminder that she would someday be great. How? She wasn't too good at the piano, she agreed, nor much of a writer, and the pencil sketches she scrawled were too close to ad drawings. But her throat kept bubbling, gently nudging her toward heights, great one way or another, she had no doubt, maybe as a suffragette or an actress or a great courtesan like – what was her name? – Lily Langtry.

No one else we knew had a nonstop prophetic bubble, but some of us English majors had been sufficiently seduced by books to dedicate ourselves to dreams of lives that echoed the 'infinite variety' of Cleopatra; withering and staling as our grandmothers and mothers did were to be avoided at the profoundest costs. We would live heroic sorrows and great pleasures as we learned them in Shakespeare, in Greek dramas and French novels, as we learned them from the daring, tough, begging-for-the-knife-in-the-bodice Carmen. And there were the lush, toothsome Belle Époque women, all pearls, plumes, and rose satin, as introduced to us by the Goncourts and Proust. If not the Odettes, the gallant unfortunates, semi-loved and thoroughly discarded, of Zola and Dreiser, and, closer to our own time, the burners of candles at both ends: Edna St. Vincent Millay, Genevieve Taggard, Elinor Wylie.

The need to be in love or connected in some way to love also sculptured almost three-dimensional, almost in-the-flesh, Hamlets to moon over, Shelleys and Keatses to worship and mourn, Byrons to spy on in their Italian villas, to want and fear their swift words, to make despairing jealous hags of their wives and mistresses. The need for loving often moved from literary fantasy to pairings in intense friendships, charged with jealousy, with demands of constant attention and affection, with strident fighting and humbling tears. Those of us who were spectators were divided on whether the passions included overt sexuality. Were our frenetic friends possibly lesbians in the fullest sense? I somehow doubted it, but there were those who were titillated by the presence of Sapphos among us, an advanced, mysterious society, imagined as Amazons and frail, peplumed girls.

Since I was nearer self-supporting than the rest, with several jobs to run among, there were periods when I was absent, regretfully, from the gossiping marketplace of the Exchange. During my absences, a naive, crush-inspired legend attached itself to me, almost naturally for the atmosphere, stemming from my extraordinary, boundless freedom and abetted by the clouds of fantasy that painted the gray air of that cellar. As mentioned, I was at least a year older than most of my friends, had worked in the real commercial world, wandered as I would, lived as I could. No parental supervision strangled me, no mother wrung her red, wash-swollen hands over my delinquencies, no father roared that I was not to go out and to give him back his keys. The keys I had were my own, to a place that was my own. In short, I was not a girl but a woman, to be envied, and idealized, as Isadora Duncan was idealized, or Mabel Dodge Luhan and Emma Goldman. Of the glamorous universe I inhabited, touched up with lies dropped lightly about my elaborate love life – in spite of faithful Davy – concerning this poet, that actor, a painter, a composer, the girls of the small tight lives constructed a portrait of me as wildly licentious, a frenzied dancer in Dionysian revels. One imaginative portrait of the Great Kate had me dancing at night in Central Park, solo and frenetically, surrounded by a group of boys who sat in a circle, urging me on as I shimmied and swung my hips and made the take-it-off gestures of a burlesque queen. On and on I danced, the legend said, faster and more frenzied, until I suddenly dropped to the grass and burst into tears (a nice literary touch that might have been invented by the imaginative seeress of the bubble). Two boys consoled me, stroking, patting, kissing, and, in consoling, entered me. I couldn't or wouldn't say no to the other boys, so we had what later became known as a 'gang bang'. The realities were that I rarely danced, I never shimmied because I didn't know how, and, having not yet seen a burlesque show, knew none of its gestures. However, there was pleasure in this elevation to minor goddess, this ascension to utterly uninhibited sexpot and total free spirit. I neither confirmed nor denied the story but for a while tried to look secretive and cynical, then forgot about the whole foolish entertainment.

Gossip had a way of seeping up from the Exchange to the first-floor offices of the directors, and one day I was summoned to a meeting with a large, disconcerting woman with doughy skin who kept glancing down at the lace insert in the V of her neckline, apparently to assure herself that she was modestly covered. (The nasty eye of youth said, Never mind the modesty; no one would think of assaulting you. But pull the lace higher, real high, to cover the stippled, wrinkled flesh, so ugly.) The woman found it interesting that I lived alone. Were my parents dead, perhaps? No. Did they live outside the city, in which case I should not be attending a city college? No, my parents lived in the Bronx and I lived alone in Manhattan at the address indicated in the records. Did I live altogether alone? Or with another girl? (It was unthinkable, impossible, to ask whether I lived with a boy.) No, I lived alone, I kept saying. When she asked how I could afford it, I told her I rented a room in the house of a poor family, that I had several jobs, and that my mother sent me money. There was clearly more searching to do, but she didn't know what wedge to use or where to pierce with it. After hesitating over my record, she dismissed me. She summoned me two or three times later to answer the same questions, but the inquisition stopped when an outburst of student demonstrations at City College threatened to excite Hunter, requiring her full alertness and attention.

(Reviving Hunter brings back not only another time but, compared to university life now as I hear and read it, what seems to be part of another universe. We rarely drank, since we were products of poor, abstemious households and very few of us had access to prohibition liquor, the right of the worldly. The only drugs we knew of were the glue inhaled by some unknown boys, the opiates of Coleridge and De Quincey, and the valerian and light infusions of opium taken by Victorian ladies, among them Elizabeth Barrett Browning, who would not be broken, even by her otherwise persuasive husband, of the comforting habit. We knew about reefers – a word for marijuana that seems to have left the vocabulary – and a small few of us had tried them. But we had no wish nor the wherewithal to continue. As for the rest, we sequestered them in incomprehensible literary lives and fabled opium dens in Port Said.)

23
Summer, Light and Dark

Whan that Aprille with his shoures soote
The droghte of March hath perced to the roote,
And bathed every veyne in swich licour
Of which vertu engendred is the flour;
Whan Zephirus eek with his sweete breeth
Inspired hath in every holt and heeth
The tendre croppes, and the yonge sonne
Hath in the Ram his halve cours yronne,
And smale foweles maken melodye,
That slepen al the nyght with open ye . . .
Thanne longen folk to goon on pilgrimages . . .

As often, a writer I revered told me how to feel. Chaucer said to me, one fragrant spring, that I was the young sun and the tender crops and, like the wakeful birds, too merry to sleep, that I was spring, the adolescence of the year. Like myself, like Davy, our friends had also felt the pricking in their hearts that told them to plan pilgrimages for the close of the spring semester. Those with parents who would rescue them if they were stranded penniless in Broken Bow, Oklahoma, were planning to hitchhike across the country and back. The less privileged would have as their Canterburys camps in New England where they might teach swimming or crafts – a crude leather pouch for each relative. The still less blessed would tutor slow children in the city; the absolutely damned were those who had to take makeup summer courses.

Summer pilgrimages were in the planning all around us, the planners including my stalwart English student Mrs. Katz, still trying to say 'the' instead of 'zee' and to take the big burr out of 'rrrun'; she was going off to stay with a cousin on a farm in the Catskills, the Green Pastures of a couple of my piano pupils as well. Vito could do without me for a couple of months; his daughter would ticket the laundry bundles. Davy, too, was entering slow seasons in a couple of his jobs and eager to leave them altogether for a while. But where to go and what to do on the sixty dollars we had saved?

One late-spring holiday, we hitchhiked up to visit the Bergsons, about whom I had told Davy a good deal, describing them as an auxiliary set of parents in my fated style – mother pretty good, father terrible, except that this one knew fascinating people and owned good books; to complete the picture, a little brother and sister to take care of. During the visit Laura told us that one of her nephews had hired a patch of land for next to nothing near a filled quarry – a wonderful big swimming hole, Bill had said – from an Italian who owned the land around the quarry, an hour's walk from the Bergson summer house.

The next afternoon, toward evening, we climbed the hill toward the quarry. At the top, where the path flattened to a plateau of bushes and tangled grass, we called, 'Guido, Guido,' politely, tentatively, in several directions. We had been told that the Italian drank a lot of wine, didn't like company, and sometimes carried a shotgun. As we kept calling warily, not moving from our spot, a clump of bushes to our right suddenly parted and there stood the laird, broad and dirty, with a large nose and a thick mat of curly black hair. Bloodshot eyes glared into the dimming light. He had no shotgun but, instead, his hand was attached to a rope that circled the neck of a white goat. Keeping our distance from him, we asked if he had some quarry land available for July and August. We had our own tent and equipment (borrowed from one of Davy's innumerable tribe) and all we wanted of him was the rental of a piece of land and the use of the quarry. He beckoned us to follow him as he walked unsteadily, supporting himself by grasping low branches of trees and the tufts of hair on the back of his goat. The shack he led us to echoed its tenant, unkempt, disheveled, stinking of soured wine and the acrid odor of unwashed bedclothes. He poured for us jam-jar glasses of wine that was heavy and rough, the sort of wine the Italian neighbors of my childhood nursed in stained barrels each fall; it was referred to as 'Guinea red'. He drank from a mason jar in one hand while he caressed his goat with the other. His hand moving smoothly along her head

and sides, playing absentmindedly with her nipples, he discussed
our business of space and price. He thought five dollars a week
would be OK. No, he didn't want any deposit. When we came to
stay would be time enough to pay the first week's rent, unless we
wanted to pay by the month, but it wasn't necessary. Come and
see the place. We stumbled with him up a gentle hill and into a
valley where there were a few tents and beyond to a dense copse
that bordered a meadow on three sides and then opened on the
wonderful quarry of gray Cézanne walls and blue-green water. We
could pitch our tent at the far end of the meadow, Guido said. We
told him it was perfect, beautiful and wondered silently if he would
remember the place and the promise that it was ours.

At a slow wobbling pace, supported by whatever was at hand,
including Davy's shoulder, he led us back to his cabin to sign a
lease Davy improvised on a page from a child's worn copybook.
First Davy signed, then he asked the old man for his signature.
The Italian made a cross and then ceremoniously, with a tottering
bow, gave the paper to me to sign. The paper went into a table
drawer full of corks, can openers, a few spoons and forks, and
other scraps of paper. We could not leave before the ritual of
another glass of wine to seal our contract and new friendship.
Although neither Davy nor I was accustomed to much wine and
didn't like this metallic stuff, we drank and drank some more on
our host's insistence, and watched him love the goat. 'Cara', he
called her, and 'Bella'. '*Vuoi fare l'amore, tesoro?*' he asked her,
stroking her head, her sides, her belly, staring into her still, dumb
eyes. Although I had read and heard stories about the common
practice among lonely shepherds of buggering sheep and goats, I
didn't think I wanted to witness the copulation of a dirty man and
his four-legged lover, yet I was also pulled to stay, to see how this
antique act as old as sex and loneliness was performed. Would the
goat enjoy it? How would she manifest pleasure? Would she have
an orgasm or was that possible only with a he-goat? Repelled and
attracted, I sat awaiting developments. Suddenly realizing the
potential direction of events, Davy, frowning and pale, jumped
from his chair, grabbed my hand, and pulled me out of the
cabin. Having had the preparation of a too-much-handled little
girl, I wasn't as shocked as he. In any case, this was one more
experience in a world of experiences I had to live, this only one of
an infinite number of wide explorations I had promised myself. But
I had to skip it because Davy was dashing down the hill yelling at

me to follow. When I reached him at the bottom of the hill he was vomiting. I wondered why.

My rose-lit memory probably plays me tricks, but I remember no rain that summer and that I made an exquisite costume of a secondhand tank suit which I cut down to *here*, front and back, and edged with crochet stitches in pretty colors. The swimming was cool and fresh, as silky as flying into a cloudless sky; the meadow a carpet of tender flowers; the shapely rock walls were a large palette of subtle colors, almost ours alone. We were a faun and his naiad playing ancient measures, I liked to think, while our drunken old Bacchus pulled berries and vegetables out of his disordered, overflowing garden to feed us. The only disturbing notes came from a tent across the meadow, as big clattering masculine laughter and shrill female scolding. We met the couple – tall, raw young Marty and his tiny sharp-faced girl friend, Marie – at the quarry a few times and one evening went to visit their tent: they were having a party, why didn't we come? The beds had been taken out of the tent and the table and benches laden with bottles of liquor and bowls of peanuts and popcorn. There were no introductions; we simply milled around together and danced to the raucous music of an old phonograph. When the mass became individuals, I noticed a short, fat young man following Marty around with a fixed, adoring smile. Every now and then Marty put a tablet or powder (it was done quickly and I couldn't see precisely what the substance was) into Fatty's drink, absorbed in one long gulp. As the evening grew noisier and merrier, Marty called, 'Stop, everybody. Fatty and I are going to do our trick.' The phonograph was silenced. Marty brought in a chair and stood on it. 'Now, Fatty, get in back of the chair and kneel down.' Fatty staggered over and fell to his knees, as commanded, back of the chair. Marty then bent over from his height and between the rungs of the chair called softly, 'Hey, Fatty, how do I look? Upside down? No. You're the one who's upside down. I'm upright.' Fatty began to whimper and cry. 'Don't do that, Marty. Please don't do that. Don't mix me up. Don't be upside down. Don't make me upside down. Please.' The whimper became shrieks: 'Take me out, take me out of this cage. Make me straight. Take your crazy upside-down head away. I'll die if you don't. Marty, you're my best friend, I love you. Please, please, get me out of here.' It was tiny Marie who pulled Fatty away and pushed him, stumbling, shivering, out of the tent. I started out too, furious with all of them. Davy immediately followed, asking what I was so upset about. Angry with him too, I shouted that using Fatty for his cruel act, doping him to perform it, made Marty – witty, imaginative, and maybe even a pretty good poet – a vicious beast.

Davy, who admired and probably envied Marty's swaggering, defiant life, couldn't understand why I thought him beyond contempt and yet accepted Guido and his goat without criticism. I wasn't quite sure, but in the course of several conversations we decided that it was a question of who victimized whom and the ensuing destructions. Guido's goat was well cared for, well fed, and, in several senses, well loved. She showed no ill effects from Guido's repetitions of the relief and pleasures he had known as a boy left alone for days to wander with grazing animals in frightening emptinesses of land. Marty, a so-called evolved man, was using his superior intelligence to make a beast of a frail being, to make, by persuasion, drugs, and the creature's own debilities, a nonperson, a slave, of Fatty. '*Es is doch a mench*' (Yet he is a human being), my mother's clarion call when my father reviled wops, micks, and niggers, rang in my ears; it was her short hymn to the wonderful uniqueness of human life, an expression of the respect, to the degree of religious awe, every person owed his fellow man. This emotion which was also her law settled deeply in her children and, as repeated to Davy, explained to him why I found Marty so loathsome. Though at least partially understanding my reaction, Davy remained fascinated by the high life in the tent across the meadow and visited a couple of times without me.

A couple of weeks after we had settled in, I telephoned my mother from the Bergsons' and invited her to come one Sunday, to rest and breathe some fresh air after a hard week's work. (We had, gradually, cautiously, become quite friendly.) She arrived in the car she had recently bought and which my father drove; she had, she said, no interest in or talent for such sophisticated machinery as autos; only sewing machines. She descended from her car as aristocratically and languidly as her short, plump body would allow and, having greeted us, looked around with pleasure at our trees and our wildflowers. She wanted to put her toes in the quarry and meet the old Italian who loved a goat. Did he? *Really?* She was as curious about this new mode of love as she had been about homosexuality when my brother and I enlightened her and when, with sudden recognition, she remembered a woman in Warsaw who dressed like a man and kept another woman as a kind of wife. My father said 'Pheh!' and stayed silent. The irregularity of our situation, Davy's and mine, was beyond his capacity to understand and difficult to endure. He had already interfered with my most innocent dates, like going to an afternoon movie with a boy; he had dragged me away from groups that included boys; he followed me when he suspected I was following or, more exactly, spying on a popular boy on whom I had a despairing crush. Here, now, sat his crazy wife beaming at the *shmendrick* Davy and street girl me, living 'free love' like wild anarchists. He couldn't protest much, however. The car was hers, the new carpet for the living room was paid for by the earnings of the corset shop she had finally achieved after years of door-to-door selling. She could now afford two skilled helpers and a Persian lamb fur coat and the diamond ring she never before owned. She had already told him, I found out later, that if he didn't like life with her, he was welcome to try it without her, but she never told him flatly to leave. She didn't want the aloneness, nor the sexlessness, nor the absence of light quarreling; they still argued, in a desultory way, out of habit. He hung on, also, because he liked to watch the ringing cash register in the store when he was not on his job. He enjoyed checking inventory and would go down to lower Broadway on Sundays to buy replacements of corset material, bones, hooks, and ready-made girdles and bras, swaggering, ordering people about, being the entrepreneur he wasn't. He had his uses, she conceded, including driving the car which gave her a great freedom she never had before. It was, like their domestic life generally as they grew older, a fairly good symbiotic arrangement.

After the exploration of our Elysian Fields and a view of the quarry and the wide country sky, she proceeded to lift out of the car a heap of grocery boxes. He never helped. It was his form of protest, and anyhow, no self-respecting man ever carried so much as a small paper bag of groceries, no matter how desperate the need. The grocer's cartons spilled and kept spilling gorgeous things, food for at least a week: bagels, eggs, cans of salmon, sardines, and tuna fish, big lumps of cheese, canned soups, two roasted chickens, cakes like palaces, only half of which we could cram into our small cupboard and icebox. (I can't remember where we got the ice, unless our landlord supplied it; he performed a surprising number of services when he shone with wine and love.) One of the ornaments of the prodigious Sunday meals we consumed was the abominable cheese-cement turnovers my mother made every Friday and with great pleasure. These, she felt, contradicted her reputation for being a lousy cook. (They didn't; rather, fortified it.) For dessert, also, a bounty of fruit with an injunction to Davy to eat, while I looked and looked before I reached. She rarely forgot to comment on the fact that since I had been a child I loved the colors and shapes of fruit almost more than I liked the taste. This one of my oddities pleased her; it indicated that I was artistic.

When we had absorbed as much of the fruit and the homemade little monsters as we could, we stretched our blankets out on the grass and talked. We told stories of our endlessly fascinating landlord, we talked of our few young neighbors and of the doings in the Bergsons' community on the other side of the highway – who was chasing whom in the fashionable games of changing partners, threatening to the older women and hard on the older men, too tired for the game. We talked about the corset store, and my mother, always a fine mimic and raconteur, told the week's story of Mrs. Greenberg, a frequent visitor though never a cutomer.

My father and the neighbors dismissed her as a 'Bellevue case'. My mother was sorry for her, while she was entertained by her costumes and her extravagant, dramatic monologues. She always made her welcome when Mrs. Greenberg chose to come into the shop, setting a chair for her as if she were a Romanoff grand duchess. The neighborhood scuttlebutt on Allerton Avenue, where my mother's shop was located, had it that Mrs. G. once owned a seven-room apartment on the Champs Élysées of the Bronx, the Grand Concourse, that she once had a *shvartzeh* – a black woman – to do her housework, her laundry, and cooking every day all day, that she had had a beaver coat and one of karakul and a fox cape. long. She once had, they said, two automobiles and a chauffeur and two long ropes of real pearls with earrings to match. Mrs. Greenberg was the stuff of legend until her husband took her furs and jewels and, leaving her without a cent, ran off with a singer of the Bronx Opera House. Where he had gone she never knew, nor did the police take much trouble tracking him down; after all, he had run off with his own property. Her children? She never got along with her daughter, who married a Canadian salesman – of what she couldn't remember – and never wrote her from Toronto, where she now lived. Her son, the lodestar of her life, had married a *shikse* who made fun of her accent

and her worn, out-of-fashion Bergdorf Goodman clothing. He sent
her money regularly, a miser's pittance, which just about paid for
her room and board with Mrs. Heller, who poisoned her bitter life,
threatening to throw her out if she played the radio early or late,
or whatever Mrs. Heller decided was early or late, or if she hung
her washed stockings in the bathroom or over a chair in her room,
wetting the rug a few drops. And that shrew, that cholera, twisted
out of her tenants double the money they should have paid for the
Gehennas she rented them.

The few times I saw her sitting in my mother's shop she
appeared sick and gaunt and of high dignity. In my habit of giving
valid reality to people by identifying them with literary characters,
I saw Mrs. Greenberg as Queen Hecuba, 'the winter-frozen bee' of
The Trojan Women. My mother's response was less literary and
more lively as she recited to us, while my father napped on a cot
under a tree, Mrs. Greenberg's latest soliloquy. Although it was a
hot day, my mother began, Mrs. G. was wearing an old fur piece,
rubbed down to a band of leather, except for the balding sharp fox
head whose eyes gleamed malevolently off her chest. On her head,
a broken garden-party hat of pink straw with two daisies dripping of
the brim (my mother's eyes, like her ears, rarely missed a detail); on
her feet, the shapeless sandals she had ordered many years before
in Greenwich Village so she could look like Mary Wigman, in one of
her early flights of artistic aspiration. The loose, ragged, peplumed
dress my mother described was probably of the same vintage, of
the same dream. Having settled herself in the chair my mother
placed for her and refused a cup of tea – she never accepted
anything – she slowly perused row on row, shelf on shelf, all
the boxes in the shop, then studied the three sewing machines and
the women, including my mother, who made them whir and speed.
After the unhurried studies, she rose. Walking to the center of the
shop, imperiously pushing aside a customer who was in her way,
she proclaimed in a rusty, cawing voice, one long arthritic finger
pointing at the shelves and piles of boxes, 'In all those boxes,
those hundreds of boxes, what do you say is in them? You say
it's laces and corset cloth, fancy brassieres, big surgical girdles
with straps to hold tired *kishkas* [entrails] together, fake titties to
put in bathing suits to fool men who think they're seeing the real
thing. Those boxes could even be stuffed with money and diamonds
and sables; your store could be bigger than Macy's and you could
live in a palace on Fifth Avenue like a Rockefeller, you could have

a dozen maids – white, Irishers – to serve you imported lox and keep a dressmaker who works only for you. But if you haven't got your health, ladies, or children who love you – never mind love: children who care whether you die or live – in those boxes, in all the boxes and in the palaces, is shit, only shit, nothing but shit. Believe me, I know.' She turned, pushed the droooping daisies of her hat away from her eyes, and stalked out. Like a proud old cat, my mother said.

Gossip and annals exchanged, the chicken bones and orange peel gathered and wrapped, dusk coming on, my mother summoned my father and they drove off, she completely contented with her Sunday and us, he still dour and disapproving but not free to express it. Davy, though a *shmendrick*, was a good boy, a smart college boy who might be a doctor someday, or a lawyer; anyhow, someone who didn't work in a factory. As for me, I was so completely out of my father's control that although he continued to mutter, he no longer complained clearly or loudly about me, or at least not in my hearing, since our encounters were few.

On several Sundays they brought with them my little sister, at the time about nine years old and very happy to pick flowers and splash around the edge of the quarry. I noticed with some interest how solicitous my mother was of her, more like the nervous Jewish mothers of my childhood. She was tensely watchful that the child didn't go too far into the water, that she didn't shiver with cold; wrapped her in towels, rubbed her, and made her put on a fresh, dry dress, not hang around until the sun dried her, as we did. When I asked my mother about this special solicitude during one of the quiet autumnal afternoons we occasionally spent together, she said it was because my sister had been a sickly child – did I remember that she had to be fed bacon, of all things, on the doctor's orders? – who had anal pinworms and was very sick, with a high fever, with each tooth she cut. Surely I remembered the weeks we ran wild in Coney Island because she needed so much attention? Mostly, she said, it was guilt that made her so attentive. This one she didn't want, really didn't, especially since my brother and I were quite grown, six and a half and eight, when she became pregnant, and old enough to care for ourselves while she took on longer hours of work. And here this pregnancy, her fourteenth, and Dr. James (a New England aristocrat whose mission, now that he was retired from ordinary practice, was to perform abortions for

immigrant women at no fee or little) would not, to her amazed
disappointment, perform another abortion on her. He tried to help
women, he had said sourly, not kill them. She was stuck, she didn't
want this baby, not at all, not for a moment. Did I remember how
tired she was, and how easily she cried? Now, of course, she loved
the child, had loved her from birth, such a pretty and frail baby,
but she never could forget the terrible feeling of not wanting her
and begging Dr. James to change his mind, to try just one more
abortion. For that she would feel forever guilty and, afraid that
the little girl might in some way sense that early unwantedness,
was especially indulgent and affectionate with her. And it was so
nice to indulge her now that there was the corset store and money
to spend on her, not like having had to be so stingy with us.

I once made a rough count of thirteen abortions between the
time we came to America, when I was not quite five, and the time
of my sister's birth; it came to about four abortions a year. My
mother must have picked up some birth control information after
my sister's birth, probably had learned about condoms and insisted
my father use them. That there was some diminution in their sex
lives after my mother's first, early heart attack I discovered when I
found her giggling as she opened her door for me. She was amused
because her doctor had told her that there was to be sex no more
than twice a week, and she was anticipating the look on my father's
face when she told him the black news. It has since occurred to me
that a woman who had undergone so many abortions would have
shrunk from or even cut off all sexual contact. Although it was
dictated by her tradition and those of her friends and neighbors
that she acquiesce to 'men's needs', there were yet thousands
on thousands of women who found some way out, headaches
to hysterics. Since she resorted to none of the dodges, it would
seem that my mother enjoyed sex and was fatalistic and stalwart
about abortions, among women's common ordeals, and infinitely
grateful that there was the old Yankee crane Dr. James to perform
them. In my still naive years I sometimes wondered that my
mother could tolerate men at all. She clearly could, playfully
and delicately flirtatious (learned from the showgirl customers in
her corset shop in Warsaw?) in her encounters with the husbands
of her customers, many of them Italian and, in their peasant way,
courteously responsive.

One of the injunctions of her doctor insisted that she walk a
certain distance every fair day and she did, to Bronx Park, not

far away, where she could rest on a bench before she returned. Shortly after the walks began I heard about Mr. Giordano, a retired butcher who also had heart disease,who also had to take walks. He was a nice gentleman, she said, who once in a while brought her cannoli and sfogliatelli, delectable Neapolitan cakes they shouldn't have eaten, but who could live on cottage cheese and lettuce all the time, so what the hell. They talked about their children, about his dead wife, Rosa, about how boring it was to be retired (she wasn't, and continued working until her death), about the flowers and trees around them and the garden he was planting for his grandchildren. I asked her if she ever met him outside the park, in a room, in his house maybe. She laughed and said, 'I think we might if we could. But we're both broken crocks and what a terrible joke it would be if we killed each other in his bed, maybe under a picture of the Virgin Mary, like many Italian bedrooms have. No, we just walk and talk and that has to be enough.' She would add wistfully, 'Sometimes it feels like a lot. I haven't had such nice talking with a man for a long time.' My mother died with an Italian text in her bed. The family story is that she was studying Italian to be able to speak with immigrant customers, to ascertain where there might be excessive pressure of steel or bone, to understand where straps on surgical girdles compressed the flesh painfully. That was quite true, but I never relinquished the thought that she might also have been learning Italian to flatter and please Mr. Giordano, to suggest a light shadow of being in love – my bit of spangle sewn on her short, narrow life.

She was still quite well, however, at the crest of her might and merriment, that quarry summer, tottering on her small high-heeled shoes as she scrambled, held on either side by myself and Davy, down the loose-stoned path to the quarry. She never went swimming; she didn't think short, fat women like herself should appear in bathing suits; it was ugly. She dabbled her feet in the water and kept a ceaselessly vigilant eye on my sister while Davy, holding her firmly, taught the child to swim. Shoes and stockings on again, Mama permitted us to pull her up the hill, laughing all the way. At the top, near the car, enclosed in his fief walled by the newspaper, sat my immobile father.

After the ceremonial 'piece fruit' which marked the beginning or end of Jewish conversations, my mother announced, one day, 'I have an idea. Why should we keep the baby' – so my sister was referred to until she went to college – 'in the hot city? I can't leave the store to take her away and it would be, if I could do it, only for a week, no more. Her best friends are away in the Catskill Mountains or Far Rockaway, or someplace, and the poor thing wanders around and doesn't know what to do with herself. So she stays alone in the house and reads too much. So – why don't I bring her up here, to you? Of course I would pay her board and give you a salary as mother's helpers.'

That is how we teen-agers became the parents of a nine-year-old and earned enough to keep ourselves comfortably at the quarry for the rest of the summer and something left over for a new pair of shoes and a heavy sweater in the fall. My sister, always a winning child, was developing a pretty little wit; she was a speaker of odd, arresting phrases and a maker of tunes which she sang in a true, limpid voice. We taught her other songs, which she learned with talented ease, and thus we spent many evenings singing blues, cowboy songs, spirituals (which I had learned on my visits with Joe to the Hall Johnson Choir in Harlem), the old Irving Berlin songs – 'All Alone,' 'Remember' – of my childhood, songs we had learned in school, and snatches of Jewish chants we half knew, into the night. We sang with a few neighbors at times, but most often as a trio, in praise of the moon and the march of stars across the dappled sky. We took her with us to the settlement across the highway, leaving her with friends who had children her age. She enjoyed the visits but was just as pleased to leave when we began the trek back to our summer estate, completely contented to swim, to pick blackberries, to stroke the family goat when Guido let her, to be with us constantly, parted from us only by the India-print curtain which separated our cots at night.

Her presence was, in spite of the curtain and her deep child's sleep, an inhibitor and a welcome one. We had, with our small knowledges and lack of experience, with Davy's fear of hurting me and my inability to encourage him – to reassure him that the pain of tearing through a hymen was not great and that I wouldn't mind – reached a discouraged state. It was easier to avoid sex than to admit that the best we could do was stroke each other, penetration avoided. Another inhibitor was the large, dark shadow of pregnancy. Davy had learned the names of condoms and knew the pharmacies that sold them. He had also learned that there were tears and holes in them sometimes, that semen could seep through dried-out 'rubbers.' He rejected the condoms, it seemed to me, also because they solved nothing about forcing a hymen, which he had begun to think of as an impenetrable wall. I had heard of thick, rigid hymens and maybe mine was like those. We couldn't afford to consult a physician – and what kind? – nor were there hospital clinics to help us, and there were no adults we could turn to for advice. I might have asked my mother, but I didn't know how to open the subject, nor could I easily confess failure of any kind to her. I needed the stance of knowing what I was doing at all times in order not to crumble. As the self-conscious cage of failure imprisoned us both, the affectionate and gratifying stroking stopped although we stayed close, devoted friends, pleased with each other's company and lonely without it. We never actually discussed it, but we must both have felt that sex that was too much like 'feeling up' and had gone on too long was immature, inadequate, and we were profoundly ashamed not to be capable of the full adult act.

In spite of the embarrassed, frozen nights, the days were garlands of pleasure. Had we found the courage – Davy less frightened, I more thoughtful – to deflower me (a curious old euphemism, less graphic than the later 'breaking the cherry'), I might now be Mrs. Davy or, as things go, the former Mrs. Davy. In a sneaky, subterranean way, I was preparing myself for the full, grown-up experience, with someone else if necessary, possibly a less talkative and younger Jones. I was determined that it would happen, not so much out of sexual hunger as from the need to know what the experience held, not to be ignorant, not to be left out. Ultimately what had to happen happened, but not for a while.

24
Siblings Refound

Summer, as summers faithlessly do, left and we said good-bye to Guido, presenting him with a strongly odoriferous Italian salami as a farewell gift, patting La Bella's back affectionately, a farewell, as it were, to an old friend. In exchange he gave us a bottle of his cutthroat wine and, for my sister, a bagful of narcissus bulbs and instructions about how to nurture them. That fall we lined up enough jobs among our several semiskills to pay the rent on a one-room street-floor apartment near Fourteenth Street and the First Avenue market. The furnishings were a couch that opened into a bed, a bridge table that could hide in our one closet, two chairs, a two-burner stove that sat on a small icebox, two rows of open shelves; beyond the kitchen space was a bathroom, its door studded with hooks for coats.

The bulbs on the wall in their paper caps were enchantments and so were our lumpy couch and my own stove and, on a shelf, two elderly pots, a frying pan my mother gave me, and a few dishes we bought in the market. I was enamored of it all and Davy swelled like an English squire as he counted out our money to pay the rent. We lived there for over a year, in our Paul and Virginia fashion, smitten with everything around us, with ourselves and each other. We loved the market and its big cans of burning flames that warmed winter nights and blazed the faces of the vendors, making stunning chiaroscuro paintings. We loved the pastries sold us cheaply by the local Sicilian baker because they were a bit smashed around the edges. We learned to make good spaghetti sauce from the tomato lady in the market and Swedish meatballs from a painter neighbor. Surrounded with crusty chunks of Italian bread, these were the culinary offerings we fed our friends, a number of them teachers and neighbors older than we. They always seemed to enjoy the food hugely, not that in itself it was remarkable but, possibly, because it had as an ingredient the courage and contempt for convention of two young lovers: 'Romeo and Juliet', insisted one of Davy's teachers, grayly, soddenly married.

But I didn't immutably feel like Juliet. I had no nurse to pet or cosset me, no choice of princely suitors, no bejeweled mother, no rich damasked father. I worked hard, running from lessons to modeling to filing, to this job and to that, to do any work that came my way, and just sufficiently attentive to school to achieve, in time, the privileged English major. And I was troubled, when I allowed myself to think about it, by my peculiar sex – or nonsex – life. No one, of course, knew of this, and my heroine portrait painted in the Exchange at Hunter accrued ever bolder colors. My independence had moved me into an ultimate mastery of life: a real, full apartment in Manhattan, a short walk from Greenwich Village, the haven of free love. Some of my coterie became formally respectful, tongue-tied when I addressed them. The loss of intimacy, the fading of the earlier slapdash ease, bothered me very little. I hadn't much time to hang around: too many jobs, a house to clean, I boasted (actually quite casually and quickly done, since both Davy and I were accustomed to the crowded disorder of not quite enough closet space, too much bed in one small bedroom, heaps of dishes in the sink, books piled on the floor). The very best of my envied possessions was the full-time devoted boyfriend, who more or less lived with me except when his straight-spoken mother commanded that he stay at home; he was a member of her family like his brothers and sisters until he was married, she said, and he wasn't ready to get married yet, not by a long shot. Never mind his mother. To the girls we were a wondrous thing, princes of Eden and Xanadu, deserving of adulation and gifts. Millie brought a big curtain her mother had discarded for us to cover our discolored couch, Edith brought some forks, a knife, and a dish that her mother thought had been unkoshered by her careless son the 'apostate', who used them for meat when they were meant for cheese, or some such mortal misdeed which I didn't follow while I happily accepted the gifts.

Our apartment added a new dimension to my brother's life. He had for some time called on me, in one room or another, to deliver the money my mother occasionally sent me. His habit had been to look around quickly and curiously, then take the money

out of his pocket, hand it to me with a laconic 'Here,' and leave.
Eleventh Street and its sociabilities made him slower, a lingerer.
He had returned tall, muscled, and suntanned from a voyage to
Cuba and back as a cabin boy. The trip had improved not only his
looks but his manner and confidence; he had the cockiness to flirt
attractively with college girls while he was still struggling through
the infantilism of high school. His visits took place early in the
evening, after school was over and he had finished his deliveries
for the local drugstore. He had supper with Davy and myself
and whatever friends hung around, friends reluctant to leave our
charmed circle, reluctant to return to the Bronx or East Harlem,
to half-crazy, unemployed fathers and testy mothers: 'Where were
you all this time? Downtown with your bum friends, their parents
should be ashamed for allowing they should live together like that.
Why don't they make them marry? What will they do when that
crazy girl becomes pregnant? Who's going to keep her? With what?'
And so endlessly on. Most often, the spur to go home finally was a
paper unfinished. If the analysis of *The Winter's Tale* was submitted
late, it was marked with a low grade, no matter what the quality.
(The scares and woes of attending stern Hunter were many and
the ultimate practical rewards limited. About the only jobs in fair
supply were those in the welfare system then being established.
Girls who might have been inventive physicists and inspiring
teachers and critics, skillful translators in several languages,
became and stayed throughout their lives – spinsters or
married – social workers.)

Back to my brother: He loved all my friends – the young, the
older, the short, the tall, the fat, the skinny – and at sixteen was
not only an adroit flirt but an inspired dancer. And my friends were
by no means immune to the 'kid's' charms; they managed to make
dates with him as they rode the subway together on their journeys
home, and there was considerable gossip about the Baby Wonder
in the Hunter Exchange. He didn't mind when I recounted it to his
satisfied face.

My brother and I had stopped fighting for some time. Though
we still argued, we had ceased battering each other's orbits. For
long periods separated, we were no longer the classic siblings; we
were joined in a spiky friendship, rather. No longer each other's
close concerns, both of us now challenged the world in different
ways, with even wider separate arenas to do battle in. I was free
of responsibility for his dirty shirt and ripped knickers and he no

longer had to obey when I screamed at him to stop playing stickball and come up to supper, right away.

The childhood wars over, I found myself mildly interested in him as something other than adversary, a hundred thorns in my life. First, he was droll, almost as droll as he was at two and rachitic, unable to walk but a cajoling, irrepressible talker and inventor of imaginative mischief. It was a revival of old nutty times to find him in the bathroom, during one of my visits to the Bronx, plucking at his armpits, trying to pull at a hair or two he thought he saw in the recalcitrant pink, smooth surface. Eventually they came, but he had a long, anxious time in front of the bathroom mirror, searching, pulling, willing the hairs to grow. On an invasion of the bathroom to catch him at yet another 'How does my garden grow' search, I found him struggling with one of my discarded brassieres, which, since his back was considerably broader than mine, he couldn't close. I asked him if I could help. Rather than pull it off, surprised and embarrassed, as I expected, he muttered, 'All right.' After strenuous pulling, I managed to hook the bra and we both looked and laughed at the futile cups barely filled with unsuitable chest. 'You won't make it,' I said. 'I don't want to. I wanted to know how it feels to be tightened all the time in a straitjacket like girls and other crazy people.' 'Oh, it's not so bad, no worse than having to shave every day' – a subject of some trouble to him at this time, since his cheeks were as slow as his armpits. 'I suppose you're right,' he said. 'Shaving every day must be terrible. Movie actors probably have to shave two and even three times a day.' My sophisticated response: 'That's nothing. The worst thing is menstruating, feeling bad and angry and hateful for three or four days, then bleeding for about a week, with cramps and never knowing if you've stained your skirt and is everybody looking. And things like that.' This usually led off, when we had the time for it, not running in several directions, to discussions of who suffered most, the shavers or the menstruators. In retrospect it seems a strange debate, which we kept going, with accretions of details and variations, for some time. We were educating each other and declaring a unity as maturing equals; no more big sister, no more little brother.

It was my mother who told me of an earlier stage in his sex education, long before he became obsessed with armpit hairs. She had given him permission to invite a dozen or so friends to celebrate their graduation from elementary school. My father was all for staying in the living room and seeing that the thirteen- and fourteen-year-olds behaved properly. My mother, having helped arrange the cream soda, the Baby Ruths, the cookies, and the chocolate kisses my brother bought out of his salary earned at the local drugstore, made vigorous efforts to get my father and herself out. She finally induced him to go to a movie, assuring him that these were good kids and would behave. If they really wanted to, they could get into trouble in the cellar or on the roof, or in someone else's apartment. 'Come on, you like Jeanette MacDonald.' After the movie she took him walking, he still eager to tear back to the house. Not yet, she said, and asked that he buy her a hot chocolate. He wouldn't walk anymore after she had finished. It was a cold night, he was tired, he wanted to go home. There was no way to keep him out after midnight, and they returned. The empty soda bottles strewn all over and the candy wrapper clogging the kitchen sink, the crumbs of cookies in the corners of the couch, didn't disturb her; it was all to be expected. A glance into her bedroom stopped her short. She called my brother to her. He appeared with his hands full of cupcake papers meant for the garbage pail, looking foolish and frightened. She said, 'Take it easy, I'm not going to do anything to you. You're too big a boy to punish and I don't want to spoil your graduation. But just look at that bed; there were bodies on it – you can tell by the crumpled cover. I don't want to know who was on it or what they did.' Long pause, and then: 'I just want to ask one thing: Do you know that the girl has the baby, not the boy? Don't ever, ever forget that.' He was slow and quiet for days after, my mother said.

My brother's curiosity and gossip about his drugstore clients, the amusement they afforded him (several insisted on calling a popular laxative, Feen-a-mint, 'Shit Gum', he informed us gleefully), and the scared faces of the boys older than himself begging that he sell them condoms, appealed to his nascent sense of power. For his affability, for his vast collection of arcane little facts (which kid wet the bed at twelve, which store was selling bargain pants), for his links of knowledges and gossip that made a tight and amusing village of the neighborhood, he was called, as he strutted down the street swollen with inside dope, 'the Mayor of Allerton Avenue', Keeping my mother's short, crisp bedroom lesson as a guiding rule, and as if he had imbibed a certain primitive courtliness from that lesson, he never in any way mistreated his girls, nor slighted them, except when there were too many for one boy to juggle.

Not all the girls who ran at me for help, for influence with my brother, wanted adult sex; too scary. They wanted movie love, soft-eyed, surrounded by heart-shaped boxes of candy, a rose or two, walks in the park, and bashful light kissing under apple-blossom trees – a Lillian Gish–Charles Ray idyll. Though he tried to be considerate, the shyly romantic was not my brother's style, nor was he often inclined, in the promising excitements of variety, to concentrate on one girl. He seemed to like them all equally and prized himself in the courteous, playful pursuer role, like Robert Young, more than he prized the girls. It was one of my duties, when I visited my mother, to tell the tearful ones who haunted her apartment that he was never serious, that he would never attach himself to anyone, too footloose, and they were to find someone else. What was wrong with good-looking Benny around the corner, or that new new boy, Tommy? So he *was* a *goy*. Her mother didn't have to know, and anyway she wasn't going to marry him. 'Stop crying, it's making your nose red and swollen. Where's your handkerchief?' I liked the role of adviser to my brother's weepers, something like being a social worker or a teacher, more like the big sister I had been throughout my childhood, a role I thought I hated but apparently missed.

Besides being, as of old, but in a new light manner, my brother's keeper, I sometimes slipped into the surrogate-mother role of being my young sister's mentor, not always an unqualified success. We had gotten to know and like each other during our quarry summer and it was later reasonable that, when I had the time, I would take her shopping, introducing her to the charms of Klein's and Ohrbach's on Union Square. Here matters went smoothly, she trusting my judgement, voicing very little dissent. She became her own woman in the public library, where I tried to help her pick out books. After several visits in quiet acquiescence, she stopped me, protesting: 'I don't want any more fairy tales, not the Green, nor the Blue, not the Red, and no more books about Dutch Twins or Belgian Twins or Japanese Twins. I want to read harder books, about real people, about real girls like me, and please don't try to find them. I will, thank you.' On my next visit she flourished a library copy of *My Ántonia* by Willa Cather at me.

We explored the Metropolitan Museum, where the naked ladies and gentlemen entranced her; she stood for a long time with the nude Greeks and an even longer time before the late Renaissance goddesses of Venice. Both she and I were smitten with the tawny supermasculine Etruscan warrior of the huge staring eyes who was later discarded as a fake; we wouldn't believe it except as a dreadful injustice. Because she had a pretty voice and learned quickly, I tried to sing Schubert songs with her, picking out the accompaniments on the piano in my mother's apartment, the piano I wouldn't touch years before. This was another occasion when I pushed too hard and failed; the German words baffled her and she would not sing that which was incomprehensible. We remained close friends, though; I too often putting on the old childhood mask of the guide, she as frequently, tactfully, rejecting my suggestions, until subtle changes made of me, at times, the younger sister and she the older and wiser. We exchanged these parts, a useful and happy arrangement, for the rest of our time together.

25
High Life

One Christmas vacation promised to be a stinker. Davy had to
go to Florida to help his uncle Moe, who paid him well to take
care of the clients in his Miami boardinghouse. I had time for
extra hours on jobs and for overdue class papers, and time to
enjoy the smell of bundles of fir trees and their country green,
staring meekly, like rows of prisoners, out of street lots. There was
time to enjoy the shiny, brittle ornaments in Woolworth's and the
glittering tinsel. The rest – the angels and lights, the beribboned
boxes, the black Salvation Army pot, the interminable repetitions
of 'Silent Night' and 'Jingle Bells', were, as our Jewish parents and
grandparents said, '*Goyim naches*', and who needed it? (We did, but
couldn't say so.) Being alone in the apartment was uncomfortable,
and besides, I was having landlord trouble. Our landlord, a pleasant
man who called himself Garibaldi and wore a swooping, discolored
hat to tighten the link with his hero, had informed me that though
I was a nice, *bella* girl, he needed my downstairs apartment for his
nephew Riccardo and his wife, who was far advanced in her first
pregnancy and couldn't climb the five flights of stairs to their
present apartment. Concetta got dizzy, she said, from the height
and from dragging her big belly; she was afraid she would faint
and fall and mash Riccardo junior. Also, she couldn't anymore go
to the toilet in the hall. She didn't make it fast enough with the baby
pressing so hard that she almost peed in her pants before she got
there. And if there was another tenant in the hall toilet? She might
die trying to hold it in, which she couldn't most of the time, or if she
did, her bladder might break. A patient, inexhaustible nagger, she
frightened Riccardo into nagging Garibaldi who nagged me to give
her my ground-floor apartment and its private toilet. I had seen
a good number of bellies in my childhood, worried about them,

hated them, especially my mother's before it pushed my sister out
and when I heard that I was pulled out with 'instruments' that cut
and tore at my mother. None of these images or fears attached
themselves with any sympathy to Concetta, who could dree her
own weird – a phrase picked up in my Anglo-Saxon class and
vengefully useful.

I would go away. Garibaldi wouldn't put my stuff out into the
street while I was gone; he was too nice and too lazy. I couldn't
go with Davy, his uncle was paying his fare and certainly would
not pay mine. He didn't like me much; none of Davy's family did
except his sweet, slow father. After some thought, and dispelling a
faint stickiness of distaste, I decided to accept an invitation that
had been pressed on me for weeks.

One odd, unexpected time in the semester, a stranger, not of
Hunter, had walked into my Shakespeare II class, sat herself under
the professor's eye, opened her genuine leather notebook, extracted
a gold-capped fountain pen from her alligator bag, and begun to
make rapid notes. It became obvious, after a week or two, that her
interest in Falstaff and the Richards was considerably less than her
need to impress those around her. She had little success with the
professor, whom she approached with questions, not always inane,
at the end of class. A dry old scholar immortally in love with Portia
and Ophelia, Beatrice and Viola, finding no facsimiles in any of us
bundles of ungraceful flesh and no elegance of spirit, brushed off
all questioners, muttering 'Another class,' and rushed out. A few
of the girls the newcomer approached were apprehensive; she was
too ardent in her courtship. We didn't quite know what to make
of her. She was eight or ten years older than most of us and
spoke of having attended, for varying periods, Vassar, Oxford,
Bryn Mawr, and the Sorbonne, her schooling interrupted by a
mysterious ailment. (At this point of her stories we were taken
to Swiss sanatoria that closely suggested *The Magic Mountain*.)
Her coats were too expensive – one of real fur – she had
too many dresses, good ones, her shoes were made by an Italian
craftsman and looked it, her pocketbooks were cut of rare skins.
She was far too upper class for us, and furthermore, her body and
looks were disturbingly inappropriate to her glamorous adventures
and queenly belongings. She was short and emaciated. Her brown
hair crept down to a forehead of thick, matte skin like blotting
paper, almost to meet heavy masculine eyebrows. She did have
compelling eyes, flat gray and large, the blotting paper under

them gathered around a thin mouth and short chin – hardly a face at all except for the eyes. Some of us found it repellent when she came very close and stuck her face under our chins, looking up pleading and expectant as she tried to seduce us with her gifts of an enchanted past and privileged present.

She was a designer, she said, and liked to photograph her models in the nude and then in the clothing she created for them. Hunter? Oh, with only a year to go, she might get her degree this time. Anyhow, she was going to be married soon. Her father was one of the most prestigious lawyers in New York, she said, and kept her in Hunter only because he wanted her near home. (Why not Barnard, NYU? leapt simultaneously and unspoken to our minds.) On the fee her father had earned in a big case some years ago, he had bought a big house in Brooklyn, probably designed by Stanford White, some experts said. Why didn't we come to Brooklyn to see the house, really unusual, have tea there, and meet her interesting father and mother? A family legend had it that Mama was, when young, the mistress of a Polish nobleman (each classic cheap-novel detail distanced us increasingly from her; she might have known it, but couldn't stop). And we would love her dear, darling brother, who was a little sick right now – nothing much; he would be fine soon.

Rejected by the others, Sandra Rubinstein laid heavy siege to me. She had learned that I lived away from my parents and could go where I liked, and being more worldly and older than the rest, might not altogether disbelieve her stories of elite schools and worldwide travel. Between Davy's absence and Concetta's whining, she caught me at a weak moment and I agreed to go to her house for Christmas, to be photographed. The pay would be my keep plus a model's fee of ten dollars a day. So I packed some books and clothing, called my several employers to say I had to leave town for a while, and moved to Brooklyn for the holidays. The generous Middle European meals prepared by Sandra's mother and served on a well-dressed table were nectar compared to my usual meatballs and spaghetti or hot dogs with potato salad. Which fork to use for what course was a matter of watching the others; there was more difficulty in deciding how to handle the serving tools, how much to take off a large platter offered by the Negro maid. Sitting at the table as the brown arms slid toward me and away felt Hollywood and yet shameful, unnatural. The rich meat borscht and the stuffed cabbage, however, the homemade cheesecakes and nut cookies, soon dispelled the awkwardness of living beyond my habits.

The father, Mr. Rubinstein, was a slender man with a Phi Beta Kappa key on his chest and the high, shouting laugh of a fat man. Mama was good-looking in a ponderous way, never quite properly buttoned or arranged when she came to the table, having to be reminded that her dress had too much neckline, that her breasts were poking out of her brassiere. 'Well, all right, all right, it's because I'm openhearted,' and, laughing, she pulled the offending gaps to. She was preoccupied with several medical discoveries she had made, abetted by home medicine volumes she studied assiduously. Any pause in the conversation was ground for one of her discourses; a favorite: 'The cause of cancer is worriment and grief, too much worriment and grief.' During my encounters with her I also learned that 'Headaches is nervousness that runs from the body to the brain and makes mixtures that fight and hurt.' Compared to my controlled, neatly dressed mother, she was a wilderness thing and aware of it, explaining her uninhibited speech and careless impromptu dress by the fact that she was born in Cossack country, where everyone was wild. She liked me only because I listened attentively to her psychosomatic revelations when no one else would. I liked her because of these eccentric enlightenments and her staccato, dramatic narratives. She would burst through the front door, trailing a Gypsy assortment of blouses, coats, and scarves, flowing, unbuttoned, her hand on her gasping, excited breast, spilling breathlessly, without a pause for hello: 'Ay, did I just meet a lady, a friend of Mrs. Franks from across the street. She's so beautiful, with real blond hair and skin like white roses. She was wearing a stylish English tweed suit and a mink jacket and a string of pearls on her neck, real. I tell you, a beauty! She has her own millinery store and doesn't take any money from her *shlimazl* husband. Her children go the Pestalozzi school and music camps. She speaks German and French, and her children, too. She wears a high-crowned silk hat she made herself; she looks gorgeous, like a czarina, like a queen, I tell you.' Without a pause: 'What am I saying? Pheh! There's nothing to her.' I could never anticipate or understand the sudden paeans of praise and the swift falls, but waited for them and marveled.

For a few days Sandra and I were busy at photographic sessions, with intervals for good meals and Sandra's long telephone conversations. I found it all deeply absorbing: the once ambitious library of matched leather bindings that stopped with *War and Peace* and *Dombey and Son*, the variety of lounging robes dripping lengths of boa, worn by mother and daughter much of the day. To one who had never had a proper bathrobe, these were the gowns of princesses in grand palaces. But how to think of a Jewish family with a dog? The Rubinsteins were not observant, they ate shrimp and pork chops, but a *dog*? Dogs were for Polish janitors and English lords in the red jackets of 'Do ye ken John Peel' sort of pictures. Jews didn't feed dogs – there were too many hungry humans – and furthermore, dogs were malevolent assistants in pogroms. Many Jewish children of my generation were afraid of dogs, as I was, having been fed on indelible stories. This one, however, was too cowardly and small and pathetically ugly – bulging eyes, crooked teeth, and bowed legs – to be anything but a caricature, and drooling constantly at that. The women of the family adored and cosseted him, the father loathed him and kicked him lightly, surreptitiously, when the women weren't around. Then the terrified dog ran for safety to the frail son, the one with the unidentified disease, who hung around, more and more, during the clothed photographing sessions, making no comment, looking, looking. His silence and pallor, his thick eyeglasses and the scarf wrapped around his throat, made me back away from him as if he carried an unnamed plague. When the photography slacked off after a few days, he invited me to a movie and proved more talkative than in the presence of his family. His conversations – actually monologues – on the walk to and from the movies were chillingly morbid, concerned mainly with monstrous births. Educated out of his mother's books and old medical volumes bought secondhand, he was well informed and graphically detailed in his information about spina bifida and hydrocephaly, even stopping to sketch quickly, in the notebook he always carried, the dreadful contours of these unhuman babies. When I begged him to stop, threatening to walk away if he didn't – he became, at times, more monstrous in his enthusiasm than his subjects – he turned to music and the new recordings he had bought for his extensive collection. He couldn't stay away, though, from his prime obsession, 'birth mistakes', and in the course of describing a Schnabel performance of a Beethoven sonata, suddenly said, 'Here's something interesting, not too morbid. Do you know that some people's bodies have cysts that contain human hair or a tooth? You know what that is? It's a twin that never developed but became incorporated in the body of the baby that did. Sometimes – and this is even more interesting – they take a baby out and find a kind of extra skin sticking to it. The skin has the full form of another baby. The healthy cannibal sucks it dry, blood, bones, and all, to feed itself.' It was impossible not to think that somewhere, he felt, a twin had half consumed him, that he was a feeble, emptied envelope, and that with study and observation he could remedy his situation, become strong again, or at least resigned to his anomalous state.

I consented to go to the movies again with him only after he promised not to talk about birth defects. He didn't, but bought me a soda and expensive English mints to eat during the show. In the following days, he became more courtly and flattering, his apogee of praise the mumbled statement that I reminded him of the Spring Song of Siegfried's meeting with Sieglinde. (Not until I became a mild Wagnerite did I appreciate the warmth of the compliment.) Papa presented me with a bunch of flowers – 'Sweets to the sweet', and he guffawed in his fat man's bellow. Mama consulted me about dinner – would I like veal chops with sour cream or chicken in lemon sauce? I was introduced to relatives and distinguished friends, among them a leading obstetrician of Brooklyn, whose spring and summer costume, he boasted, was an outfit for golfing, including clubs, to impress his patients with the fact that he tore off some fictitious golf course or other to be immediately with them in their painful need. When I sneezed, there was quick solicitude from Mama and Papa – was I catching a cold, God forbid? How pretty and unusual I looked in my earrings. How smart I must be in school with such an intelligent face; surely I would make Phi Beta Kappa.

Sandra brought me little presents – a wallet, a scarf – and the family presents came faster and faster, increasingly expensive, as if to display the delights I would enjoy as a member of this prosperous, generous family. They were crowding me, urging me to love them and Sam, who needed a strong, healthy girl. I didn't want to live here, to be part of them and under their control. I had been invited for work and that was all. Though only several days of the holiday were gone, the sickly sweet praise, the forced attention, Sam's mania becoming heavily oppressive, Mama's medical inventions no longer amusing, I wanted to go back to Eleventh Street to brave Garibaldi and Concetta's belly. But the bed and board in Brooklyn were sybaritic and the promised salary

munificent as compared to the wages I received for much rougher
work in my screaming laundry. I stayed; waiting, wary, preparing
for some sort of overt proposition that would probably first come
from wild Cossack Mama in her stained blue velvet dressing gown
with the stringy boa.

It came one evening over the nuts and fruit on the round
dining table. Mama led off, asking if I liked Sammy, her son.
Ready as I was, I still found the question annoying and hated
them all. I said I liked him but not very especially. Papa clattered
his loud laugh – how cute I looked blushing – and pushed
Sam's hand nearer mine as they lay on the table. Sam grew uneasy
and dropped his hands in his lap. Mama went on: Sandra was
going to be married soon – she supposed I knew – to a
successful young accountant, Rick, but unfortunately she couldn't
have children: her bones were too narrow and her health too frail,
the doctor had said. So, Mama went on reasonably, why shouldn't
I marry Sam, whose sickness would be over in a short time, he
only needed some rest. We might marry in the late spring. I liked
children, didn't I? I had spoken so affectionately about the kids I
baby-sat. Such a fresh, young, healthy girl like me could have lots
of babies. So-o-o- – a sententious pause – my first would go
to Sandra and Rick because they were older, the next I could keep
for myself and Sam; the third would be theirs, the fourth ours, and
so on.

Since I had left my parents' house to live with others –
as mother's helper, as companion, as tenant, as tutor – I
had learned to anticipate strikes of madness, when ordinary
rooms become crooked, surrealistic, when smiles were suddenly
carnivorous, issuing from frightening maws. I had also learned
control and an accompanying degree of politeness. Instead of
flaring up as my head and limbs urged me to, screaming 'How can
you – Jews – talk about giving and taking babies, like dirty,
thieving Gypsies? You're not only crazy, you're immoral!' I laughed
a little, not too difficult since somewhere in my anger was a strand
of amusement over these madmen. 'What makes you think I'm a
baby machine? How do you know I want children and how soon
I want them if at all? When I came here it was on hire, only for
modeling, not as a permanent purchase of a one-woman obstetrics
ward. Good night, I'm leaving tomorrow morning.' Sandra ran after
me to the spare room I used, a place of boxes and chests of drawers
and a decent bed attached to a small bathroom. She pleaded with

me not to leave, wouldn't I please, please stay until the end of the vacation, when she would give me all my money, one hundred dollars. It would be terrible to break into her project, which was going so well. I agreed to stay after she swore to get her family off my neck; no more talk of marriage or babies.

I couldn't find her the next morning, and leaving a message with the maid that I would be back in a day or two, took myself off for a short break of movies, pastrami sandwiches, and comfortable friendships. When I phoned the Rubinstein house the next day, I was told that Sandra had flown off to visit friends in Atlanta and would be back in a couple of days. Back to my footloose friends. When we ran out of movie money we walked and walked, exploring Hester and Essex streets, streets of Greek stables, of huge round cheeses and long, fat logs of Italian sausages, the dim sinister alleys that hung off Canal Street toward Chinatown, vowing there that some moneyed day we would feast of the myriad dumplings that misted and perfumed the air of Doyers Street.

The night of my return, Sandra still absent, the Rubinsteins had a party whose star attraction was an animated, coquettish woman who played small roles in the Yiddish theater. Her effects were good: bobbing, burbling under auburn curls like Shirley Temple at one moment; sloe-eyed long looks under drooping lids and a muted drawl the next minute. Another design was to be mysteriously silent for a while and then, pointing herself at a male target, to bombard the speechless object with eloquent high praise. Early in the evening there was no one to engulf: Papa knew her too well and laughed, Sam was afraid of her and despised her, Rick, Sandra's fiancé, whom I hadn't yet met, was working late and would arrive after dinner.

While the dessert was being served, a stocky young man with a high complexion burst into the dining room, a telegram shaking in his right hand. 'What's the matter, Rick?' came from several directions. 'I'll tell you what's the matter. This telegram came from your darling daughter Sandra. She's having such a good time with her friends, and I suppose their brothers in their white linen suits and their mason jars of moonshine, that she thinks she'll stay a little while longer. What kind of while? For going to bed with all of them? And come back to me with Dixie gonorrhea?' Turning to Mr. Rubinstein: 'You can phone her and tell her to stay on and on. She won't find me around when she gets back.' Mama and Papa ran to him, patted his hands, caressed his cheeks, stroked his

back, begging him not to be impulsive. He knew how mischievous
Sandra could be; she was only playing games with him, trying to
make him jealous, that's all. A sophisticated man like Rick should
understand a silly female impulse that meant nothing but a bid for
extra attention.

Into the excited huddle came our minor Molly Picon, Francie,
who took his manicured, ruby-ringed hand and led him into the
living room, the salon of red plush drapes and chairs, the blue
Oriental rug, the Steinway grand, the inlaid Chinese tables and
the glass cabinet of chinoiserie, a room for serious discussion, or
seduction. Francie chose her surest field. Settling herself close to
him on the velvet couch, she lifted Rick's hand and, looking around
saucily, said, 'Has anyone seen before such an aristocratic hand,
a thinker's hand, an artist's hand? And look at that profile' –
turning his chin cradled in her red-tinted fingers – 'just look
at that profile; it's much better than John Barrymore's. And the
full face is more sex-appealing than that drunkard's. There's
Italian heat in those deep brown eyes. Your grandmother was
Sicilian, a passionate Silcilian beauty, wasn't she, Valentino?'
Her elderly husband was snoring softly in a dim corner of the
room, the Rubinsteins weren't enjoying the seduction, they were
too worried, and I soon had enough of the foolishness of the whole
scene, including Rick's descent into calm, then purring pleasure
and a taut crotch. I went upstairs to the library to read. But
Francie's sinuous voice kept sliding over the pages. She was now
shamelessly extolling Rick's charming personality, his acumen as
a businessman, his generosity to his parents and grandparents.

Her voice faded away into last good nights at about midnight,
and the snap of the safety lock on the front door. Rick came up
the stairs and stood before me, close. He was drunk and intensely
agitated, feral and threatening, looming over me like a great buck
ready to dig his horns into me. Anger, liquor, and sensual stroking
words had set him trembling in a menacing ecstasy. I slid away
from under him and dashed to the bathroom, where I stayed until
I thought he had gone into Sandra's room and to bed. I found him
standing at a window of the library staring out at the garage, far
back in the yard. 'Come here,' he said. I obeyed. Pointing at the
boxes in the open upper story of the garage, he said, 'Wanna see
me shoot those boxes down, every one of them? That's more than
a hundred yards away, isn't it?' I said nothing and still nothing
when he pulled a small gun out of his pocket and began to aim at

the boxes. 'Please don't; they'll hear you and be scared.' 'No, they won't; there's a silencer on this gun.' I, still trying to hold back time and threatening events, said, 'How come you've got a gun? Isn't that illegal?' 'No, sweetie, I have a permit. I got it through some friends.' The veins stood out on his head, he became again the plunging, aggressive animal as he leaned out the window and shot, unfailingly, box after toppling box. I kept whispering, 'Stop, please stop!' He kept on shooting, then suddenly turned, his gun pointing straight at me. 'You saw what happened to those boxes. That'll happen to Sandra if I find out that she's fucking those Atlanta boys. And if you say a word about the gun – or anything – I'll shoot you, too. Maybe I'll fuck you first.' As I stood motionless with fear, he shot into the books on the shelves above my head and into a sofa pillow near my arm. Then he turned the gun in his hand, examining it intimately, affectionately. He put it back in his pocket and closed himself in the bathroom.

I slept fitfully, listening for the soft splat of his gun. Quite different sounds came through my door at about four in the morning. Opening the door a crack, I could see him standing before the mirror of the open dressing alcove we shared, wearing only the bottoms of his blue silk pajamas. As he hummed softly, contentedly, he tweezed hairs from his nose and from the clumps in his armpits. He stroked his chest and followed the slope of his sides to the curve of his ribs with satisfied fingers. He opened the cord of his pajama trousers, dropped them to lift his penis, and inspected it carefully with a look of approval. He plucked a few hairs with his tweezers, pulled up his pajama pants, and like a mother powdering a baby, he tenderly patted talcum powder on his torso. He then turned out the light and disappeared.

The next day was Saturday and I assumed that Rick, his alcohol and self-love, would rest long that morning. Quite early I went down to warn Mr. Rubinstein to get Sandra home quickly and be prepared for Rick's gun when she did get back. Mr. Rubinstein phoned Sandra, told her to be back the next morning, Sunday, without excuses or delay. Then I took myself off, books, clothing, and all, to Eleventh Street, safe from Mr. Garibaldi, who spent his Saturdays playing boccie on Houston Street. When we met in Manhattan the following Monday, Sandra told me with a proud smile that her father and his partner had met her, holding Rick tightly by either arm. Impatient with the story she was expanding in length and drama, I broke in to tell her that I was no longer going to stay at her house and would like the money I had already earned. School was going to start in a few days and I needed the money and the time to catch up on neglected school assignments. Sure, sure, she would give me the money, but she was a little pressed now with all that partying in Atlanta and the fare and presents to her hostess. She would have it soon, though. In the meantime, couldn't we take some of it out in entertainments, like paying for my admission and drinks in some famous Harlem speakeasy clubs, like Dickie Wells's and another that was owned by friends. I had begun to doubt that I would get the money and this suggested arrangement offered novel diversions, experiences that would make balls of fire as I told of them in the Hunter Exchange – not to Davy.

I learned a good deal more about Harlem with Sandra. If you were a regular patron, your waiter could buy you a reefer for fifty cents on almost any nearby corner. I learned that it was possible for a female entertainer to pick up a stiffly folded ten-dollar bill between her labia. It was a wow of an act, additionally rewarded by a bill tucked into the ribbons of a bra – money at the bottom and the top made a nice balance. The great climax of one show was the appearance of a man wearing a small contraption equally adept at the female money-eating trick. (My attempts at home with a crisp dollar bill and my own authentic equipment were dismal failures; it was a skill that required long practice, and were I to master the trick, where would I perform it? This would clearly not be one of my showpieces.)

Another delight of those evenings was the possibility of being picked up, for one drink or an evening of drinks, by a Broadway notable. One husky-voiced actress, enamored for the drunken moment of my storm of multi-yellow hair and what she called 'Tibetan' cheekbones, invited me to sit with her for a drink. I accepted. She worked quickly, no time for subtleties, for the slow sensing of mutual rhythms. As I sipped my drink, she stroked my cheekbones for a moment or two and insisted I go home with her for the night. No longer awed or made shy by liquor-soaked luminaries, I answered (with too much icy poise, I suspect), 'No, thanks.' She spat 'Bitch!' at me, roared at the waiter to take away my half-finished drink, and with her strong, agile behind pushed me off the bench we had been sharing. One night Sandra invited her brother Sam, who threatened to leave almost as we arrived; the waiter who helped him off with his coat had scrabbled at his anus while seemingly adjusting his jacket. We calmed Sam that night but not another, when we went to the apartment of two of Sandra's friends. In one of the dim rooms, bare except for large reproductions of the Belvedere Apollo and other soft Grecian youths, two young men were flicking at each other with light whips, gracefully, caressingly, giggling. Sam took off and I after him. Sandra stayed.

26
Life of Crime

As school and jobs again engulfed me, high life in Harlem closed its tantalizing, educational doors. I wrested no more than twenty-five dollars from Sandra; Concetta had her baby in her Aunt Rosa's house and moved next door to stay with her. Garibaldi and I became friends again.

The new semester offered promising explorations – the Cavalier poets, the Scottish Chaucerians, a second term of that Anglo-Saxon earl, Abraham, with his holdings of lands and ceorls, the now and then mystical mazes of Blake, the ornate mind and word games of Browning, and the sort of masturbatory verbal pleasures that were Swinburne's. I had a new Saturday job in Woolworth's, selling lipsticks, and a couple of my old ladies remained faithful in their English lessons. (I often wondered why they wanted to learn English, since their families addressed them in Russian or Polish or Yiddish. The answer when I questioned them did not betray so much intellectual ambition as avoidance of the dread word 'greenhorn' and causing the daughters-in-law to think they understood every critical word spoken in English.)

In the dingy Exchange, a flatness of no new romances, no new slavish crushes; no one flunked out, no one threatened with Phi Beta Kappa possibilities, nor had the place been painted as promised. After I told my stories of life in a Stanford White house in Brooklyn and high adventure in Harlem, conversation settled into the mundane. The few excitements we could muster came from the classroom, where one of the habitual pleasures was to stump professors as nastily as we could. One of the science girls, a pre-med – if her father gave her the money for medical school, if she did well in chemistry and physics and biology, if medical school quotas limiting women would allow it – spent a fair amount of

time positing and rehearsing the most effective puzzles with which
to confront her biology teacher, the one who wore her Phi Beta
Kappa key belligerently like a platelet of armor, on her high bosom.
One day, during a lecture on the digestive system, Becky raised her
hand and asked guilelessly why the stomach didn't digest itself. Let
her answer that in front of the class, the Phi Betnik. The teacher
fumbled and mumbled but had no answer. Later a few of us raised
our voices in protest: 'That's plagiarizing, it comes from Thomas
Mann, he asked that question. You can't!' 'Oh, can't I? Not in a
million years would that illiterate read Thomas Mann. It's a very
tiny chance and my stock may go up one thousand percent as an
astute biologist, an original thinker, or maybe she'll just really
hate me. I'll take the chance.' In one variation or other, we bolder
girls, most of us well-read, with the uncanny memories of youth,
staged these little scenes, for fun, for wrapping the Olympians
in discomfort. One linguist sharpie asked in class for a precise
translation of an ambiguous line from the medieval French of the
Romance of the Rose. The professor did not know or had forgotten.
Palpably hating her questioner, she admitted defeat but was fair
enough to credit the girl with meticulous scholarship, a victory for
our side. I was interested, I told a Romantic poetry professor, in the
life and works of Hartley Coleridge, the neglected son of the great
Coleridge, who was for a while Wordsworth's charge. It seemed to
me that he had had a brother who published his letters and poems.
What was the brother's name and where might I find further
references to him? The professor couldn't help me and didn't
care to. To a lover of the pristine spirits of Shelley and Keats,
the degenerate, drugged, and drunken Coleridges were beneath
contempt, the detritus of literature. I lost that minor foray, without
resentment, since I enjoyed this lissome, fawn-gloved, very minor
poet-professor, who read to us weekly, as if it were religious litany,
'La Belle Dame Sans Merci', with lovely shades of terror in his
countertenor voice. (We didn't think he had to display his fear
of women quite so blatantly while we admired wholeheartedly the
infinite sadness he put into 'The sedge is withered from the lake,
And no birds sing!' These, he added, were among the greatest lines
in all poetry. He convinced us and we stayed convinced.)

One mode of winning over professors was to be utterly,
idiotically honest during a short-lived experiment that instituted
an honor system like that enjoyed for many years by Virginia
gentlemen in Jefferson's university at Charlottesville. It was

announced in classes and halls that no proctors would be present at examinations; grown women, serious students, did not require monitoring. The gesture proved a shaming mistake. An indifferent mathematician hanging on to a C by short-bitten nails scored ninety-two on a trigonometry exam by copying from a gifted friend. A mediocre German student translated a subtle piece of Goethe amazingly well, helped by a prepared card lying in her lap, and earned an astonishing A-minus. Everyone became a wunderkind except myself.

I had requested a year of classical literature and philosophy instead of the alternative Latin, but for a forgotten reason I was forced into Latin, in which I had less than minimal interest. Read *Medea*, Plato, salacious Roman comedies – yes, heartily. But I was too disappointed and angry to study Latin and too much a snob to cheat. I would not copy from the baby whiz who knew all the rules of Latin grammar and apt examples for each, nor sequester bits of paper covered with Latin verbs in my bra or sleeve, nor allow myself to be distorted by a subject of which I knew, and was contented to know, nothing, nor diminish myself to follow the practices of hoi polloi, my frightened, competitive Hunter friends. While the others were nervously rummaging for little papers inside their blouses or copying the papers of experts, I answered what I easily could and let the rest go, making the exam period short enough to allow for a couple of cigarettes in the Exchange before the next exam began. When the end of the term came, a few days later, I expected a failing grade; never mind, maybe then I would be allowed to register for the classics course. Grade cards were issued at the end of the last class; quite sure of an F on my card I found a C, a passing grade. 'There must be some mistake; this can't be my card,' I said to the young instructor. 'It's your card, all right. Honesty should be given some reward. My respects and congratulations.' (The honor system at Hunter was shortly dissolved, and never mentioned again.)

At about the time the teetery honor system was elevating Hunter's dignity, many Hunter girls were playing a simple, crooked game on Saturdays and the busy shopping days before Christmas in a popular department store. We English majors, companions of Beowulf, could rarely play the game; we were sequestered in a 'rare'-book niche, where *The Last of the Mohicans, Little Women, Huckleberry Finn*, were sold in matched leatherette groups, ordered as 'two feet of red with gilt lettering, no more than ten inches high'; room decorations, in short. Who could, if she wanted to, steal a green leatherette copy on thick paper of *Great Expectations*? Friends in other departments did much better: a pair of stockings, a fine handkerchief, a bracelet, could be slipped into stocking tops. But there were obvious dangerous limitations there; no matter how adroit, a girl might be observed by a store detective and arrested. The most profitable and safest Saturday game was for Hannah at the glove counter, for instance, to sell to Minna a pair of long opera gloves whose price was $16.50. Hannah accepted from Minna and rang up $1.25, the price of the cheapest gloves. Several days later Minna returned the opera gloves in the original wrapping and asked Hannah for a refund. Sorry, the gloves didn't fit her mother and since they were a gift she had discarded the sales slip. The fancy gloves went back into their drawer and Minna received $16.50, a handsome return for her expenditure of $1.25. Hannah was by far the best partner to work with. She was experienced and quick, having worked in several sorts of shops. Noticing her speed and poise, the personnel department made her a Saturday 'floater', capable of learning speedily the goods and systems of any understaffed department. In order to know where and what she was selling, we arranged to meet with her at a given time in one particular toilet and began foraging – not in clumps, but discreetly one by one. Over several Saturdays, we bought bath sheets for the cost of washcloths, reclaiming the higher price on a later day. An ordinary syrup pitcher yielded the price of a costly vase, a cotton scarf brought proceeds from a Kashmiri shawl. Always the story was, 'This was meant to be a gift, so I discarded the sales slip.' We ate full lunches those weeks and bought extra pairs of stockings. Until store accountants began to study minutely discrepancies in slips and disbursements in several departments. The fat days were over, except for one last piece of mischief which earned no money. Nettie, who had never worked at anything before and inclined to easy agitation, was put by some malicious spirit into the toy department on the Saturday immediately before Christmas. She was deafened by questions, pummeled by children climbing up on her counter to pull down dolls and belled push toys. Their parents, sadists, she said, insisted on paying with checks, others with large bills for which she had no change; yet others presented her with long lists of purchases from various departments to which she was to add her own sale, with a special notation. There were foreigners whose requests she couldn't understand at all and always

there were the agile, twelve-armed kids. Out of her mind with the
confusions and her own helplessness, she quickly swept checks,
slips, dolls, puzzles, wagons, musical tops, checker games, sales
books, to the floor under her counter and fled, leaving a mess that
might have cost the shop more than our assembled crookedness
had.

Our thefts were often explained, particularly by those who
were members or groupies of members of leftish youth groups,
as small but telling skirmishes in the battle against capitalism.
One skeptic countered with the fact that big shops lost huge sums
to shoplifters but they were still flourishing, how come? Well, the
idealogues with strong voices and convictions responded, thirty or
forty bucks stolen from the capitalists would not make them fall,
but we should at every opportunity, petty as it might seem, try to
undermine them; thinking of them as the enemy to be victimized,
no matter how, was proper practice for the revolution.

Sandra did not return to school for the spring semester and it
was a relief not to have to listen to her autobiography begemmed
with high living and multiple Don Juans. But I was still curious
about her. Had she finally succeeded in making Rick so mad that he
shot her? Were they getting married? Actually already married? On
the excuse of asking for a misplaced book, I called Sandra's house.
She was out, but I spoke to Mama, who knew nothing about a book,
but why didn't I come for supper one night soon? 'I bet you can
use a good meal. I'm fixing calves' foot jelly and stuffed peppers
for Thursday night. Come.' I accepted, and arrived at about seven.
The house looked startlingly beautiful. The rugs had been cleaned
and their Oriental lozenges and paisley leaves shone like jewels;
the small tables had been dazzlingly polished; the curtains hung
white and stiff, flanked by the glowing red drapes. The shine, the
smell, the color, appeared as intensely appealing as my mother's
Friday night living room with the china closet glistening and the
ceremonial tablecloth with the fat red roses spread on the round
dining table. I was homesick, but life in the Bronx had been so
prickly and unhandleable that I would not, could not, admit it
and instead translated the homesickness into admiration of this
house of strangers, another shade of longing. As I stood there
dazzled by the beauties of the room, which I had once dismissed
as overheavy, kitschy Middle European, it seemed that I *could*
live here. I could marry Sam and have many babies to divide
with Sandra. The family would take good care of me, feed and

clothe me well, buy me rings and bracelets, and the maid would iron my blouses. I would finish Hunter and maybe the Rubinsteins would help me go on to graduate school between babies. It was an alluring picture for a girl often frightened and made lonely by her independence.

Tearing myself with reluctance from the seductions, I decided that life with the Rubinsteins was not really on my roster, their plump country was not for me. I visited rarely thereafter, and then not at all, my last picture that of Mama in one of her philosophical searches. One of the guests at a Friday night dinner was a young Chicago relative come to meet her fiancé's parents, who were New Yorkers. Mama: 'Who is this boy you're going to marry?' 'He's a boy I met at the University of Chicago. He's now studying law here in New York, at Columbia.' 'Can he support you?' 'He will soon, when he graduates next year.' 'So then you'll get married?' 'Of course.' 'Why of course?' 'Because then we'll be happy.' 'So you'll be happy. And so what?'

The girl looked shattered, her security blanket taken from her. Mr. Rubinstein and Sam apologized for Mama – she doesn't often know what she's saying – and urged the girl to finish her dessert. She did, head down, troubled. Mama came clearer in my mind. Anyone who could say, 'So you'll be happy. And so what?' had no measure for happiness or unhappiness – what did it matter? – nor concern for anyone's feelings, capable of taking babies and placing them where it suited her, if she was permitted. I said my farewells, forever farewells, to the Rubinsteins and returned to more innocent, less brutally cynical Hunter friends.

Birth control clinics existed, as witness the pessary of the foxy-faced girl, our infertility goddess, who offered it to anyone with a weekend date. The rest of us didn't know where the clinics were and didn't try to find them, much too afraid of potential trouble since we had heard that they were from time to time attacked by the law. Some of us took chances sexually because it was the brave, wiggling-finger-at-the-nose stance and because an abortion was an achievement of full, worldly womanhood. There were very few of us who used potential pregnancy to ensnare and marry our sexual partners. It would be an immoral act and, as a practicality, futile. Our boys worked at all sorts of odd jobs – as delivery boys, as shop clerks, as tutors, as movie ushers, as blood donors – in order not to burden their families while they attended college classes. Support a wife and child? Forget it, babe.

Most of our sexual encounters were truncated, gasping ventures made jumpy by the sound of a neighbor's step, an imagined turn of a key in a lock, or the cry of a child with whom one was baby-sitting. The semen spilled on stocking and underpants and inside trousers or, more awkward still, on trouser legs; kitchen rags and towels, hastily grabbed, carried off more semen than the girls did. Virgins were rarely deflowered under these circumstances, and knew an orgasm as an explosion set off by teasing touching and a warm spill of thick moisture on the thigh, the coitus interruptus method of birth control – a matter not so much of conscious control, however, as of inept haste. We knew only one girl who held the rope that led from pregnancy to marriage with a good-natured, acquiescent boy she had pursued, and raped, according to her friends. During the anxiety and turmoil of an unsuccessful search for abortion money, he married her. The marriage held up, as far as I know, maintained by her stubbornness and the forbearance that made him silent and bent-shouldered by the time he reached thirty – someone out of Yiddish folk tales of *shlemiels*. The rest of us played the field, not wildly, since there weren't enough candidates for dating in those hard-working, penniless days.

Whether I actually loved Davy or not, I am not quite sure. We loved our friendship and mutual admiration, we loved playing house and wandering the city together, we liked shopping in the market and cooking together; our united possessiveness and dependency made us feel large and strong. Bed was tender, considerate, sad, fumbling, and in time it faded into total discouragement. Davy would never consider infidelity with a more experienced woman, as a matter of romantic principle and probably because of his fear of failure. Back, not too far back, in my mind was a sureness that life with Davy was a beginning, a walking hand-in-hand in a spring garden of pink primroses and white daisies. In time, I knew, I would wander in darker copses with thorny bushes and strange flowers.

Experimenting once or twice, finally unvirgined – no great opening of the skies and no earth moving – I joined the worriers. Brave as we were, and as brightly, offhandedly *New Yorker*ish our manner when we mentioned it, our stomachs turned to burning knots as one week and a second and a third passed without a period. Money, money, money – where were we to get it? The fear of not finding money almost obliterated the fear of the operation itself. A decently performed abortion would be attended by a nurse who administered an anesthetic for a white-coated doctor in a brownstone on Irving Place or Stuyvesant Place. Appointments had to be made well in advance, and one departed in a taxi whose driver always knew when to raise a jump seat: 'Put your legs up here, honey; I know you'll be most comfortable that way. I get a lot of girls like you around here.' The cost? At least one hundred fifty dollars and more frequently two hundred. Appealing to parents for money even if they had it was hardly fruitful. A weeping, distraught mother: '*Gottenyu*, what happened to the nice girl you used to be? Who will marry you if you're not a virgin? Men can tell when a girl has had an abortion and some girls die from abortions.' 'No, Ma, people die of abortions only when they do it themselves with wire hangers and dirty scrapers and poison medicines. This is like going to a dentist's or a doctor's office, everything clean and careful, Ma. Don't cry, but see if you can find me some money, please.' Only in extremis did one approach a father, who controlled the money. As my friends told it, the response ran: 'Money for an abortion? Let the bum who knocked you up pay for it; he got the pleasure. Why don't you earn the money on the streets doing what you stupidly did for nothing? Even if I had the money to throw away, I wouldn't give it to you, you black plague.' As in childhood, the less parents knew, the better. One's friends were more reliable.

I was hardly one of the dependable lenders since I had to pay my share of rent and food out of my earnings, but I could occasionally lend the five dollars my mother sent me now and then. Others lent what they could as the strangling days and weeks went by and the fear mounted that the safe period for an abortion would pass before the money was collected. Fears that sharpened with exam nerves – exams that required concentrated study of chemical formulae, exams that demanded precise recall of experiments in physics, exams that asked for long quotations from 'The Parlement of Foules', all tortured times – should have helped serve as imperative warnings, but didn't. At almost any time a distraught friend would dash to our Exchange table, ashen faced: 'I missed my period, it's two weeks already.' 'Maybe it's one of those irregular months.' 'No, I'm always regular and Joey said he thought his condom might have slipped. He saved fifty dollars and he's going to borrow twenty-five from his little brother's bar mitzvah loot – he told him that now that he was a

man he had to help out with men's troubles – and his bachelor
uncle, with his usual snide remarks and taking his own sweet time
with stupid jokes and bathhouse wisecracks, finally consented to
lend him thirty. We need at least another fifty or maybe a
hundred. How about you? You? You? Please, I'm going crazy
and so is Joey.' (It should be recorded that in my knowledge
no City College boy ever denied his responsibility or removed
himself from the money gathering. They were an honorable crew
and were, somewhere under the fear, pleased with the knowledge
that they were biologically ready to stop being 'boys', ready to join
or possibly displace their fathers as men.)

Though illegal, abortionists were not difficult to locate; everyone
had a friend who had a friend who had an address and telephone
number. And the address was not always Stuyvesant Square and
its guild vicinity. Those who couldn't raise the larger sums could
find a faceless room, a table, and a washbowl in Staten Island or
the Bronx, or Jersey, no refinements assured or expected; price, one
hundred dollars. My first was a New Jersey abortion, the result of
drinking deeply of synthetic gin and romping with an anonymous
beauty over house roofs and down some stairs or other, to roll on
the grass in a nearby park. One effect of this minor Saturnalia
was being transformed into a red shapeless thing, disfigured by
poison ivy; the other was the pregnancy. My party hosts tracked
down the young man; I hadn't wanted to because the fault was
mine: I had designed the chase and led it off. He came through,
though, with fifty dollars and I borrowed five dollars here, seven
dollars there, another fifty, to pay for the arrangements made by
an experienced friend's friend. My young man, no longer Adonis
but a frightened pre-law student, borrowed a car and we drove out
toward somewhere in Jersey, I too scrambled with fear to read the
map and be of any help to him. After a couple of hours of driving
onto highways and off, into rough and rougher roads, we came to
a foursquare, unadorned stucco house standing alone in a field.
When my feller rang the bell, a stout man in a creased shirt
greeted us but didn't let us in until he had his hundred dollars
in hand. He directed us to the back of the sparsely furnished
house and indicated a chair for the boy to sit in and wait. I was
taken to a kitchen with a large rectangular table in the center. The
man told me to take my panties and stockings off and to get up on
the table. There was no pad on the table, nothing but a wrinkled,
coarse sheet and a shallow pillow which was removed as I climbed

up. The man, whose face looked like soiled marzipan, said he was
going to give me an anesthetic; lie still. I saw no needle, no vial
of drugs, no mask, only a bulb syringe. This he inserted in me,
letting loose a flood of icy water, the anesthetic whose effects
lasted a few seconds. The man began to pull and cut at me,
tearing, scraping, with a violence that threatened to rip out my
intestines and stomach, everything in me to flood the table and
floor and leave my body empty and dead. To remove myself from
the pain I entered a delirious world of conjecture. How much pain
must make madness? But maybe madness would go on and on as
its own different, dreadful pain? But that, too, must ultimately end.
In death. But what if death were again endless pain? Around and
around I went, pain to madness with pain, to death with ceaseless,
forever, pain. Until I felt the shock of another infusion of ice water.
The man pushed my legs to the floor, gave me two sanitary pads,
and said I could go, telling me to watch out for the basin on the
floor. I knew what was in the basin and, without looking down,
felt my way around it. As I stumbled to the door the boy asked
me how I was. I didn't answer. I didn't want to talk to him. I had
no connection with him except as a wavering figure in a gin-washed
dream I wanted to forget. He drove me home, we murmured good
night, and never met again.

My grand abortion was the result of an encounter with a young
poet, Arthur, whose techniques were erratic and uncertain, the girls
told me, though he was fun – and for that reason I felt safe.
Confident in his lack of skill and underestimating my receptivity
(one of my friends said that a kind smile could make me pregnant
and I was rather proud of that; it equated me with the great earth
mothers of mythology – Demeter, Isis, and even O'Neill's Nina),
I missed a period and another. Arthur had ninety dolllars that he
was saving for a flivver and I had forty saved for a good warm coat.
He managed to borrow some money from a cousin and I from my
mother, who was worried but not censorious. After all, wasn't it she
who had advocated a life of lovers and had herself survived many
abortions?

Like rich people, we bought the two-hundred-dollar abortion on
Irving Place. The room my friend Minna and I entered was guarded
by a nurse in white shoes, costume, and cap, the real thing. She took
my address and name (both false), age and weight, and invited us to
sit on a settee that already held two women. We were all young, we
in that room full of chairs and couches and a table that held worn

magazines, some of us twisting Woolworth wedding rings bought the day before. A few girls picked up magazines, turned the pages quickly, and put them down; a few girls held books whose pages didn't turn. Mainly, we stared at each other's pale faces. There wasn't anything to say to Minna that I hadn't said before. I wanted nothing but to push two or three hours away, to be out of the room of the stricken girls and their whirling rings, of the idiotic prints that supremely insultingly featured women with babies – Japanese women with babies, French women with babies, Italian women with babies – laughing at us off the walls.

After about an hour of waiting, I was ushured into a room that looked satisfactorily surgical: a table draped in sheets of thick leatherette and towels, on movable, adjustable wheels. The doctor, a smooth young man in horn-rimmed glasses, introduced himself, assured me it would all be over swiftly and without pain. He then settled my head on a pillow, strapped my arms to my sides, and quickly placed a cone over my nose and mouth. He told me to count slowly to one hundred. I sank at sixty, sank completely and was gone, how long I don't know, until I felt someone stroke my cheek and kiss me on the mouth. I was dreaming; as reality this was impossible, insane. But I could hear his voice: 'This is a pretty one. Come on, sweetheart, get up, it's all over, you'll be able to go home soon.' He continued to kiss me, gently, then fervently, and slipped his hand under the sheet to my breast. A wave of wonder and rage woke me fully. I pushed his hand away. How could he? After mutilating my insides, how could he want to touch me? How could he? As I glared at him while he washed his hands and put his instruments into an autoclave, the nurse helped me off the table. She then accompanied me into a back room to rest on a cot among two or three other girls. Minna was still in the waiting room, I assumed, as I fell into a doze.

I was awakened by a rhythmic dripping sound. There were no sinks or toilets about that might make that sort of faucet sound. The dripping was close and it gradually occurred to me that I was the source. Lifting myself to look at the underside of my cot, I saw that it was spilling bright drops of blood, steadily, regularly. The window showed twilight, the girls on the other cots were gone. I was spiked by terror. Had everyone left – nurses, patients, doctor, Minna – and forgotten about me? I got up and found towels to clean myself with and bleed into. Had they locked me in? Was there any way to get out? I walked through the rooms.

No one in the operating room, no one in the small adjoining office. In the waiting room I found a cleaning woman, who gave me my panties and stockings and unlatched the street door. Minna was sitting on the stone stairs, sallow and looking elderly. She had been waiting all the long hours since noon and knew something terrible had happened, that I was too sick to be released, or worse still, that I had died. It was shockingly inhuman, she said, that no one had checked up on me. What if I had bled to death? What would they have done if they found me dead the next morning? They couldn't report a death in the ordinary way because the operations were illegal. Maybe they had a deep back garden for their burials or sold their dead late at night to medical students, who dragged them away to work on in hospital morgues. Maybe dead women were bound into sacks for highly bribed special sanitation men to pick up and dump surreptitiously with the rest of the city's garbage and filth. As Minna's immaginative indignation mounted and soared, I drooped in exhaustion, too tired to be angry.

The taxi, which was Minna's financial contribution to my abortion, took us back to her house, where she explained to her mother that I was having a small hemorrhage as the result of a polyp operation. Mrs. Speller looked skeptical but fed us a large dinner before I took the bus, still bleeding, back to my own apartment, to be comforted by the noises of my neighbors, the banging of crates and cellar doors as the market around the corner closed for its short night, pleased that Davy would spend that night in his parents' house. I thought again of what might have happened had I bled to death, how my corpse might have been disposed of, how Minna would spread the news of my death. I never once thought of the fetus – neither as an object nor as a potential baby. It was nothing, only a forbiddingly expensive nuisance, a thing that signaled passage into my mother's painful, gallant world.

Postlude

In her *Human Condition*, Hannah Arendt, speaking of the end of adolescence, says that 'in word and deed we insert ourselves in the human world and the insertion is like a second birth', a swift abstraction with a suggestion of volition and the rational. A fuller, more detailed picture of my own adolescence draws a long, erratic labor, alternately pulling away from and pushing toward a vague new condition, a faint goal reached with difficulty since the second birth dragged with it vestigial forms that were slowly, reluctantly discarded, a few leaving indestructible shreds and stubborn shadows.

As I look back at the labor of my rebirth in its wayward progress, there appear long, contemplative pauses for unaccustomed thoughts and new, firm decisions, clean of hesitancies and vacillations. To replace the hindrances of fat, I drove it off, and in congratulating myself on my new shape as reasonably acceptable and maybe even sexy, threw off the shabby old gray raincoat that had been 'I' for a couple of years. (The Borsalino stayed, no longer a hat but a treasure of faded Renaissance gold and a witness to important times and events.) I lost completely the flapping nostrils that had been appointed the antennae of my sensitivity. Lipstick, rouge, and powder were not yet for me, a symbol of plain living and high thinking, it once seemed, and now a welcome form of vanity, a conviction that I didn't need Woolworth's help to enhance my charms. The deep contralto voice forced its way up to an ordinary nonoperatic level and the overcareful, actress speech contented itself with being a fair imitation of the teachers to whom I listened carefully when I was an immigrant child. In any case, I had acquired the wisdom, during my rebirth passage, to know that job interviews for full-time work after college would go badly if I was judged too odd, too affected, a prickly object among smooth office anonymities. The fast quips, like those of Dorothy Parker and Robert Benchley, that I had traded with friends in Hunter's basement lost their little stings and whips and ultimately died when I became fond of a girl who didn't hear well; it was cruel to ask her to strain and to try to lip-read the bright nonsense at which I had been so quick, a skill that no longer gave me pleasure since I saw it give pain.

Telling transitions sometimes came when the rebirth struggle left me skinless and unprotected, not quite ready for the new human world. In one night's meanderings I saw and felt like a woman standing in a doorway, howling at a running man, 'Come back, please come back! I won't say it again! Please, please!' On the next corner a drunk with a battered face put out a shaking hand for a few coins. My hand shakes as I give him a couple of dimes. I bump into cripples and dwarfs and blank-faced idiots who look a little like me in this Walpurgisnacht engraving. Earlier I would have made this night an exercise for toothsome description with a touch of literary hyperbole to distance the experience. Now it hurt, as the unhappy children in the castle school had hurt. When I was a child it was constantly puzzling that when my brother punched me I felt the pain, but when I punched him I felt nothing. That was changed; skinless and all nerve endings, I was subject to a universe of punches. Newspaper stories of floods could drown me, earthquakes strangled my breath and buried me, forest fires burned off my hair and boiled my eyes. I was no longer immune, no longer the mythical, separate, and privileged entity I had tried to design. I was earthbound and vulnerable, like anyone and everyone else.

The girl of the singular destiny melded with other young women, who tried to look like happy, bright birds as they fearfully approached job interviews, who had to search for places to live, enduring dank cellars and cold lofts when the money was low. My wide, fanciful travels in any corner of the globe I happened to choose would have to sink to hitchhiking, my intellectual entertainments among the cultivated elite would have to live in library books, in museums, in the movies, and in conversations with equally earthbound, unexotic friends. Now I could listen with patience and sympathy to their sorry tales of lousy bosses and thwarted loves, as I had found myself sympathizing with old Mrs. Sonntag in her loneliness, as I found myself heartsick and furious that I could do nothing to hold back my mother's decline.

I could only listen when my mother lightly complained about the endless cartons of dull cottage cheese she had to consume to keep her weight down, weight that burdened her prematurely worn-out heart. I could only listen as she spoke about aging as an overlong good-bye, like guests who stood and talked at the door long after one was ready to close it. Yet she was pining away for life as everything, she said, was going down, down, toward death; the breasts, the belly, the behind, even the front – you know where I mean – hang down like useless rags. Her slow, flat voice, once musical and lilting, kept intoning, 'It's not nice to get old, it's not nice and there's nothing I can do about it.' (I heard the same notes much later in a poet's sentence: 'For the bleakness of December there is no solution.') My mother, who had once slept well and noisily, now slept little. Maybe she didn't want death to catch her unawares and preferred to take light catnaps in the back of her store with other people around who might – foolish, superstitious peasant idea, she said – warn her or hold death off altogether. It wasn't only that she couldn't do certain things; she had no wish or will to do them. Even if she could dance the mazurka without stopping her heart, would she want to now? There was the mandolin in the closet; she didn't want to play it, and – with a return of her gay laugh – there were those shiny dentures and she couldn't chew on a fresh, forbidden bagel with their strong, expensive whiteness. She hated the notion that they would still be shining and new, almost unused, when she died and that her new fur coat would still be new and the new rug hardly in need of cleaning. It was someone's idea of a joke, a terrible joke, that she should start dying when she could, finally, afford to start living.

There was nothing I could do with my pity. I could not relieve her anger and her fear, nor take the smallest part of them as my own burdens, a frustration as cruel as loss and death. When I began to leave her in the deepening twilights, plumping up yet another cushion, feeding her fish, watering her big rubber plant, reluctant to go except that I chose to avoid encounters with my father, who would shortly be returning from work, I, too, felt old and exhausted, angry and despairing. Almost, I was my mother and like her an intimate of death, no longer the invulnerable girl, responsible to no one and for no one.

The girl who was to be immortal, the bright fantasist and loony wanderer, was lost in the struggles of the second birthing –

and not quite. Like Sam Rubinstein's dreadful twin who sapped his embryo companion, she, too, carried an envelope of earlier shapes: of the me as I would never again be and of my friends and mentors – puzzling, kindly, brutal, narcissistic, stimulating, and destructive people who were washed away in the second amniotic flood. Not altogether washed away, as the girl was not altogether lost. Like an old string of beads slipped from their broken thread, like a loose pile of fading snapshots, they rattle around with the golden Borsalino hat and the volume of Heine verse in a box rarely opened but palpably there; not transferable, not inheritable, immutably mine as testaments of once-upon-a-time me.